THE IRONCLADS OF
CAMBRAI

THE IRONCLADS OF
CAMBRAI

THE FIRST GREAT TANK BATTLE

BRYAN COOPER

CASSELL

Cassell Military Paperbacks

Cassell
Wellington House, 125 Strand
London WC2R 0BB

First published by Souvenir Press 1967
This Cassell Military Paperbacks edition 2002

British Library Cataloguing-in-Publication Data
A catalogue record for this book is available from the
British Library

ISBN 0-304-36363-4

Photographs courtesy of the *Royal Armoured Corps Tank Museum*
and the *Imperial War Museum*

Printed and bound in Great Britain by
Cox & Wyman Ltd, Reading, Berks.

Contents

5

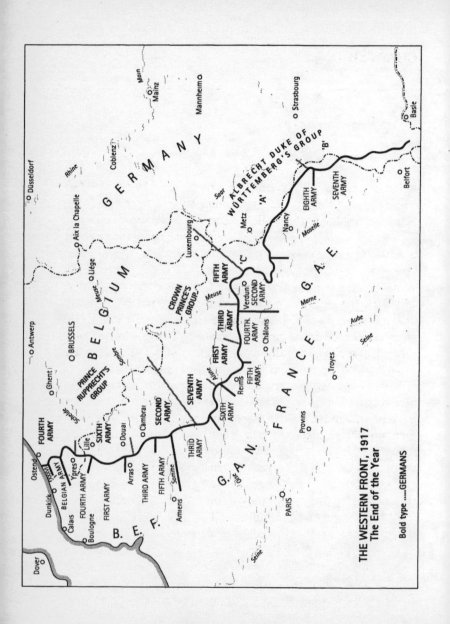

THE WESTERN FRONT, 1917
The End of the Year

Bold type .....GERMANS

CHAPTER ONE

The First Victory

ON the morning of November 21, 1917, the church bells of London rang out for the first time since the start of the Great War. They were celebrating a sudden and dramatic victory which had taken place the day before near the town of Cambrai, in northern France. For the first time since the two opposing armies had become deadlocked in the trenches of the Western Front, the mighty German defensive system of the Hindenburg Line had been broken. The Third Army of the British Expeditionary Force had advanced five miles along a six-mile front, and in a matter of hours had accomplished more than in any other single operation during all the months of fighting on the Somme and in Flanders.

It was a stirring victory, and gave the public at home their first chance of jubilation since the early days of the war. For by now, the initial flush of enthusiasm had waned. Young men no longer queued up in their thousands to volunteer for the Front. The eager, adventurous ones had gone anyway, most of them never to return, and conscription had now become necessary. No longer did elegant young ladies tour the streets of London, handing out white feathers to any men who were not in uniform. The flag waving and the jingoism had been replaced by a deep sense of depression. The heroic phrases did not seem to ring true against the rising tide of casualties, the lame and the blind, the shell-shocked and the gassed, who were straggling back from the Front. Food was becoming scarce as a result of German submarine activities. Bombing raids were becoming more frequent. Many people were, for the first time, beginning to ask themselves just what the war was all about.

The news was no less welcomed on the Western Front. The year had opened with a certain degree of hope and optimism, with Haig and his commanders confident that their tactics would win the day. It was ending as the worst year of all for the Allies. Men wondered if the war might go on forever. The Western Front had stagnated into the horror and futility of trench warfare in which no side was able to break the deadlock. Troops of the British, French and Commonwealth armies faced the Germans across a No Man's Land that was no more than a few yards wide in places. Each side had burrowed into the ground, and the two great defensive lines of barbed wire, trenches, dug-outs and machine-gun posts, stretched side by side in a wavering barrier right across Europe, from the Belgian coast to Switzerland. The Germans were particularly well entrenched. During 1916 and early the following year, while the two monolithic armies had been locked in fruitless combat, they had been hard at work behind their front lines, building one of the greatest defensive systems the world had ever seen. The Siegfried-Stellung, or the Hindenburg Line as it became generally known, extended some 45 miles from the British front near Arras, down past Cambrai and Saint Quentin, to a point six miles north-east of Soissons. It was more than four miles deep in places, and made up of three distinct lines of trenches, with fifty yards or more of barbed wire massed in front of each one. Concrete positions were built for machine-guns, and a network of railways constructed so that troops and supplies could be brought right up to the front. The Line had been chosen for its strategic position, rather than to retain the few miles of captured territory between it and the existing front lines. The Germans considered this massive barrier to be impenetrable, and so it was, apart from a partial breakthrough during the Arras campaign, until the Battle of Cambrai. Behind it, they planned to stand on the defensive, to enable divisions to be sent away to other fronts and to be a position of rest and recuperation for troops who had been fighting in Flanders. Also, it gave them time for their submarines to continue the destructive work against British shipping.

When in March, 1917, the Germans had fallen back to the Hindenburg Line, they left behind an area of utter devastation. Everything had been destroyed—towns, villages, even trees. In their place were planted mines and booby-traps. Slowly, the Allied forces made their way forward to re-establish contact with the enemy. And then had begun the furious assaults to try and flank the Line, the British in Flanders and the French further south around Saint Quentin. Men were hurled in their tens of thousands against well-defended positions, only to be mowed down by fire from machine-guns which some British generals had previously considered " overrated weapons ". The casualties mounted to terrifying proportions, of a kind never before, or since for that matter, experienced in war. Often, men were expended for no other hope of success than that of wearing down the enemy's reserves, the fatal policy of attrition ordered by generals who rarely, if ever, left the safety of their rearward head-quarters to see for themselves the hell of the front line. They might have learned a lesson from the five months of fruitless fighting on the Somme the previous year, when the British lost 420,000 casualties—60,000 on the first day alone—and the French nearly 200,000. But no—the same kind of campaign had to go on. The battles followed the same pattern— days or weeks of artillery bombardment, and then a blind rush forward into a curtain of machine-gun fire. The bombardment seemed to be the only apparent way of destroying the barriers of barbed wire and giving the infantry even half a chance. It certainly enabled the enemy's front lines to be taken during the initial attack, which was why, by 1917, both sides had learned to keep their forward positions only lightly held, with the real defence in depth at the rear. But it also gave ample warning of a coming attack. Every time the British and French made such an attempt, the Germans knew what was coming and had time to bring up reserves to strengthen their defences.

And so the slaughter continued. During the Third Battle of Ypres in the summer of 1917, the British casualties over three months were nearly 400,000—for the gain of no more than a few miles of cratered mud-flat and the ruins of a village that was called Passchendaele. The Hindenburg Line remained unbroken and unflanked.

By the end of the campaign on the Somme in 1916, even the generals were aware that something was wrong. Grand battles in the old style just did not seem to work, no matter how many men were thrown into the slaughter. But still they were continued in Flanders the following year. Passchendaele was the most senseless disaster of them all. It was, as it happened, the last battle of its kind, although no-one realised this at the time. For on the horizon was a new kind of weapon, being developed by a small band of devoted visionaries against official indifference. It was a weapon which was to revolutionise warfare and which was ultimately responsible for the final victory of the war. It was the tank. And it was at Cambrai that tanks were used for an attack en masse for the first time in history.

Those who fought in the battle were taking part in the first great cavalry charge which Europe had seen for centuries. This was the kind of attack which had dominated warfare from the time when William the Conqueror's horsemen routed Harold's foot soldiers at the battle of Hastings until the longbowmen of England had turned the tables at Crécy, defeating the French cavalry by long-range, accurate marksmanship. Later, the invention of gunpowder and the rifle made even more impossible the charge by armoured knights on horseback. Only now, instead of the thunder of horses' hooves, the ground was to tremble with a new thunder as the iron horses, awesome fire-belching monsters of iron and steel, rolled forward on grating tracks.

The location chosen for the first great battle of the tanks was the Front near Cambrai, a medium-size town some forty-six miles south of Passchendaele and seven miles behind the

Hindenburg Line. There had been little fighting here, and unlike the shell-pitted quagmire of Flanders, the ground was hard and firm, ideal for tanks. So was the open, rolling countryside, covered by uncultivated grass. The objective was to break through the German lines and seize Cambrai. From then on, the plan was vague, but if the first part was successful, it was thought that it might be possible to spread out on either side and attack the German flank.

The tanks had been brought into position behind the British lines by five o'clock on the dull, misty morning of November 20. For days past, they had been secretly transported to the Front on trains, travelling by night. It was one of the best-kept secrets of the war. By the time they were ready for battle, 376 of them strung out along a six-mile line, even most of the British infantry did not know they had arrived.

At 6.30 a.m., as dawn began to break, the British artillery started to bombard the German trenches. Had the attack followed the previous pattern of the war, this bombardment would have started days before and millions of pounds worth of ammunition would have been expended on cutting down the barbed wire. This time, the tanks had already begun to move forward ten minutes before, crossing the British lines and heading onwards into No Man's Land. The infantry followed, for once protected from the deadly machine-gun fire.

From the German trenches, the sight of the great machines lumbering forward was electrifying. Nothing like it had ever been seen before. Many German soldiers fled in panic before the monsters, others surrendered immediately. Within minutes of the attack, the tanks were crushing through the front-line defences, flattening the barbed wire, bridging trenches, destroying machine-gun posts, leaving wide paths for the oncoming infantry. Standing up in full view in the tank Hilda, leading the attack, was General Elles, commander of the newly formed Tank Corps. Brandishing an ash stick carrying the brown, red and green flag of the Corps, he led his tanks into action like some mediaeval general leading a cavalry charge.

The surprise was sudden and complete. By midday, the tanks had broken through the three trench systems of the Hindenburg Line, penetrating five miles into enemy-held territory. Over 8,000 prisoners had been taken and more than 100 guns captured. So fast was the advance that the German Supreme Command, knowing that they could not bring up reserves for two or three days, were seriously considering an evacuation of the Front. For a while, it seemed almost as if it might be the beginning of the end of the war.

In the town of Cambrai itself, the civilian population heard the opening of the artillery barrage from the south with astonishment. They crowded on to the streets to witness the confusion that was taking place among their German invaders. Ever since August, 1914, they had been under occupation. Their chief industry, that of weaving fine fabrics which had given the name of cambric to the world, was in ruins. Now, as the sound of the battle advanced, liberation was at hand.

Among the first to hear the news in London was Lieutenant-Colonel E. D. Swinton, one of the few men who had fought to make the tank possible. He was told of the victory by Lord Hankey, his chief at the Committee of Imperial Defence. Swinton was delighted at first. Then he looked out of the windows of his quiet Whitehall office, and frowned.

" What's the matter? " Hankey asked. " You don't seem too pleased."

" I'm pleased all right," replied Swinton. " But I'm wondering. I bet that GHQ are just as much surprised by our success as the Germans, and are quite unready to exploit it."

They were prophetic words, as the next days were to prove. For the moment, however, the first hours of the Cambrai attack marked a great victory. But more than that, it was to go down in history as a turning point in warfare. It showed that forever afterwards, horses would be replaced by a new kind of cavalry—an armoured cavalry on wheels and tracks. For some, it was a lesson that was learned painfully and slowly, particularly by those cavalry officers who still saw the " horseback charge with drawn sabres " as the gentlemanly way to conduct a war. Even as late as 1923, an officer writing in the Cavalry Journal could still extol the virtues of a horse-back charge at sword point, and, describing one of the incidents which actually took place during the battle of Cambrai, could write: " the small German rear-guard appeared astonished and cowed by the galloping horsemen and showed no fight." Other squadrons of cavalry did not have the luck of such astonishment, and were cut down by more modern weapons. And although at this time the tank was actually an infantry support weapon, many senior infantry officers were just as reactionary as the cavalry.

But for official opposition and indifference to the idea of tanks, they could have been available to the British Army soon after the war started. Even as it was, after the first pioneering experiments had been made in England in 1914, the French took up the idea more enthusiastically and actually manufactured more of them than the British, although they were mechanically inferior. Only towards the end of the war did the Germans begin to make tanks themselves—and by then, it was too late.

Tanks were certainly a revolutionary new weapon, but they were hardly a new concept. Perhaps Hannibal's elephants were the real predecessors of the modern tank. As far back as the 16th century, Leonardo da Vinci had designed an armoured fighting vehicle which was in the form of a shallow metal bowl, with slits cut in the bottom to take the wheels. These were to be turned by eight men inside the vehicle, operating by hand a system of gears and cranks. During succeeding centuries, various attempts were made to harness this idea for practical purposes, but it was not until the Crimea War in 1855 that the advent of steam power provided a means of driving such a vehicle. An assault car was invented, a formidable machine very similar to the da Vinci design but with cannons fitted through loopholes in the sides and retractable scythes on the outside framework. It was not used, however, and many thought it to be too brutal for civilised use.

The development of the internal combustion engine in 1886 gave new impetus to such ideas, and a few years after the first motor car appeared on British roads, an experimental armoured car was built by Frederick Simms and exhibited at the Crystal Palace in 1902. Two machine-guns were mounted in turrets, and the driver steered with the aid of a periscope. The vehicle was not a big success because of its weight and low power—but it was the forerunner of the armoured fighting car.

Such vehicles as this and others which followed were handicapped by the fact that they could only be used on roads. They could not cross rough country, and therefore offered no alternative to cavalry in battle. But the answer was available, if only there was someone who could see it. Soon after the turn of the century, tracks had been developed for use on tractors, which were mainly steam-driven in those days. The firm of Richard Hornsby & Sons was responsible for much of this work, and in 1905 the War Office bought one of their tractors, fitted with tracks, for experimental work. Interest in the idea waned, however, although Hornsby and others continued their research. Eventually, as there was no financial support available in Britain, Hornsby sold the American and Canadian patent rights to the Holt Caterpillar Company of New York. This company went ahead with further development work on tracks, and by 1914, they were being used extensively on farm vehicles in the United States. It is perhaps ironic that tractors did not begin to become popular in Britain until after the war, and then as a direct result of people having seen how effective tanks were at the Front.

These two developments, the internal combustion engine and tracks, provided the ingredients with which to make a tank. And by this time, interest in such a fighting vehicle was coming from other sources.

CHAPTER TWO

Birth of the Tank

IT was late in the afternoon of October 8, 1914. Alone in the flat Belgian countryside outside Antwerp was a pilot of the Royal Naval Air Service, Flight Lieutenant R. L. G. Marix. Behind him, in a ploughed field, was the Sopwith biplane in which he had just crash-landed. Although it was riddled with bullet-holes, these had not caused the crash. The plane had simply run out of petrol. Ahead of Marix lay twenty miles of enemy territory, regularly patrolled by German infantry units, which had to be crossed before he could reach his base. It was cold, and it was raining.

The lines in those early days of the war were not yet established as the barriers of trenches and barbed wire of the Western Front. That was to come later. Now, after the battles of Mons and the Marne, both sides were engaged in the " race for the sea." The depleted ranks of the British Expeditionary Force were withdrawing towards Dunkirk, while the Germans were sweeping through Belgium to cut them off. Already, Antwerp was under heavy fire, and in fact, plans were being made to evacuate both the town and the air base. In this confused situation, in which movement by infantry and cavalry was necessarily slow, fighting was local and sporadic, as patrols from either side ran into each other. It was in the middle of all this that Flight Lieutenant Marix crashed.

Earlier that day, he had left his base to carry out one of the first-ever British air raids into German territory. Faced with the threat of Zeppelin attacks on London, the British

War Cabinet had ordered the Royal Naval Air Service to attack and bomb the sheds in which the great airships were being built. Marix's target had been Dusseldorf. From a height of 600 feet, he had bombed and destroyed the airship sheds on the outskirts of the town. It was later discovered that one of the sheds contained the biggest and newest of the German Zeppelins, the Z.IX, making the raid one of the outstanding aerial achievements of the early part of the war. Heading for home, Marix found himself under heavy rifle fire. His plane was severely damaged—but it was still flying. Then it had run out of petrol some twenty miles from base, and Marix was forced to land.

There was just one chance. The squadron retained a fleet of cars which were used for darting into enemy territory to pick up pilots who had crashed. It was often possible to get through without meeting German patrols, but if they did, the cars were at least equipped with machine guns to give some protection. But to Marix, there didn't seem to be much possibility of being picked up so far from home. So he set out on the long walk back to Antwerp, keeping a sharp lookout for enemy patrols. After a while, he came to a farm and managed to persuade the farmer to lend him a bicycle. It meant faster travel, but was also more dangerous as it was by road. It was while on the road that he suddenly saw a German patrol ahead.

He quickly hid in a ditch, but there was only a slim chance that he hadn't been seen. He lay there on the damp earth, trying to resign himself to being taken prisoner. A depressing end to what had been, until then, a highly successful day. But it was at this point that he heard machine-gun fire. Peering over the embankment, he saw a car coming towards him, exchanging fire with the Germans. His rescue had arrived—but what chance did a car have in open country like this? Then, as the car came nearer, he found himself staring in astonishment. What kind of strange vehicle was this, with metal plates slung over the sides and a machine gunner firing from a kind of turret on top? It was like nothing he had even seen before. He stood up as the car pulled to a halt.

" What the devil is that? " he asked the Sergeant who was in the driver's seat.

" Better jump in first, sir. Things are warming up down the road."

Marix clambered aboard, and the car turned and headed back towards Antwerp. Once inside, Marix saw that it was certainly one of the Rolls Royce cars with which the squadron had been equipped. But improvised metal boiler plates had been slung all round the sides, protecting the wheels and the bodywork. The bullets from the German rifles simply glanced off.

" Whose idea was this? " Marix asked when they had passed out of fire of the astonished Germans.

" The Chief's, I think. Pretty useful, isn't it? "

It was not only useful, but although the occupants of the car didn't know it at the time, they were sitting in one of the direct forerunners of the tank, that was to have such an impact later in the war and, twenty-five years later, to become the main assault weapon of the Second World War.

The Chief referred to by the Sergeant was a fiery, unconventional naval officer, Commander C. R. Samson. He had joined the Air Service of the Royal Navy shortly after it was formed in 1908, and in the years just before the war, had worked on bomb dropping experiments and had flown the first seaplane to be equipped with wireless, sending messages up to a distance of ten miles. Following the creation of the Royal Flying Corps in May, 1912, the Admiralty reviewed the whole policy of using aircraft in naval operations, and a special Air Department was set up under the directorship of Commodore Murray Sueter to be responsible for all the activities of what was first known as the Naval Wing of the Royal Flying Corps, and later, the Royal Naval Air Service.

At the outbreak of war, the Service had a strength of some 830 officers and men, ninety-one aircraft, of which fifty-two were seaplanes, and seven airships. Air stations had been established along the eastern coast of Britain, from Dundee to the Isle of Grain and Eastchurch. During the crisis in August, when the British Expeditionary Force was under such pressure, Winston Churchill who was then First Sea Lord, decided to attempt a naval diversion by sending a brigade of marines to Ostend, under the command of Brigadier General G. Aston. In order to support them, an R.N.A.S. squadron from East-church was also sent over, under Commander Samson. They landed on August 27—three B.E. biplanes, two Sopwith bi-planes, two Bleriot monoplanes, one Henri Farman biplane, one Bristol biplane, and a converted Short seaplane with a land carriage instead of floats. The marines stayed for only three days before being recalled. The squadron was supposed to return as well, but this didn't suit Commander Samson. With a Channel fog as an excuse, he landed his squadron in Dunkirk, and enlisted the aid of the British Consul there in arguing to stay on to support the French. Churchill saw the establishment of a naval air base on the French coast as a means of protecting England from German airship raids, and so " Samson's boys " became a permanent feature in Dunkirk.

The little force began operations at once. In order to set up advanced air bases inland and to pick up any pilots forced to land outside the aerodromes, the squadron was equipped with motor cars. Shortly after Samson had landed in Ostend, he and his brother, Lieutenant Felix Samson, had accom-panied General Aston on a reconnaissance trip by motor car. It was during this trip that the idea had been put forward, probably by Felix Samson, for adding armour as well as guns to such vehicles. When the squadron became established in Dunkirk and long-range motor patrols soon became a regular feature of their work, Commander Samson took up this idea, using improvised boiler plates from a local steel works. At the same time, as a result of his requests to the Admiralty, Com-modore Sueter arranged for proper armour-plate to be fitted at the Rolls Royce factory where the cars were being made. The first two were sent to Dunkirk on September 19, and thirteen more were delivered in October. It was during this period that part of the squadron, including Flight Lieutenant Marix, was transferred to Antwerp to aid in the defence of the port. But the unit was evacuated on the evening of October 8

—minutes after Marix got back to his base, in fact. Antwerp was overrun by the Germans.

Meanwhile, back at home, Commodore Sueter was increasingly impressed by the activities of the armoured cars, some of which had by now been attached to the 3rd Cavalry Division and the IV Corps under Sir Henry Rawlinson. They played an active part in the struggle for Ypres during the last part of October, and by the time the various R.N.A.S. units had been brought back to Dunkirk, the " Dunkirk Armoured Car Force " had come into being. Although protected from the sides, the open design of the cars left the crews exposed to snipers firing down from trees. And so Sueter developed a new type of car which had overhead protection and a revolving gun turret. Several of these were delivered in December. But by then, the fighting had reached stalemate and the opposing armies were digging into the trenches that were to be a permanent feature for the rest of the war. There seemed to be no use now for the armoured cars, and they were all shipped back to England.

However, the germ of an idea had been born, and from several quarters there came the suggestion that if the armoured cars could be put on tracks instead of wheels, they would then be able to cross trenches. One of the first to see this possibility was Lieutenant Colonel E. D. Swinton, who was in Dunkirk at the time. Swinton had a unique job. During the first months of the war, there was complete censorship in Britain, imposed not only by the Government, but also by the patriotic restraint of the newspaper proprietors. Only those facts were presented that would bolster the confidence of the public in the country's political and military leaders. As far as the Army was concerned, the Press had virtually ceased to exist on the outbreak of war. Not one correspondent was allowed near the fighting zone or with the Fleet, and the public was expected to be satisfied with the cryptic communiques issued from time to time by General Headquarters. But this did not prevent the rumours which filtered back from the Front, and no-one could hide the thousands of wounded who were being brought back home. The demand for knowledge and real facts became in-

sistent, and eventually, early in 1915, a few selected corres-
pondents were allowed with the Army. After a complete
eclipse of Press freedom, the power of the newspapers rose
again. But already, during that interim period of censorship,
Churchill had suggested to Lord Kitchener the establishment
of an official observer at General Headquarters, to write
material for the Press. Because of Kitchener's dislike of news-
papermen, a serving officer was to be selected for the job. The
choice fell on Lieutenant Colonel Swinton, and during the
months he acted as a kind of official war correspondent, he
wrote under the pen-name of " Eyewitness ". During this time,
he saw at first hand the valuable work done by the armoured
cars, and he also saw the kind of deadlock that resulted from
trench warfare. It so happened that before the war, he had
received a report on the Hornsby tracks tested by the War
Office but in which they had then lost interest. If armoured
cars and tracks could be combined, thought Swinton, they
offered exciting possibilities for a new kind of weapon. In
October, he put the idea forward to Lieutenant Colonel
Maurice Hankey, the Secretary of the Committee of Imperial
Defence.

Hankey talked about it to various people. But there was
little interest in the idea, particularly in the War Office. Lord
Kitchener thought that " these armoured caterpillars would be
shot up by the guns ", and most of his staff took the same line.
Little was done until, in a long memorandum to Churchill
and others in the Cabinet, Hankey suggested that such vehicles
might be used to overcome the impasse of trench warfare.

At the time, there was another factor which came into the
picture. As far back as 1903, H. G. Wells had published a
short story in the Strand Magazine, entitled " The Land
Ironclads ", in which he had described a fictional weapon of
war which had a turtle back and was a hundred feet long and,
what was most important, by means of huge wheels, could
climb ditches and cross trenches. It was a remarkable vision
of future warfare. The story had been widely read and then
forgotten, but it probably lay dormant in many minds, need-
ing only an imaginative spark to bring it to life. Whether or

not Churchill had read the story is not known, but he was already thinking along similar lines. As First Sea Lord, he was well aware of the success in Dunkirk of Samson's armoured cars, and he had supported the design and building of more efficient vehicles. After receiving Hankey's memorandum, he wrote on the subject to the Prime Minister, Mr. Asquith. With such weight from high quarters, the War Office had to do something, but with a few notable exceptions, what they did was without enthusiasm. There was still a general feeling that the war would be over quickly. What was the point in developing such a new and revolutionary idea which was unlikely to work anyway? The idea was bandied about by various committees and eventually, the matter was referred to the Master-General of the Ordnance, General von Donop, who was then, and was to remain, one of the main antagonists of tanks. He decreed that before going any further, a trial should be held, using one of the Holt Caterpillar Tractors which had previously been brought over from the United States.

An obstacle-course was prepared at Shoeburyness, and on February 17, 1915, the trial took place. It was pouring with rain, and the ground was sodden. The tractor was given the handicap of drawing a truck laden with sandbags weighing 5,000 lbs., which were supposed to represent the weight of armour and armament. In front of a delegation of high-ranking officers, the tractor began the trial. It broke through the barbed wire entanglements which had been set up, but when it came to the trenches, it not surprisingly got stuck in the mud. This was enough for the War Office. The idea was impracticable and a waste of time and effort. It was dropped.

But Churchill was not prepared to give up so easily, after such an impossible and unscientific trial. If the Army was not interested, he could at least make sure that the Navy retained the initiative. Three days after that first trial, he set up a Landships Committee at the Admiralty, under the chairmanship of Tennyson d'Eyncourt, Director of Naval Construction, to look into ways of further developing the idea.

And it was on to this committee that there came another of the pioneers, Albert G. Stern. A City banker before the war, he had heard about the armoured cars being built by Sueter at Wormwood Scrubs, and offered not only to pay for the cost of one, but also his services as an administrator. The upshot was that he was appointed Secretary of the Landships Committee, with the temporary rank of Lieutenant. For some months, this committee explored further ideas, and carried out tests on another type of American tracked vehicle, the Killen-Strait Caterpillar Tractor.

Although the War Office had no interest in what was going on, Swinton was still trying to convince his superiors that the idea was practical. When he heard that the Admiralty had taken the initiative, he sent for Stern.

"Listen, Stern," he said. "This is the most extraordinary thing I have ever seen. The Director of Naval Construction appears to be making land battleships for the Army, who have never asked for them and are doing nothing to help. You have nothing but naval ratings doing all your work. What on earth are you? Are you a mechanic or a chauffeur?

"A banker," Stern replied.

"This makes it still more mysterious," Swinton concluded.

Meanwhile, Sueter was carrying out experiments on tracked vehicles with the No. 20 Armoured Car Squadron. His idea really was for a land battleship, a 300-ton monster mounting 12-inch naval guns and moving on three 40-foot diameter wheels. Its measurements were 100 feet long, 80 feet wide, and 46 feet high, and the whole contraption very much resembled the landship of fiction created by H. G. Wells. The idea was completely impractical and never got beyond the design stage. But when Sueter began working on smaller vehicles, mounted on caterpillar tracks, it began to make sense.

After a while, the Admiralty began to tire of the project. As one of the Sea Lords had said: "caterpillar landships are idiotic and useless. Nobody has asked for them and nobody wants them." The Armoured Car Force was disbanded and the cars turned over to the Army, although at the last minute,

Sueter managed to retain No. 20 Squadron for his tracked vehicle experiments. Luckily, at about this time, renewed interest was shown by the War Office. This was not due to a change of heart by the military authorities, but because of promptings from General Headquarters in France, to which Swinton had returned and was continuing to campaign for his idea. He was helped by the failure of the Allied offensives in the spring of 1915, when it seemed that a new solution would have to be found to the problem of trench warfare. On June 1, Swinton presented a memorandum on " The Need for Machine-Gun Destroyers ", part of which drew attention to the performance of some caterpillar tractors which he had seen being used to haul heavy howitzers. The suggestions were accepted by a GHQ committee and forwarded to the War Office, which now had to take some action.

So just when it seemed as if the idea would founder in the Admiralty hierarchy, the War Office again became active. The Landships Committee became a joint naval and military affair. Stronger and more enthusiastic now, with financial support allocated to it by Churchill, the Committee took over an office in Pall Mall, and arranged a demonstration with the Killen-Strait tractor. This was far more successful than the previous trial, and at last, actual plans were put in hand for the building of an experimental machine on tracks, that would be armoured and able to cross trenches and climb parapets. The work was given to the firm of William Foster & Company of Lincoln, and the two men most responsible for the design were Mr. William Tritton, managing director of the company, and Lieutenant W. G. Wilson, a naval officer who was later transferred to the Army with the rank of major. The contract was placed on July 24, 1915, and construction of the first prototype began on August 11. It was really a mock-up, using parts that happened to be handy. Named at first the " Tritton " and later, " Little Willie ", it was driven by a 105 h.p. Daimler engine, giving a speed of about two miles an hour. Steering was achieved by throwing one of the tracks out of gear. The body was made of boiler plate, and the turret was, for the time being, a dummy. In order to make the machine more stable, a pair of tail wheels dragged behind. The body rested on special nine-foot Bullock tracks which had been brought over from America.

While this vehicle was being given its trials, both Tritton and Wilson were working independently on new designs. Tritton continued with the method of resting the vehicle on tracks, but Wilson hit on the revolutionary idea of taking the tracks right round the body. The shape of the body was rhomboid, pointed at the top front and sloping down at the back. It was to be the basic shape for years to come.

" Little Willie " emerged for trials in September, 1915. But when Wilson's machine made its appearance later in the year, it was obviously the better design, and from then on, both men worked on it. To begin with, it was known as the " Centipede ", but shortly afterwards named " Big Willie ". Eventually, after tanks had become well established, it was affectionately called " Mother ". It was a remarkable vehicle. Although its shape was different, it still retained the tail wheels at the back, kept in contact with the ground by springs. Its overall length was 33 feet 3 inches: width 8 feet 3 inches: height 8 feet. Two 6-pounder guns were mounted in large sponsons, sticking out of each side of the hull. On the top were two fixed turrets, at front and rear. In the front turret there was room for the commander and the driver, sitting side by side, with a machine-gun between them. There was another machine-gun in the rear turret, and semaphore arms extending to the outside, the only means of communicating from one vehicle to another. There was a manhole at the top, and doors in the rear and on both sides. The total crew numbered eight, the others being four gunners and two gearsmen. The total weight, with ammunition and crew, was over 28 tons. The engine was again a 105 h.p. Daimler, giving a speed of just over 3·7 miles an hour. Steering was similar to that of " Little Willie ", in which the differential was locked on the side to which it was desired to turn. This was the function of the gearsmen, who carried out the instructions of the driver. The armour was between 6 m.m.

and 10 m.m. thickness, reckoned to be sufficient to provide protection against a reverse bullet fired at ten yards. This standard of measurement was used because of the discovery that if a bullet was reversed, it had greater armour-piercing qualities.

A problem had arisen as to what to call the vehicle. As it was essential to maintain secrecy, it was felt that the names "landship" or "landcruiser" gave too much away. But the name had to be roughly consistent with the shape of the vehicle, in case it was seen during transit. Various ideas were considered, such as "cistern", "container", and "reservoir". Eventually, it was decided that "tank" was short and ambiguous enough not to reveal its purpose.

"Big Willie" was the first real tank. As with any new idea, its birth had been difficult and due to the drive of a few men of vision. Had it been left to the normal channels of the War Office and the Admiralty, it would probably not have been born at all. After the war, when it had become apparent that here was one of the most important weapons ever devised for warfare, many people laid claim to having invented it. A special Commission was set up to examine these claims, many of which turned out to be exaggerated or untrue. The fact was that no one person could be given the entire credit for the idea. Swinton and Sueter had certainly seen the value of combining armoured cars and tracks, arriving at their conclusions independently, but Stern had been responsible for much of the drive once the idea got under way, and nothing would have been possible without the backing and support of Churchill. The seeds had been germinating in the minds of many people at the same time. The ultimate development of the tank was a combined affair against the weight of official indifference and contempt. But the biggest irony was that while work was going ahead on the project, with the War Office and the Admiralty alternating between scepticism and reluctant acceptance, there was all the time lying in a War Office pigeon-hole a design for a tank which had been sent in as far back as 1912. This had come from a private inventor, Mr. E. L. de Mole, of North Adelaide,

South Australia. It was ignored both then and again when Mr. de Mole resubmitted his idea in 1915, while serving as a private in the 10th Battalion, Australian Imperial Force, although it was in fact a better design than either " Little Willie " or " Big Willie ". When in 1919 the Royal Commission on Awards to Inventors met to consider the many claims for the invention of the tank, they said of Mr. de Mole

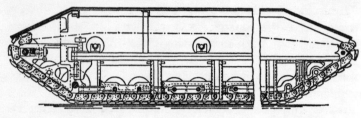

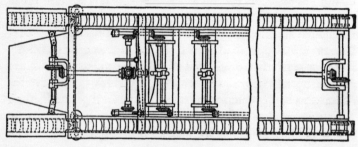

DE MOLE'S PLAN

Drawing of an endless track vehicle submitted to the War Office by Mr. E. L. de Mole, of North Adelaide, South Australia, in 1912 and again in 1915. Unfortunately the plan, although it was officially admitted that it would have made a better machine than that which went into action at the Battle of Somme, was pigeon-holed and therefore not used at all in the evolution of tanks. Mr. de Mole served as a private in the 10th Battalion, Australian Imperial Force.

that: " he is entitled to the greatest credit for having made and reduced to practical shape as far back as the year 1912 a very brilliant invention which anticipated and in some respects surpassed that actually put into use in the year 1916. It was this claimant's misfortune and not his fault that his invention was in advance of his time, and failed to be appreciated and was put aside because the occasion for its use had not then arisen."

But in 1915, the tank still had a long way to go. There were still many who regarded it as useless. And there was still the problem of how it could be used most effectively. It took two years, and the Battle of Cambrai, before the military authorities were finally convinced.

The day of decision for " Big Willie " was January 29, 1916, when the first trials were held at Hatfield Park. With a great deal of secrecy, a battlefield obstacle course had been laid out on what was once a private golf course. The tank was brought by train to a nearby station, and driven to the park under cover of night. In front of selected War Office observers, it tackled the " official tests "—climbing a four-and-a-half feet high parapet, crossing a trench five feet wide, crawling through dug-outs, shell craters, and marshy streams. All these obstacles were overcome, and to the relief of the little band of pioneers who were present, the trial was judged a big success. By coincidence, the two men who had done so much in their individual ways to promote the idea, Swinton and Sueter, met each other for the first time at this trial. Sueter apparently commented that " three thousand of these vehicles should be ordered at once," to which a senior Army officer who had overheard retorted, " what's it got to do with this damned naval man? Who says we want three thousand tanks? " There were many in the War Office who were to agree with him.

A few days later, on February 2, " Big Willie " was again put through its paces before a larger audience of top-ranking generals, including Lord Kitchener, and political leaders like Lloyd George and Balfour. All went well—the tank even achieved the feat of crossing a ten-foot trench. But in spite of the enthusiasm of the ministers, who went for rides in it and who declared that if the military agreed, all the necessary money would be made available for developing the tank, Lord Kitchener remained sceptical. Even when the King himself came down on February 8 for a command performance and declared that " it would be a great asset to the Army possessing a large number," Kitchener regarded the machine as just a mechanical toy and considered that the war would never be won by such vehicles. The advocates of the tank, especially Swinton, Stern and Sueter and the design team of Tritton and Wilson, who had all argued and struggled so earnestly against the wall of obstinate bureaucracy, were naturally disappointed. They waited anxiously for the decision of the War Office and General Headquarters as to the numbers of tanks that would be ordered. They saw that to be of any real use in an offensive, large numbers would be required. They hoped for the order to make hundreds at the very least. When it came, the order was for only forty. Despite further arguments with the War Office, particularly by Swinton, they could only succeed in getting this raised to one hundred.

The politicians were not as short-sighted as the professional soldiers, however. Lloyd George was impressed by what he had seen, and from then on he took a great deal of interest in the new invention. A Tank Supply Committee was formed under the chairmanship of Stern, now promoted temporary Lieutenant Colonel, and Lloyd George was instrumental in getting this incorporated in the Ministry of Munitions. While work went ahead at the firms of Fosters and the Metropolitan Carriage Company to manufacture the hundred tanks ordered, experiments were made into the construction of a more advanced tank which would not only be proof against bullets but also field-gun shells.

The " Big Willie " prototype became known officially as the Mark 1. Equipped as it was with two heavy 6-pounder guns for offensive action, it was felt by Swinton and others that it lacked sufficient defence against an attack by the enemy infantry. It was proposed that each of these tanks should be accompanied by a similar vehicle which, however, would carry machine-guns instead of 6-pounders, to provide covering fire. This was agreed, and at the same time, with the help of Lloyd George, the initial order was increased to 150. As the tanks would move in pairs, the one with the 6-pounders being engaged in attacking enemy artillery while that carrying machine-guns would fight the infantry, they came to be known as " male " and " female " respectively. These definitions lasted until well after the end of the war.

It was obvious that a new force would have to be trained to man the tanks, and this responsibility was given to Swinton, the man who had done so much to develop the idea. He was not, however, to lead the force into battle. It was felt that command in France should be given to an officer with experience in warfare on the Western Front, and accordingly, Lieutenant Colonel Hugh Elles, a Royal Engineers officer, was chosen. Elles, later to become General Sir Hugh Elles, already had some knowledge of the new weapon. At the beginning of the year, as a major in the Operations Branch at General Headquarters, he had been sent to London by Sir Douglas Haig to make enquiries about the " caterpillar " project. Haig had just taken over as Commander-in-Chief from Sir John French, and read about the project in a memorandum on " Attack by Armour " written by Churchill. This had come about when Churchill, following his resignation from the Cabinet War Council after the Dardanelles failure, had gone to France for a period as a major in the Yeomanry. His memorandum had contained references to the tanks which were being developed in Britain, and this seemed to be the first that Haig had heard of them. He was interested, and so Elles was instructed to find out all he could about them, being present during the eventual trials at Hatfield Park.

The new force was first of all called the Tank Department, but for reasons of secrecy, this was changed to the Armoured Car Section of the Motor Machine-Gun Service. In the May of 1916 this was again changed to the Heavy Section, Machine-Gun Corps, and it was not until June of the following year that it became the Tank Corps. The prefix Royal was added after the war, with the decision to retain it as a permanent part of the British Army.

Swinton didn't think there would be any problem in recruiting for the new force—but he was wrong. As soon as a base had been established at Siberia Camp, Bisley—which was also the training school of the Motor Machine-Gun

Service—Swinton began casting about for recruits. The obvious choice to begin with was the Armoured Car Division of the Royal Naval Air Service. A few officers volunteered, those who knew something about the work on tanks, but as Swinton couldn't reveal to others the secret nature of the force, the expected rush to transfer did not occur. It was only by a slow process of persuasion and cajolery that he slowly built up the framework of an organisation which in its early days was known as " Fred Karno's army, the ragtime A.S.C.". General Headquarters had laid down that instead of large battalions, companies were to be the tactical units. This was the first of a long series of mistakes in making the most efficient use of tanks. Each of the six original companies had 25 tanks, and comprised 28 officers and 255 other ranks. Training was a make-shift affair. Few tanks were available in the early stages, and there were problems in finding a suitable range. And it also became apparent that a major difficulty was going to be in communications for controlling tanks in battle, and providing liaison between tanks and infantry. The wireless transmitters of the time had a limited range of three miles, and in any case could not be used while a tank was moving because of engine noise and vibration. The methods adopted were semaphore, with metal arms sticking out of the sides of the tanks, and morse-code flag signalling out of the trapdoor in the roof, but these were hardly ideal—as was to be found out later in battle.

Swinton had been giving a lot of thought as to how the tanks could best be used. In a memorandum " Notes on the Employment of Tanks ", he urged that they should be kept secret until a large number were available for one great attack, combined with an infantry assault. The element of surprise would also contribute to the chance of success. This was in February, 1916. But it was not until late in 1917, at the Battle of Cambrai, that the keypoints of Swinton's argument were taken into account. The memorandum was circulated within the War Office and General Headquarters, and to begin with, Haig expressed his complete approval— much to Swinton's relief. But then Haig went on to ask for some tanks to be made available for the Somme offensive he was planning and which was due to start on July 1. It was only a few months after the initial order for forty tanks, and showed a complete ignorance of the time necessary not only to build the vehicles but to train the crews. Having been lukewarm to the project all along, the planners at GHQ were now preparing to rush blindly into using tanks while the force was still ill-equipped and under-trained.

Swinton managed to hold off for a while the growing pressure to send tanks to France, and work on training the crews continued. On July 1, the Battle of the Somme began, and on the first day resulted in the heaviest loss of life ever encountered by the British Army in one day of fighting. Sixty thousand men were mowed down by machine-gun fire from defences which the Germans had been strengthening for the past year. Over one-third of these men were killed. As the battle raged on, the list of casualties mounted, to the accompaniment of growing criticism at home. Haig and his staff pressed even harder for the tanks, seeing in them a means of raising the morale of the troops and perhaps tilting the battle in their favour. Lloyd George, who was now War Minister, saw the danger of prematurely disclosing the new weapon and urged that, while 150 tanks might be made available in September, many more could be ready in the New Year if an order for them was immediately given by GHQ—enough perhaps to have a decisive effect. But Haig was still arrogantly confident that he could take the German positions by the autumn and insisted that even a few tanks would help, despite the disadvantage of revealing the secret weapon to the enemy. The French by now had seen something of the tanks, and were going ahead on production of their own. They also urged a delay until sufficient numbers were available. But Haig was adamant, and in mid-August, the first tanks arrived in France, shipped from Avonmouth to Le Havre and designated as " His Majesty's Landships "— H.M.L.S. An improvised training centre was established at Yvrench, near Abbeville, and by the end of August, two companies of fifty operational tanks and ten spares had arrived.

No clear plans had been laid down as to how the tanks should be used. Not only did the crews still lack sufficient training, but there was no time for any training at all in the co-operation necessary between tanks and infantry. In addition, the tanks were such a novelty that Yvrench became a kind of circus, in which the tanks were required to perform for the benefit of visiting staff officers from GHQ, taking up what little time was left for preparation.

It was under such circumstances, with untested machines, ill-trained crews, some of whom had never seen fighting before, and with only the scantiest understanding of what tactics might be employed, that tanks went into battle for the first time ever.

CHAPTER THREE

Baptism of Fire

THERE were three distinct phases to the Battle of the Somme. From July 1 to July 14, a heavy assault was made by the British Fourth Army, under General Sir Henry Rawlinson, along a fourteen-mile frontage north of the Somme, while at the same time the French Sixth Army attacked alongside on an eight-mile front. A week of intense artillery bombardment preceded the offensive, during which, in a single day, more ammunition was expended than could have been supplied by the British munitions industry in the first eleven months of the war. But the Germans had been given time to prepare their defences, and despite the severity of the attack, it failed. Only in a few localised sectors were slight advances made of up to one mile. The repulse was so severe and the loss of life so great that even the commanders most eager for this kind of warfare were shocked. During the next two months, the second phase of the battle consisted of a number of small attacks in which the British High Command pursued a strategy of attrition while planning another large-scale offensive for the middle of September. It was to take place along the front between Combles and Thiepval, and it was in this third and last phase of the battle that Haig decided, almost as an act of desperation in face of the enormous numbers of casualties suffered for little apparent gain, to throw in the tanks. As Rawlinson noted in his diary: " The chief (Haig) is anxious to have a gamble with all the available troops about September 15, with the object of breaking down German resistance and getting through to Bapaume."

Amongst those who disagreed with Haig's decision was Winston Churchill. As he later wrote in his war memoirs: " The ruthless desire for a decision at all costs led in September to a most improvident disclosure of the caterpillar vehicles. . . . Fifty of these engines, developed with great secrecy under the purposely misleading name of ' tanks ', had been completed. They arrived in France during the early stages of the Battle of the Somme for experimental purposes and the training of their crews. When it was seen how easily they crossed trenches and flattened out entanglements made for their trial behind the British lines, the force of the conception appealed to the directing minds of the Army. The Headquarters staff, hitherto lukewarm, now wished to use them at once in the battle. Mr. Lloyd George thought this employment of the new weapon in such small numbers premature. He informed me of the discussion which was proceeding. I was so shocked at the proposal to expose this tremendous secret to the enemy upon such a petty scale and as a mere make-weight to what I was sure could only be an indecisive operation, that I sought an interview with Mr. Asquith, of whom I was then a very definite opponent. The Prime Minister received me in the most friendly manner, and listened so patiently to my appeal that I thought I had succeeded in convincing him. But if this were so, he did not make his will effective, and on September 15, the first tanks, or ' large armoured cars ' as they were called in the Communique, went into action on the front of the Fourth Army attacking between the Combles ravine and Martinpuich."

The plan was to concentrate the weight of the Fourth Army against a three-mile sector on the right wing and try to break through the German defences, past Combles to Morval on the right, and through Flers and on to Gueude-court on the left. Forty-nine tanks were to take part in the attack from C Company under Major Holford-Walker and D Company under Major Summers. But instead of being used en masse for one big drive forward, they were spread thinly along the front. On the right, seventeen were allocated to the XIV Corps, ten with the Guards Division and seven with the 6th and 56th Divisions, the objectives being Ginchy and the Quadrilateral. On the left, eight tanks were allocated to the III Corps, to operate east of Martinpuich, and seventeen to the XV Corps. The remaining seven were attached to the reserve army, the 5th Canadian Corps, which was to attack between Pozieres and Martinpuich.

During the nights of September 13 and 14, the tanks, which had been camouflaged, were moved up into position under a cloak of great secrecy. Driving at night was extremely difficult, and white tapes were laid on the ground to guide the vehicles. But even during this preparation for the battle, the first casualties occurred. Moving in the pitch dark through mud and deep shell-holes, some of the tanks broke down or became irretrievably ditched. And one tank commander reported that his driver refused to go down a narrow sunken road that was strewn with dead bodies. In all, only 36 tanks reached their positions on the front line.

Equipping the tanks for battle order had been a major problem in itself. Each member of a crew, the officer and seven men, carried two gas helmets, one pair of goggles, and a leather " anti-bruise " helmet, as well as the usual equipment of a revolver, haversack, field-dressing kit, water-bottle and iron rations. All this was dumped on the floor of the tank as the crew came aboard. But there was more. In addition, each tank carried thirty tins of food, sixteen loafs, cheese, tea, sugar and milk; drums of engine oil and grease; a spare Vickers machine-gun and four replacement barrels, together with 33,000 rounds of ammunition; three flags for signalling (which were often lost amongst the stores just when they were needed); a lamp-signalling set; a crude telephonic contrivance with a hundred yards of cable which could be unwound as the tank advanced so that messages could be sent back; and a more reliable means of communication in the form of a basket of carrier-pigeons. The purpose of these was to release them at intervals as the tanks progressed through villages or other main points so that the battle commander could know how far the tanks had advanced. The tank commanders were supplied with little printed forms on rice paper, on which the messages were to be written in code and put into metal tubes attached to the pigeons' legs. They did not always work, however, and in some instances, where a tank commander had forgotten in the heat of battle to send the pigeons, he chose pigeon pie as a way of destroying the evidence.

Soon after 5 a.m. on the morning of September 15, after three days of incessant artillery bombardment which had worn the nerves of the tank crews lying close up to the batteries, the attack began with the advance of one solitary tank, D.1, under the command of Captain H. W. Mortimore. Zero hour for the main body was 6.20 a.m., but D 1 was ordered forward in a small preliminary operation to clear the enemy out of a pocket just ahead of the British front near Delville Wood. It was to be followed several minutes later by two companies of infantry. The effect on the Germans was electrifying. As the monstrous vehicle crawled towards them out of the gloom, its tail wheels bumping on the ground behind, shells firing from the turrets on either side, and machine-gun fire spitting out from the front, they took one look and fled in terror. It was a scene to be repeated all along the line at those positions in which tanks were used. The following description was written by a German newspaper correspondent who witnessed the first tanks in history to go into battle:

"When the German outposts crept out of their dug-outs in the mist of the morning and stretched their necks to look for the English, their blood was chilled in their veins. Mysterious monsters were crawling towards them over the craters. Stunned as if an earthquake had burst around them, they all rubbed their eyes, which were fascinated by the fabulous creatures.

"Their imaginations were still excited by the effects of the artillery bombardment. It was no wonder then that imagination got the better of these sorely tried men, who knew well enough that the enemy would try every means to destroy our steel wall of fragile human bodies. These men no longer knew what fear is. But here was some devilry which the brain of man had invented, with powerful mechanical forces, a mystery which rooted one to the ground because the intelligence could not grasp it, a fate before which one felt helpless.

" One stared and stared as if one had lost the power of one's limbs. The monsters approached slowly, hobbling, rolling and rocking, but they approached. Nothing impeded them: a supernatural force seemed to impel them on. Someone in the trenches said ' The devil is coming ', and the word was passed along the line like wild-fire.

" Suddenly tongues of flame leapt out of the armoured sides of the iron caterpillars. Shells whistled over our heads and the sound of machine-gun fire filled the air. The mysterious creature had yielded its secret as the English infantry rolled up in waves behind the ' devil's coaches '."

Inside the tanks, the crews worked manfully to steer and control their lumbering charges. There was very little room to move about in, most of the space being taken up by the large petrol engine in the centre. The interior was dimly lit by a naked electric light bulb, fed from the batteries. Vision to the outside was provided through narrow glass prisms, which had a habit of splintering into a driver's eyes when hit by a bullet. While riding across rough country, the crew were thrown from side to side as if weathering a stormy sea, and the noise was so intense that it was not unknown for a man's eardrums to split. Another hazard was from the choking fumes of the petrol engine, and if an exhaust pipe become damaged, a crew could easily be asphyxiated. The armour provided protection from the hail of machine-gun fire, but if a tank came within range of an enemy field-gun, it could be a death trap.

One of the first men to go into battle in a tank, William Divall, described the experience in a letter to his sister:

"As the tanks travel over the front trench, the troops rub their eyes in wonder at their strange, cube-impressionist coats of many colours. The deck of the tank rolls and pitches like a torpedo-boat in a storm. But we are all old hands—A.B.'s in fact—and we come safely through without sea-sickness.

" Hun bullets are rebounding from our tough sides like hail from a glass roof. We just crawl over the embankment, guns and all. It is not necessary to fire a single shot. Two or three Huns are brave enough to creep on the back of the tank from behind. We open a small trap-door and shoot them with a revolver.

" It is almost like playing hide-and-seek as we travel backward and forward along the trench.

" Inside the tank is the crew, strangely garbed, as becomes their strange craft, while around them is a complicated mass of machinery. We succeed in putting out two machine-gun emplacements, the guns of which have been worrying our infantry for some time. And now the action begins in earnest. The whole crew are at various guns, which break forth in a devastating fire.

" By this time the fumes from the hundreds of rounds which we have fired, with the heat from the engines and the waste petrol and oil, have made the air quite oppressive and uncomfortable to breathe in. However, those who go down to the land in tanks are accustomed to many strange sensations, which would make an ordinary mortal shudder.

" We make a fairly difficult target as our way lies between numerous tree trunks and battered stumps, also much barbed wire. We are battling bravely with the waves of earth we encounter. But thanks to our protective headgear, we come through it all.

" The last trench proves to be the worst, for just as we are crossing a large hole, our bus stops. I believe the sparking plugs have ceased to sparkle, and it is in a very awkward place as the tree stumps now prevent free traverse of our guns.

"And now the old bus is going strong again. Only just in time, for a large lyddite bomb bursts against the armoured jacket of my gun. The flare comes in through the port-hole, blinding me for a minute or so, while splinters strike my face. But my gun is still untouched, thanks to the armour-plate, and somehow seems to work much better.

" The Germans are now scattered in small parties. After a few short runs we find no more Huns to hunt, so as our objective, the wood, has been gained, we leave the scene to the infantry and find shelter from possible stray shells in a large hole which has been made by many shells.

"After a little exercise we start to overhaul the tanks and guns, in readiness for the next joy-ride. Then we snatch a few hours of sleep."

It was another member of his crew, Private A. Smith, who on September 15 won the first award to be presented to a member of the Tank Corps. He received the Military Medal for good work during the operations to the right of Delville Wood.

Other tanks met with varying success. Some broke down with engine trouble. Others became ditched and were attacked with hand-grenades by the Germans. Direct hits by enemy shells destroyed others. But the biggest success of the day was the assault on the village of Flers. Seven tanks began the attack in the centre of the XV Corps sector, with the objective of leading an English and New Zealand infantry division nearly a mile to the German strong point there. Four were knocked out by direct hits, but by 8.40 a.m., three had managed to push on to the outskirts of the village, smashing through machine-gun posts and breaking down fortified houses. One tank, D 17 (" Dinnaken ") under the command of Captain Hastie, drove right through the village, followed by a party of infantry. The scene was witnessed by an observer in a British aircraft overhead, and was widely reported by the British Press in the words, "A tank is walking up the High Street of Flers with the British Army cheering behind." For now the secret was out, and the public came to hear about tanks for the first time. In their enthusiasm, newspapers called them " Diplodocus Galumphants " or " Polychromatic Toads " or " flat-footed monsters that perform the most astonishing feats of agility as they advance, spouting flames from every side ". *Punch* magazine had its own comment to make, and in the September issue described the coming of the tank as " a most humorous and formidable addition to the fauna of the battlefield—half battleship and half caterpillar—which has given the Germans the surprise of their lives, a surprise all the more effective for being sudden and complete. As an officer at the front writes to a friend: ' These animals look so dreadfully competent, I am sure they can swim '."

But perhaps the most moving tributes came from the battle-weary infantrymen, who had at last found a friend who could shield them from the deadly partnership of wire and machine-gun. A wounded London Territorial said: " ' Old Mother Hubbard ' they called her and lots of other funny names as well. She looked like a pantomime animal or a walking ship with iron sides moving along, very slowly, apparently all on her own, and with none of her crew visible. There she was, groanin' and gruntin' along, pokin' her nose here and there, stopping now and then as if she was not sure of the road, and then going on, very slow but over everything.

" It was her slowness that scared us as much as anything, and the way she shook her wicked old head and stopped to cough. It was a circus—my word! I only saw her for about ten minutes. She came bumping out of the fog at one end of the line and bumped into it again at the other. The last I saw of her was when she was nosing down a shell crater like a great big hippopotamus with a crowd of Tommies cheering behind."

By the afternoon, the villages of Martinpuich and Courcelette had also been captured and the line had advanced to within attacking distance of the strong line of defence in front of Morval, Les Boeufs and Gueudecourt. The whole operation was a considerable success, particularly after the preceding failures, and Haig was able to report: " The result of the fighting of September 15 and following days was a gain more considerable than any which had attended our arms in the course of a single operation since the commencement of the offensive. In the course of one day's fighting we had broken through two of the enemy's main defensive systems and had advanced on a front of over six miles to an average depth of a mile. In the course of this advance we had taken three large villages, each powerfully organised for prolonged resistance. . . . All this had been accomplished with a small number of casualties in comparison with the troops employed. The total number of prisoners taken by us amounted to over 4,000, including 127 officers."

A small but brilliant success, and Haig gave full credit to the tanks. But as the days wore on, the tanks were one by one knocked out of the battle, either by shells or engine breakdowns or ditching in shell-craters. A few helped groups of infantry as the fighting dragged on until mid-November, and it was during these sporadic operations that the first tank D.S.O. was won, by 2nd Lieutenant Charles Storey on September 26 while clearing up trenches in the region of Gueudecourt. He worked his way up and down each trench until all his petrol was exhausted and only two of the crew were unwounded, and was responsible for taking nearly 300 prisoners. A second D.S.O. was won by Captain (later Major General) Frederick E. Hotblack a few weeks later during the fighting between Beaumont-Hamel and Beaucourt. Only one tank was available, and in order to guide it into position for the attack on the morning of November 18, Hotblack as Reconnaissance Officer had laid tape over the ground. Just before dawn, however, it began to snow and the white tape was obliterated. As the only man who had reconnoitred that particular piece of ground, Hotblack volunteered to lead the tank into action on foot. He did so, walking in front of the tank while bullets hailed round him. Somehow, none of them found their mark, and Hotblack returned to the British trenches while the tank blazed away at the Germans in the redoubt in front. Then it became necessary to bring the tank back for duties in another sector. But there was no way of communicating with the crew, and so Hotblack returned to the field of fire and once more guided the tank, this time back to the British line. Again, he was miraculously not hit. This courageous incident had far-reaching results, for later in the year, Hotblack was transferred to the Tank Corps to establish a Reconnaissance Branch, and he was considerably involved in the preparations for Cambrai.

This action at Beaumont-Hamel marked the end of fighting on the Somme for that year. By the time that fighting petered out in heavy snow storms and frozen mud, it had become apparent that overall, the Battle of the Somme had been a strategic defeat. The small part played by the tanks, however successful on a local scale, was overlooked in the general sense of failure. The troops at the front, both British and German, had no doubt as to the value of the new weapon. In a secret instruction to his units, the Chief of the German 3rd Army Group had reminded his men that they must defend every inch of ground to the last man against an enemy which " in the latest fighting have employed new engines of war as cruel as they are effective ". But the potentialities of the tank were lost to the German High Command, just as they were to the British. General Erich Ludendorff, virtually the Commander-in-Chief of the German armies although holding the misleading title of Quarter-Master General, tended to dismiss the tank as an impractical weapon, and it was not until the Battle of Cambrai a year later that he took the threat seriously. Although production of tanks was begun in Germany, it was too late to catch up on the lead in design which Britain had achieved. The secret which, to the consternation of Churchill and others, was prematurely revealed at the Somme turned out to be a damp squib as far as the Germans were concerned. They ignored the lesson —luckily for the Allies. But the British High Command made the same mistake. Doubts which many staff officers had previously expressed as to the value of tanks turned to scorn. Instead of trying to plan an intelligent use of the superior weapon that had been put into their hands, the military leaders could only make carping criticisms of minor details. They conveniently forgot that it was they who had ordered so few tanks to be built in the first place, and that it was Haig's own decision, against the advice of those who were beginning to understand the nature of tank warfare, to order them into battle before their crews had been properly trained and before they were available in sufficient numbers to make a worthwhile contribution.

Haig's reaction, however, was more favourable than that of his senior staff officers, and it was at his personal request, following a visit to General Headquarters by Swinton, that an additional 1,000 tanks should be built, 100 of the Mark I type and the others of better design with heavier armour. But even this was not to go unchallenged. On October 10, Stern received an official instruction from the Army Council, cancelling the order. Stern wrote of this episode afterwards : " This sudden cancellation came as a thunderbolt. I immediately went to see Mr. Lloyd George, the Secretary of State for War. He said that he had heard nothing of the instruction. I told him that I had, with enormous difficulty, started swinging this huge weight (the tank building programme) and that I could not possibly stop it now. Sir William Robertson, Chief of the Imperial General Staff, then appeared, and Mr. Lloyd George said he did not understand how this order could be cancelled without his knowledge, since he was President of the Army Council. . . .

" The order for the production of 1,000 tanks was reinstated next day."

Soon afterwards, Stern was appointed Director-General of the Department of Mechanical Warfare Supply, with Sir E. H. Tennyson d'Eyncourt and the Hon. Sir Charles Parsons as chief technical advisers, Sir William Tritton as Director of Construction, and Major Wilson Director of Engineering. In order to keep the factories going, 150 of the Mark I's were to be built, then fifty each of Mark II and Mark III, although these differed only by having no tail wheels, thicker armour, and new cast-iron rollers. The remainder of the order was to be made up of the new Mark IVs, on which design work had just finished. These incorporated a number of changes. Lewis guns were mounted, instead of the Hotchkiss. The petrol tank was to be at the back instead of inside the tank. There was thicker armour all round, and the side turrets, which had previously been carried to the battlefield separately on trucks, were so constructed that they could swing inside the tanks when travelling by rail.

At about this time, the Russian Government asked not only for a supply of tanks, but also for the plans. Stern was strongly opposed to this, believing it very likely that the request had really come from Germany, but the War Office insisted that the plans should be passed over. So Stern had a set drawn up showing incorrect details. " I am convinced that they found their way into the hands of the German General Staff," he wrote. If they did, which is not likely, then the Germans took little notice of them. For, as early as 1912, the European representative of the Holt Tractor Company, a man called Steiner, had tried to interest the German High Command in his company's tracked vehicles. The military authorities returned the designs with the comment that there was no military application for such a vehicle. In 1916, after the tanks had appeared at the Somme, the Germans began a frantic search for Steiner and his designs, and began drawing up plans for tanks of their own.

Meanwhile, work was going ahead on the vital task of training the tank crews. In Britain, a move was made to a fresh training ground at Bovington, in Dorset, and this was to be the home of tanks ever afterwards. But at the same time, Swinton, who had done so much to father the cause of tanks, was transferred to duties in the War Cabinet Secretariat and his place taken by Brigadier General F. Gore Anley. It was a move deeply resented by the newly formed Corps, who felt Swinton had been replaced through political motives. Not until 1934 was Swinton's work officially recognised, when he was chosen to be Colonel-Commandant of what had then become the Royal Tank Corps.

CHAPTER FOUR

The Beginnings of the Tank Corps

IN France, the organisation of the Heavy Branch—Machine Gun Corps (it was not until July 1917 that it became the Tank Corps) was getting under way amidst all the chaos and confusion one might have expected in the forming of a completely new fighting arm. On November 18, after the Battle of the Somme, the little force moved to Bermicourt, a small village near St. Pol on the road from Montreuil to Arras, and General Elles set up his headquarters in the large, rambling Bermicourt Chateau. What was left of the original companies was formed into four battalions, keeping the same letters A, B, C and D. (The two which had been the first to go into battle, C and D, were later formed into the 1st Brigade.) Work started on training new recruits. The hard core of instructors were those who had seen action in the Battle of the Somme. Such men were suddenly veteran tankers. Captain Hotblack, after his experience in leading a tank into battle, found himself regarded as something of an expert and he became the Corps Intelligence Officer, responsible for instructing others in tank reconnaissance work. Officers and men volunteered from a variety of other units, for no matter what General Headquarters thought about tanks, they were popular with those who had seen them in action at the front. There were men from the cavalry and the infantry, gunners from the Machine Gun Corps, airmen from the Royal Flying Corps, and even seamen from the Navy and the Royal Naval Air Service. There was at

Bermicourt the oddest collection of uniforms ever seen at any one place—riding breeches, Scottish kilts, naval and air force blue.

Something of the atmosphere during those early, hectic days at Bermicourt was described by Major W. H. L. Watson, who early in 1917 was posted to the Corps to take command of a company of tanks.

" The usual difficulties and delays had occurred in assembling the battalions," he wrote. " Rations were short. There was no equipment. The billets were bad. Necessaries such as camp kettles could not be obtained.

" The men were of three classes. First came the ' old tankers ', those who had been trained with the original companies. They had been drawn for the most part from the Army Service Corps—Motor Transport. They were excellent tank mechanics. Then came the motor machine-gunners, smart fellows without much experience of active operations. The vast majority of officers and men were volunteers from the infantry—disciplined fighting men.

" On parade, the company looked a motley crew, as indeed it was. Men from different battalions knew different drill. Some of the less combatant corps know no drill at all.

" The company lived in a rambling hospice, built around a large courtyard. The original inhabitants consisted of nuns and thirty or forty aged and infirm men who, from their habits and appearance, we judged to be consumptives.

" Training continued until the middle of March. Prospective tank drivers tramped every morning to the Tank Park, or ' Tankodrome ' as it was called—a couple of large fields in which workshops had been erected, some trenches dug, and a few shell-craters blown. The Tankodrome was naturally a sea of mud. Perhaps the mud was of a curious kind— perhaps the mixture of petrol and oil with the mud was poisonous. Most of the officers and men working in the Tankodrome suffered periodically from painful and ugly sores, which often spread over the body from the face. We were never free from them while we were at ' Blangy '."

The men were trained in the elements of tank driving and

tank maintenance in the appalling winter of snow, rain and mud, while officers' courses were held at Bermicourt. Very few tanks were available for instruction, and so dummy tanks were provided.

"Imagine a large box of canvas stretched on a wooden frame," Major Watson goes on to describe the device. "There is no top or bottom, it is about 6 feet high, 8 feet long and 5 feet wide. Little slits were made in the canvas to represent the loopholes of a tank. Six men carried and moved each dummy, lifting it by the cross-pieces of the framework. For our sins we were issued with eight of these abominations.

"We started with a crew of officers to encourage the men, and the first dummy tank waddled out of the gate. It was immediately surrounded by a mob of cheering children, who thought it was an imitation dragon or something out of a circus. It was led away from the road to avoid hurting the feelings of the crew and to safeguard the ears and morals of the children. After colliding with the corner of a house, it endeavoured to walk down the side of a railway cutting. Nobody was hurt, but a fresh crew was necessary. It regained the road when a small man in the middle, who had not been able to see anything, stumbled and fell. The dummy tank was sent back to the carpenters for repairs.

"We persevered with those dummy tanks. The men hated them. They were heavy, awkward, and produced much childish laughter. In another company, a crew walked over a steep place and a man broke his leg. The dummies became less and less mobile. The signallers practised from them, and they were used by the visual training experts. One company commander mounted them on waggons drawn by mules. The crews were tucked in with their Lewis guns, and each contraption, a cross between a fire-engine and a triumphal car in the Lord Mayor's Show, would gallop past targets which the gunners would recklessly endeavour to hit."

Eventually, and not entirely by accident, the dummies were broken up and the canvas and wood used for other purposes. As more tanks became available, the crews were able to train with the real thing. But even this had its problems for new recruits, some of whom had never seen a tank before. A special practice course was laid out over old trenches and shell craters. Sergeant Littledale, a new recruit to the Tank Corps at that time, described his experience in an article written after the war:

" There is not one of us who will ever forget his first ride—the crawling in at the sides, the discovery that the height did not permit a man of medium stature to stand erect, the sudden starting of the engine, the roar of it all when the throttle opened, the jolt forward, and the sliding through the mud that followed, until at last we came to the ' jump ' which had been prepared. Then came the forward motion, which suddenly threw us off our feet and caused us to stretch trusting hands towards the nearest object —usually, at first, a hot pipe through which the water from the cylinder jacket flowed to the radiator. So, down and down and down, the throttle almost closed, the engine just ' ticking over ', until at last the bottom was reached, and as the power was turned full on, the tank raised herself to the incline, like a ship rising on a wave, and we were all jolted the other way, only to clutch again frantically for things which were hot and burned, until at last, with a swing over the top, we gained level ground. And in that moment we discovered that the trenches and the mud and the rain and the shells and the daily curse of bully beef had not killed everything within, for there came to us a thrill of happiness in that we were to sail over stranger seas than man had ever crossed, and set out on a great adventure."

And here is another description of that first meeting with a tank by Richard Haig:

" We looked around the little chamber with eager curiosity. Our first thought was that seven men and an officer could never do any work in such a confined space. Eight of us were at present jammed in here, but we were standing still. When it came to going into action and moving around inside the tank, it would be impossible. There was no room even to pass one another, so we thought. In front are two stiff seats, one for the officer and one for the driver. Two narrow slits serve as portholes through which we looked ahead. In front of the officer is a map-board and gun-mounting. Down the middle of the tank is the powerful petrol engine, part of it covered with a hood, and along each side a narrow passage along which a man can slide from the officer's and driver's seat back to the mechanism at the rear. There are four gun turrets, two each side. There is also a place for a gun in the rear, but this is rarely used. ' Willies ' do not often turn tail and flee.

"Along the steel walls are numberless ingenious little cupboards in which stores and ammunition cases are stacked high. Every bit of space is utilised. Electric bulbs light the interior. Beside the driver are the engine levers. Behind the engine are the secondary gears by which the machine is turned in any direction. All action inside is directed by signals, for when the tank moves the noise is such as to drown a man's voice."

Many of the ideas behind the training at Bermicourt were due to a man who was later to become one of, if not the world's greatest authority on tank tactics and strategy. In December 1916, Major (later Major General) J. F. C. Fuller joined the Tank Corps from the Oxfordshire and Buckinghamshire Light Infantry. His appointment was that of chief general staff officer. To begin with, he shared the doubts of so many other infantry officers as to the value of tanks, but once he had seen them at close quarters, he quickly became their most ardent advocate. It was an enthusiasm that was to last for the rest of his life. His writings on the theory of tank warfare between the two world wars established for him a world-wide reputation. He was far ahead of the general thought of his time. But other countries appreciated his genius, particularly Germany. It was on the basis of his tactics that the German staff colleges trained their tank commanders in the 1930s, resulting in much of their great success with tanks at the beginning of the Second World War.

Fuller's first manual of tank tactics was written early in 1917. In it, he emphasised the necessity for " surprise " in any attack, and artillery bombardment beforehand should be reduced to a minimum, certainly not more than 48 hours. This was heresy to the artillery experts at General Headquarters, and the pamphlet was immediately withdrawn from circulation. It was the first of a long series of arguments that Fuller was to have with traditionally-minded artillerymen who thought their efforts with massive bombardment the only means of softening up the enemy and breaking down the wire barriers, regardless of the warning of an attack that this gave.

In England, work was going ahead on the tank building programme, against the usual difficulties put in its way by the War Office. Modifications were made to the Mark I tank, which included the abolition of the tail-wheels that had proved so vulnerable at the Somme. Hotchkiss machine-guns were replaced by Lewis guns. These modificaitons resulted in fifty each of a Mark II and Mark III being built, but there was very little difference between these and the original Mark I. It was with the Mark IV, originally designed by Major Wilson at the end of 1916 and first delivered to France in April, 1917, that the biggest step forward was made. The tracks, rollers and links were all of a new and heavier design. Petrol was carried in a 60-gallon armoured container mounted on the back of the tank, instead of being carried inside the driver's compartment as with the Mark I. The armour was greatly improved to resist the German armour-piercing bullet. The dangerous glass prisms which shattered so easily were removed, and now the driver and the gunners looked out through pinholes in the steel plate. In order to give assistance if a tank became ditched, as happened so frequently at the Somme, each vehicle was equipped on top with a square wooden beam which, when required, could be carried by the tracks round and under the tank to give it a lift to climb out.

Production of the Mark IV went ahead slowly—too slowly. On July 16, Churchill joined the new government of Lloyd George as Minister of Munitions. What he found there appalled him. Each of the armed services was fighting to obtain every ton of steel and freight for itself in a free-for-all in which the Royal Navy seemed to come off best. The politicians were understandably worried about the effects of U-boat warfare against British shipping. But Churchill was determined to do all he could for the tanks in which he believed so vehemently. In "The World Crisis", he wrote:

"In the fight to secure a handful of steel plates for the tank programme, we encountered at first the odious statement, 'but the Army doesn't want any more—General Headquarters does not rank them very high in their priorities.'

"The War Cabinet, and particularly the Prime Minister, always took a great interest in tanks . . . But at the same time they ruled that the Admiralty demand for ship plates for the Mercantile Marine, which was several hundred times greater than would ever be needed for tanks, should retain their super-priority. Since we were unable to overcome Sir Eric Geddes (Head of the Admiralty Board) by reason, it became necessary to gorge him with ship plates. This the Munitions Council and Sir John Hunter's steel department soon succeeded in doing. The Admiralty merchant shipbuilding programme of three million tons in 12 months proved far beyond even their very great and splendid activities. We watched with unsleeping attention the accumulations which soon began of ship plates in every yard. Not until the moment was ripe did we unmask the guilty fact. The effect was decisive. The proud department condescended to parley, and eventually the modest requirements of the tank programme were satisfied."

Churchill commented that, "the one great blot upon the high economy of the British war effort in the last year of the struggle was the undue and unwarrantable inroads upon the common fund made by the Admiralty."

At General Headquarters in France, the campaigns for the spring of 1917 were being planned. But then came the German's strategic withdrawal to the Hindenburg Line. The British Fourth and Fifth Armies laboriously followed up through the devastated area, while Allenby's Third Army held the sector at Arras, where the Hindenburg Line ended.

It was here that there was seen to be a chance for a surprise attack, before the Germans could bring up reserves: an attack which could turn the flank of the new Line by breaking through the defences to the North. This was partially successful at Vimy and Chemin des Dames. But the concept of surprise was not really possible when each attack had to be preceded by weeks of artillery bombardment. An attack by massed tanks might have achieved the required result, but there were just not enough tanks available. As many as 240 of the new Mark IVs had been promised for the spring offensive, but because of indecision over the orders in France and delays in supply deliveries in England, none arrived until late in April. Only sixty of the Mark I and Mark II tanks, vulnerable to armour-piercing bullets, were available for the battle.

By now, the tank battalions had been formed into brigades. The original C and D Battalions became 1st Brigade, under the command of Lieutenant Colonel C. D'A. B. S. Baker-Carr; A and B Battalions were formed into the 2nd Brigade, under Lieutenant Colonel A. Courage; and later, a 3rd Brigade was formed from new battalions arriving from Bovington.

It was the 1st Brigade that was assigned to take part in the Battle of Arras. But instead of the sixty tanks being massed together for one big strike forward, they were once again spread thinly along the entire front. Forty were divided between the three corps of the Third Army, sixteen to each of VI and VII Corps attacking south of the River Scarpe, and eight to the XVII Corps north of the river. Another eight tanks were to co-operate with the Canadian Corps attack on Vimy Ridge, and the remaining twelve to operate in the region of Lagnicourt, near Bullecourt, with the Fifth Army.

The offensive began on April 9—Easter Monday. But even before this, some of the tanks were in trouble. During the previous night, while moving up into position, C Battalion had taken a short cut across a valley near Achicourt, south of Arras. A causeway of brushwood and railway sleepers was laid across the worst sections of ground, and it was hoped that the remaining area would be hard enough to bear the weight of the tanks. But it turned out to be only a thin crust over a deep bog, which broke when the column was only half-way across. In the darkness, one tank after another floundered into the morass until six were engulfed. That left only 26 tanks to help in the main attack south of the Scarpe.

The offensive opened successfully—certainly far better than on the Somme the previous year. The German Front-line defence system was captured within an hour. But then German reserves were brought up, and despite heavy fighting, no real advantage could be taken of the breakthrough.

On ground that had been churned up during the heavy artillery bombardment and made worse by rain and snow, the tanks as a whole were not able to contribute very much. There were a number of individual successes. Four tanks of D Battalion helped to capture the strongly fortified village of Neuville-Vitasse. Eighteen of C and D Battalions were used in the successful attacks on Telegraph Hill and the stronghold called " The Harp ", although all but four became bogged in the shell-torn trenches or were put out of action by enemy fire. One tank helped in the capture of Tilloy village. But most of the others either ditched or were knocked out at an early stage, and the eight which were to assist the Canadian Corps take Vimy Ridge became bogged down in the mud before they could even take part in any fighting. Only one important achievement could be credited to the tanks, and that was the capture of Manchy-le-Preux, due to three tanks of C Battalion. They managed to force their way into the village on their own and had the garrison subdued by the time the infantry arrived.

It was not a very successful day for the tanks—but worse was to come. On April 11, the 4th Australian Division joined in the offensive with an attack on Bullecourt, and eleven tanks of D Battalion were allotted to help in the effort. The attack was to have taken place on the dawn of April 10 without any previous artillery bombardment. The idea was for

the tanks to steal up to the Hindenburg Line and take the
enemy by surprise, crushing down the wire for the infantry
to pass through. But due to a heavy snowstorm, the tanks were
late in arriving and the attack had to be cancelled—although
not before the Australian infantry had suffered a considerable number of casualties. This had already shaken the confidence of the Australians in the tanks, but their doubts were
overruled by the Fifth Army commander, General Sir Hubert
Gough, who insisted that the attack should be carried out on
the following morning. The result was a disaster. The day
dawned bright and clear, and against the whiteness of the
newly fallen snow, the tanks stood out as easy targets. The
attempt on the previous morning had given the Germans
warning, and they were ready for them. The Australian infantry, following in lines behind the tanks, also made perfect artillery targets. Nine of the eleven tanks were knocked
out by direct hits before they even reached their objectives,
and the Australians suffered heavy losses. The 4th Brigade
lost 2,250 officers and men out of 3,000. The remaining two
tanks were captured by the Germans and enabled them to
examine the machines closely for the first time. In particular, they could see how effective were their armour-piercing
bullets. Luckily, the tanks were of the Mark I vintage, and
the Germans weren't to know that the Mark IV which was
just beginning to arrive in France was armoured against this
bullet. A German Order was issued that every man should
be provided with five rounds of this " K " ammunition, and
every machine-gun with several hundred, and these caused
heavy casualties amongst tank crews as long as the Mark I
was used.

Bullecourt was a disaster and a tragedy, and caused great
distrust of the tanks among the Australians. They felt the
tanks had " let them down ". This attitude persisted throughout the ranks of the Australian Imperial Force until 1918,
when their confidence was restored at the Battle of Hamel.

In later, limited battles during the Arras offensive, small
pockets of tanks were used. But fighting was extremely difficult over that kind of terrain, and those that did not break

down became victims of the armour-piercing bullet. One played a decisive part in the capture of Roeux by the 51st Division, and in the same action, Sergeant J. Noel, a member of the crew of another tank, won the D.C.M. when he took over command after his officer had been wounded. Finally, on May 3, another attack was made on Bullecourt, this time using thirteen tanks, but it was hardly more successful than the first, and the casualties among both the tank crews and the infantry were, relative to the numbers involved, amongst the highest of any battle of the war.

This was the last action at Arras for the Tank Corps. The 1st Brigade—or what was left of it, for there was hardly an unwounded man among the crews—returned to Bermicourt. They had fought under extremely difficult conditions and had been given tasks little suited to tanks. Nevertheless, in some situations they had proved their worth, and at least had pointed to a better way of being used in the future. But it was to be some months before they were to have their chance, at Cambrai. First, they had to suffer the worst ordeal of all in Flanders, at the Third Battle of Ypres.

The battlefields of Flanders could not have been more unsuitable for tanks. It was here that artillery bombardment reached its highest peak of the war, and the ground was reduced to swampland and quagmire. Nevertheless, it was into such impossible conditions that the tanks were sent. The first task was given to the 2nd Brigade—the attack on Messines Ridge which overlooked the Ypres Salient. It was intended to be a prelude to the main summer offensive which Haig had been planning ever since he became Commander-in-Chief in December, 1915. The French tanks had already made their debut by this time, during the opening of the Champagne offensive on April 16. But only a little over a hundred were available, instead of the 800 expected, and it soon became apparent that they were extremely vulnerable to enemy artillery fire and poor performers. Here again, there was little co-ordination between the tanks and the infantry. The whole battle became a fiasco, resulting in outbreaks of mutiny in the French Army, and as a result the French decided to suspend work on the medium size Schneider tank and to concentrate on the new Renault light tank.

The Battle of Messines began on June 7. The Tank Corps had at last begun to receive deliveries of the new Mark IV and it was these tanks which were allocated to 2nd Brigade, the Mark I and Mark IIs being used only as supply vehicles. As it happened, the Messines attack was a great success, largely due to the explosion of huge mines which had been laid in tunnels deep under the German Front lines and first class siege line preparations. The tanks were hardly needed, but they did give valuable support to the infantry. Of the forty which advanced in the first assault, twenty-five reached the final objective on the ridge. And at Messines village it-self, where New Zealand infantry were under heavy fire, it was due to the efforts of a tank in crashing through to the village that the Germans eventually surrendered.

It was later, during the main offensive in Flanders which began on the last day of July, that the tanks suffered their biggest casualties. Over 200 were brought up to the Ypres area. By the time the campaign ended, on November 6, with the capture of the ruins of Passchendaele, few of these remained in one piece. Most had been put out of action after sinking deep into the mud and presenting sitting targets for enemy fire. So many were knocked out on the Menin Road that it became known as the " tank graveyard." Those three months of bloody fighting had gained no more than a total advance of four miles at a cost of nearly 400,000 casualties.

The prestige and reputation of Britain's war leaders, particularly of Haig, reached their lowest ebb after the summer offensive in Flanders. The third year of the war had opened full of promise for the Allies, but it was ending as a year of failure and disillusionment. The revolution in Russia had weakened the Eastern Front and it was apparent that effective Russian participation in the war could not be relied upon. The announcement, in April, of America's entry into the war would in time restore the balance, but it would be many months before this power could be made effective. Meanwhile, the German submarine campaign was scoring a striking success against British shipping, and this, in conjunction with the increasing number of air raids, threatened to starve Britain into an ignominious surrender. At Caporetto, on October 24, the Germans had scored a dramatic victory over the Italian army and British troops had to be rushed to Italy's aid, troops already wearied by the attacks on the Western Front which had proved not only unsuccessful but an appalling waste of men and arms.

It was of Haig and his chief of staff, Lieutenant General Sir Lancelot Kiggell, that Fuller wrote after the war:

" They considered that their doctrine of war was infallible, that the wearing battle must succeed if sufficient reinforcements were forthcoming and that as ultimately this doctrine demands an onslaught of cavalrymen, without cavalry the battle could not be won. The truth I believe is that long before the outbreak of war their brains had become ossified and that even the terrible circumstances of this battle (the Somme) would not penetrate the historic concrete in which they were encased. If this is not the true explanation, then Haig and Kiggell must have been two of the greatest knaves in the history of war, which I cannot believe."

Unfortunately, and however unfair it was, much of the criticism at the time of the general conduct of the war on the Western Front rubbed off against the tanks as well. And within the military hierarchy itself, although some divisional commanders reported favourably on the way they had supported the infantry, the general tendency, especially in higher command, was either to blame the tanks for the failure or regard them as useless weapons. As one Army Commander reasoned:

" One, tanks are unable to negotiate bad ground; two, the ground on a battlefield will always be bad; three, therefore tanks are no good on a battlefield."

The disparaging reports from General Headquarters found ready listeners at the War Office in London and, for a while, it seemed that the fate of the new Corps hung in the balance. It was common talk among military circles that tanks were going to be abolished. No matter that they had been ordered to perform in impossible conditions. No matter that Fuller and others at Tank Headquarters had predicted the dismal results under such conditions. Someone or something had to be blamed, and the tanks were a convenient scapegoat.

Surprisingly, perhaps, the Tank Corps received unexpected support from Haig. He knew more than anyone of the difficulties that had been put in the way of the Corps. He knew of the indecision over orders, the delays created by some of his critical officers, the suggestions which had been ignored as to how the tanks should be used. In his official Despatch after Third Ypres, he stated:

" Although throughout the major part of the Ypres battle, and especially in its later stages, the condition of the ground made the use of tanks difficult or impossible, yet whenever circumstances were in any way favourable, and even when they were not, very gallant and valuable work has been accomplished by tank commanders and crews on a great number of occasions. Long before the conclusion of the Flanders offensive these new instruments had proved their worth, and amply justified the labour, material and personnel diverted to their construction and development."

They were fair words. But the Tank Corps knew all about the problems. As a result of experience in the various battles, General Elles and his staff at Tank Headquarters had issued notes on the limitations of tanks. One of these listed the following:

a) weight makes for heavy going on heavily shelled wet ground;

b) speed over heavily shelled ground is only 10 yards a minute, and over unshelled ground from 1 to 5 m.p.h.;

c) difficulty of maintaining direction because of limited visibility;

d) exhaustion of crews due to heat and difficulties of driving.

This led to the following conclusions:

(i) if the ground has been heavily shelled, tanks will cross slowly, but if soaked with rain as well, the majority will not cross at all. To employ tanks in such conditions is to throw them away (e.g. tanks with the First Army operating against Vimy Ridge);

(ii) tanks cannot keep up with infantry until the zone of heavy bombardment is crossed. This zone is about 3,000 yards deep. It is impossible for tanks to co-operate in initial attacks in this zone;

(iii) tanks cannot proceed certainly during dark or twilight over ground which is intersected with trenches or shelled unless this has been reconnoitred;

(iv) mist and smoke will bring tanks almost to a standstill; so will dust, not only that thrown up by shells but that picked up by the tracks and blown into the face of the driver. (Here it was suggested that goggles should be provided for driver and officer);

(v) on a hot day the temperature inside the tanks rises to 120° in the shade. This excessive heat causes vomiting and exhaustion. Eight hours continual work is the limit of the crew's endurance, after which the men require 48 hours' rest;

(vi) a tank's circuit of action is about 8 miles;

(vii) tanks cannot operate through thickly wooded country or over ground covered with tree stumps. Tank unit commanders are the best judges of the ground they can cover; infantry commanders should be brought to realise this;

(viii) tanks cannot pass through barrages with safety. High explosive barrages are the most dangerous. In a Creeping barrage, H.E. should not be mixed with shrapnel. The progress of tanks would be facilitated if heavy artillery and trench motors were not used on the enemy's trench system;

(ix) infantry should be warned not to bunch behind the tanks, and not to be led off their objectives if the tanks are moving diagonally across their front;

(x) the greatest assistance in the location of tanks during a battle is that provided by the Royal Flying Corps. When a tank is ditched, a white square should be spread on top to notify aeroplanes that a tank has broken down.

These and other points were part of the mass of information about the use of tanks which the Tank Corps was collecting. It was information gained from bitter experience for by the summer of 1917, the crews knew they were being strategically mis-used. In all the battles in which they had fought, the tanks had been divided up in ones and twos amongst the infantry units, and the long artillery bombardment which preceded every battle prevented any element of surprise. No tank battle as such had been fought; a battle in which the tanks would be used on a large scale as the main weapon of assault; and preferably without warning the enemy beforehand. A prime requirement for such a battle was hard, firm ground over which to operate, instead of cratered swamplands of the kind that had proved so disastrous in Flanders.

But events were moving forward, and it was not long before such a ground was found and the Tank Corps was to have a chance to prove itself. The vital test was to take place at Cambrai.

CHAPTER FIVE

Plan of Battle

IT was on August 3, 1917, that Fuller, now promoted Lieutenant Colonel in his capacity as chief General Staff Officer of the Tank Corps, returned to the Corps headquarters at Bermicourt after visiting the Flanders front. The atmosphere in the chateau was gloomy and oppressive. Most of the officers and crews had already been sent to Flanders, together with all the available tanks, and the large, stone-flagged rooms were practically deserted. When Fuller sat down to discuss the situation with General Elles, his grim expression reflected the suffering and the appalling conditions he had witnessed on the battlefield of Ypres.

" They're simply throwing the tanks away," he said angrily. " First they shell the area until the ground is churned up into a swamp. Then they send the tanks in. How can they be expected to work in such conditions? They just sink in the mud and become sitting targets for the German artillery."

" That's what we've been telling GHQ since the campaign started," Elles replied. " But what about morale? "

" It's not good. The infantry think the tanks are a failure. And even the tank crews feel they're being wasted."

The two men sat in silence for a long time. Both were tall and sparsely built, Elles in many ways the epitome of the English officer, handsome, conventional but with a touch of panache in his character. He was a brave soldier, but as events in his later career were to prove, he tended to alter his opinions in accordance with the current vogue, and was always concerned with retaining his popularity. Fuller, at 39, was the older by two years. He was sometimes gruff and certainly had no compunction about airing his views. His almost accidental involvement with the tanks changed his life. From then on, he was a devoted supporter of the new weapon. They gave his imagination full scope, and even now he was revealing that brilliance of mind for which he would later be hailed as a military genius.

Outside the lonely chateau, the late summer rain continued its incessant downpour. Fuller was well aware of what the rain would be doing to the mud of Flanders.

"What we need," he said at last, "is a surprise attack by tanks—on good ground."

Elles smiled wryly. "You know what happened the last time we put up that idea to GHQ."

This had been back in mid-June. Fuller had written a paper on the future employment of tanks, and in it he had suggested that the country lying between Cambrai and St. Quentin was ideal for such attacks. This part of the front, held by the Third Army which was now under the command of General Sir Julian Byng, had seen little fighting. The ground had not been churned up by artillery fire and remained hard and firm. Also in its favour was the fact that it was lightly held by the Germans. They felt secure behind the massive barriers of the Hindenburg Line, and this sector was used by them partly as a rest camp for troops who had been fighting in Flanders. Fuller saw that it was in this kind of situation that tanks could have their first real chance of fighting on suitable ground and being used for the purpose for which they were originally designed, that of crashing through the defences of barbed wire and trenches and letting the infantry through in a surprise attack.

The idea of tank raids of this kind had been enthusiastically taken up by some of the staff officers at General Headquarters, but at a meeting in July it had been vetoed by General Kiggell, the Chief of Staff. In fact, the idea was hardly new. It had been suggested in broad terms in a memorandum written by Swinton as far back as early 1916. But like so many other ideas that didn't appeal to Haig and Kiggell, it had been conveniently pigeon-holed at GHQ and had not even been seen by Elles and his staff at tank head-quarters.

" We were talking in generalities then," Fuller said. " But what about a specific operation. A lightning raid on St. Quentin, say."

Elles considered the proposal thoughtfully.

" Something like that would do a lot for our prestige and morale," Fuller persisted.

"And what about the French?" Elles asked. St. Quentin was on the boundary line between the British and French forces.

" They would have to co-operate, of course. It would be a joint operation."

Elles shook his head. " Haig would never accept that," he said, well aware of the Commander-in-Chief's dislike of the French.

" All right, then—how about further along the front? Cambrai, for instance."

" Over the toughest trench system in France?"

" But the ground there is ideal for tanks."

"Well—we can suggest it," Elles replied. But it was without much confidence that GHQ would accept the idea. " Put it down on paper and I'll see what can be done."

Fuller got to work right away, and so was conceived the idea for a raid on Cambrai. The following day, Elles took Fuller's memorandum to General Headquarters, housed within the dark walls of the old Vauban fortress at Montreuil. But his doubts were proved correct. Everyone there was so concerned with the Flanders campaign that Elles could rouse very little interest in the idea of a tank raid on another front. Besides, as some of the staff officers couldn't resist pointing out, the tanks weren't doing so well at Ypres. Why make a wasted effort elsewhere? Elles didn't feel inclined to make a very firm stand. But the rest of the Tank Corps were not so easily daunted. It happened that Lieutenant Colonel J. Hardress-Lloyd, who in April had joined the Corps as commander of the 3rd Tank Brigade, was a personal friend of General Byng. Since it was on Byng's sector of the front that the raid would take place, this presented another line of approach. Hardress-Lloyd put up the idea at a meeting on August 5 at Third Army headquarters. This time, the Corps met with a better reception. Byng was already considering plans for an attack in the Cambrai region, and the idea of using tanks appealed to him. Byng made the all-important decision to accept the Tank Corps suggestion. But it was at this point that the first danger signs became apparent. As originally conceived by Fuller, the scheme called for a sudden lightning raid, to destroy and capture German personnel and equipment and generally to demoralise the enemy, and then a quick retreat back to the original lines before a counter-attack could be mounted. The whole operation should not last much longer than eight hours. But the Third Army had a bigger plan in mind, and they saw in the tanks a means of penetrating deep into the enemy lines and capturing ground. What had started out as an idea for a raid was taking on the character of a full-scale battle. Fuller had his doubts even then, but no one liked to damp Byng's enthusiasm, not when the Tank Corps had at last found a supporter.

In any event, even with Byng's support, it still looked as if the idea was doomed. When Byng visited Haig the following day to seek approval for the attack to take place in the coming September, it was turned down. Haig himself showed signs of being in favour of the plan to begin with. But Kiggell rejected it on the grounds that the Army could not win a decisive battle by fighting in two places at once, and wanted every man concentrated in the Ypres area. It was this attitude, responsible as it was for yet more slaughter in Flanders without any question of a " decisive battle ", that won the day. Haig was himself still convinced that his campaign would be successful, and accepted Kiggell's reasoning. Byng returned empty-handed.

The days passed, and as the casualty rate in Flanders mounted, it gradually became apparent to even the most obstinate that the offensive was a failure. Haig and his staff at General Headquarters were coming increasingly under attacks from critics at home. By now, the total British casualties on the Western Front since the start of the war amounted to nearly two million, of whom the high ratio of over one-third were dead. The French had suffered even more, nearly four million casualties, while the Germans had lost some three-and-a-quarter million. The figures alone seemed to disprove the " war of attrition " policy. Haig looked around for some operation that could be mounted quickly to show immediate results in order to raise morale both at home and among his troops. And he found it in the plan which Byng and the Tank Corps had put forward and for which they were still lobbying at GHQ. On October 13, Haig gave approval for preliminary plans to be drawn up for an attack on Cambrai, and a few days later it was decided that " Operation GY ", as it was coded, should take place on November 20.

But the conditions for such an attack were not nearly so favourable now. The battles in Flanders had drained the Army's resources. Divisions were under strength, and the men who had survived were battle-weary. In addition, on October 24, the Italian Front collapsed suddenly at Caporetto and five British divisions had to be rushed to Italy to hold the line, leaving the British Army short of reserves. Nevertheless, in spite of all this, Byng and his staff at Third Army began planning the operation with great enthusiasm. They really had the bit between their teeth, and to Fuller's consternation, he saw that a full-scale battle at Cambrai was in prospect. Even Haig saw the danger of making such an attack with too few reserves, and told Byng that he would call it off after 48 hours if the situation did not look promising.

The Third Army plan, briefly, was to break through the

German defence system along the six-mile section of the front between the Canal de L'Escaut on the right and the Canal du Nord on the left. This was to be accomplished by the tanks followed by infantry. Then, while both tanks and infantry captured the two main features of the area, the ridges of Flesquieres and Bourlon, the Cavalry Corps was to pass through the gap and isolate the town of Cambrai, some seven miles behind the front lines. The German forces in Cambrai and in the area between the canals were to be rounded up, and the way would then be open to drive north-east towards Valenciennes, capturing the passages over the River Sensee and rolling up the German front. This ambitious project was to be undertaken by six infantry divisions, with support from another two and three more in reserve; five cavalry divisions (including the Canadian Cavalry Brigade); three tank brigades; over 1,000 field-guns of the Royal Artillery; and with the assistance of fourteen squadrons of the Royal Flying Corps 3rd Brigade, with assistance from the 1st Brigade.

Writing after the war, Fuller recalled: "The operation was in no sense a raid but instead a decisive battle. When I realised this I was aghast, because on August 4, when I had selected this area of attack, it was on account of it being advantageous to a raiding operation and disadvantageous to one of decisive intention. Further, from where were our reserves to come? I talked these things over with Elles but it was not until later on that I placed before him certain of my doubts in writing."

But there was the compensation that this area was ideal for tank movement. The country between the British lines and Cambrai consisted of smooth rolling uplands. Valleys, ridges and slopes varied the levels, but at no point abruptly so. The ground was chalky and hard and had not suffered from any shelling. In addition, the surface of the fields was covered with a strong growth of grass, which in the late autumn was a grey, withered mat, ideal for tanks to move on. Within the area in which the attack was to take place, some six miles wide and seven miles deep, were a number of villages and hamlets, of which Ribecourt, Marcoing, Masnieres, Flesquieres, Graincourt, Cantaing, Bourlon and Fontaine were the largest. The British lines ran from in front of the large Havrincourt Wood to the north-west—an ideal place in which to hide tanks and guns—and down past the villages of Trescault, Beaucamp, Villers-Plouich, Gonnelieu and Villers-Guislan. The main features of the ground which lay ahead of them were the Flesquieres Ridge, behind the Grand Ravine, and over to the north-west the Bourlon Ridge, crowned by a large wood and overlooking the main road into Cambrai from Arras. The two canals, the du Nord and the de L'Escaut, formed natural boundaries on either side of the area. The first had still been under construction when the war started and was therefore dry, but the Canal de L'Escaut was filled with water and was therefore a considerable obstacle for the tanks.

Cambrai on the River Scheldt was itself an important target for attack. Before the war it had been a prosperous industrial town, well-known for the weaving of fine fabrics—giving rise to the term "cambric". It had known many invasions and occupations in its tumultuous history, first by the Romans, then the Normans, and even the Hungarians. For a long time in the Middle Ages it was a bone of contention among its neighbours, the countries of Flanders and Hainaut and the kingdoms of France and England, and had frequently changed hands until eventually, in 1678, it had been assigned to France. Now, since August 1914, it had been in German hands. What made Cambrai important to the Germans was the fact that it was a major centre of communications. Four main-line railways converged here, as well as a number of big roads and several waterways. The railway line which ran laterally along the German front from St. Quentin to Douai, Lille, Courtrai and on to Ghent passed through Cambrai, and it was this line which supplied much of the lifeblood of men and supplies to the various sectors of the Front.

It was not surprising therefore that the German defences here were particularly strong. They lay in a wide path, up to five-and-a-half miles deep, between the British front and Cambrai, and had been constructed to take the best possible advantage of the ridges and spurs of the terrain. This formidable defensive system was made up of three main lines of resistance. First came the Hindenburg Main Line—the Seigfried-Stellung to the Germans—passing from the north-eastern corner of Havrincourt Wood to la Vacquerie, and in front of a dried-up stream bed known as the Grand Ravine with the village of Ribecourt near the centre. Part of this line was hidden behind ridges so that it was only completely visible from the air. Some thousand yards ahead of the main line was a strongly fortified forward trench system, built on sloping ground leading down from the British positions. A mile or so behind was the Hindenburg Support Line, and another three to four miles behind this lay yet another defence system, the Beaurevoir-Masnieres-Marcoing line. The trenches had been dug much wider than usual—up to 16 feet in fact—and with a depth also of 18 feet, the Germans were confident tanks, even if they should be used for attack, could not cross them. Each trench system included concrete dugouts in which were massed batteries of machine-guns, and in front were acres of dense wire, nowhere less than 50 yards deep. It was estimated that it would have taken five weeks of artillery bombardment, at a cost of £20 million in ammunition, to cut down this wire. Work on this part of the Hindenburg Line had been completed early in 1917, in time for the German withdrawal to the position in March. There were further plans to take the system of fortified trenches right back to the outskirts of Cambrai itself, culminating in a line of defensive earthworks called the Wotan Line, but in fact these were never completed. The front here was held by the German Second Army, under General von der Marwitz. It formed the left flank of the Army Group that was under the overall command of Field Marshal Crown Prince Rupprecht of Bavaria. The German Second Army was sub-divided into two groups, each consisting of three to four infantry divisions. To the North-west was the Arras Group, under Lieutenant General von Moser, comprising the staff of the XIVth Reserve Corps and the 111th, 240th and 20th Infantry Divisions. Further to the south-east was the Caudry Group, under General Baron von Watter, with the staff of the XIIIth Wurttenberg Army Corps and the 20th Land-wehr, 9th Reserve, and 54th and 183rd Infantry Divisions. Some of these divisions had recently been brought up from the Russian Front.

The British line lay parallel to the Hindenburg Main line, separated by a No Man's Land of between three to five hundred yards and following the forward slopes of a ridge from Havrincourt Wood to Villers-Guislan. Under Byng's Third Army, it was now held by IV Corps (Lieutenant General Sir C. Woollcombe) to the north-west and III Corps (Lieutenant General Sir W. Pulteney) to the south-east. The actual divisions holding the line in October 1917 were the 36th Ulster Division of IV Corps and the 20th Light Division of III Corps, both of which were to play a major part in the battle.

It was after the German withdrawal to the Hindenburg line in March that the British line here had been established. At that time, Captain Geoffrey Dugdale of the 6th King's Somerset Light Infantry had been one of those who moved forward, and recording the event, he wrote: " The next day we were ordered forward. Behind us we left a scene of great activity as roads had to be made over the shell-scarred battle-fields of the Somme. The guns were moving from the gun-pits which they had occupied for months and the routine was altered by this enemy move. They had retired in perfect order to the long-prepared Hindenburg Line. They left nothing behind them and had destroyed every house and even cut down the trees in the orchards. Soon it was dis-covered to our cost that they had set clever booby-traps for us. Steel helmets were left in deserted buildings which, when touched, sprung a mine, destroying the would-be souvenir hunter. For days we slowly advanced until finally our bat-

Sains

Wotan 2.

Bourlon

Quarry Wd.

Pronville
20

Inchy

Bourlon Wood

HINDENBURG

Mœuvres

Tadpole Copse

MAIN

Quarry Factory

Chapel

Ann

20 Ldw.

C.

56

LINE

Bapaume

Boursies

Graincourt

Or. V

Demicourt

Doignies

36

Flesqui

SU

Hermies

Havrin-court

Ribècourt

Grand Ravine

54

IV.

Canal du Nord

Havrincourt Wood

62

Bilhem

Trescault

51

Beaucamp

T
H
I
R
D

Ruyaulcourt

6

Villers-Plouich

Ytres

Neuville

Metz

A
R
M
Y

III

Gouzeaucourt Wood

29

Gouzeaucourt

Peronne

CAMBRAI—Before The B

British Front Line − − − − −
Hindenburg Main Line ▬▬▬▬▬

Zero hour, November 20.

German Support Lines:
completed ——————
uncompleted — — — —

talion came to a halt near the Canal du Nord. Our company was quartered in a sunken road which led down to the canal bank and on the other side the Australians held the line. We were on a gentle downhill slope leading to the edge of Havrincourt Wood, the trees of which covered the slope on the opposite side of the valley for about half a mile."

Later, in October, Captain Dugdale found himself back at Havrincourt as Observation Officer for 6th Division, and he was to be an important witness of the Battle of Cambrai. He described the scene before the battle after making a tour of inspection with Brigadier-General Duncan, commanding 60th Brigade.

"We walked for about half a mile down a sunken road before we arrived in open, flat country, rather like Cambridgeshire. On our left was the village of Trescault, with Havrincourt Wood beyond it and the village of Havrincourt itself about two miles to our left front. This village was just inside our line. In front of us stretched uninteresting country which looked as if it would yield wonderful wheat crops and partridge driving. On the opposite slope lay the village of Gouzeaucourt and beyond this we could see the villages of Gonnelieu and La Vacquerie in the distance. Immediately in front of us was the village of Villers-Plouich, with the wood on the left of it. During the tour of our trenches we were both lost in admiration of their work. The trenches, beautifully planned to give an excellent field of fire, were built up with sand-bags supported with wire-netting in the fire-bays and round the trenches. The whole of the system was duck-boarded and it was the most perfect system of trenches I saw during the whole time I was in France. We had an excellent view of the German lines, which were further off than usual—in fact in some places, No Man's Land was nearly 500 yards wide."

On October 25, Elles called a meeting of brigade commanders at Tank Corps headquarters to outline the Third Army plan. After discussion, it was agreed that there were three main objectives as far as the tanks were concerned.

The first was to break through the main Hindenburg Line from Bleak House to the Canal du Nord, and capture the village of Ribecourt. Secondly, to penetrate the Hindenburg Support Line. And thirdly, to exploit the area northwards to Cambrai. It was vital to maintain the utmost secrecy if the attack was to be successful. It had already been decided that, for virtually the first time since trench warfare had started, there would be no preliminary bombardment to warn the Germans of an attack. The artillery were to wait until the tanks began to move forward before opening up, and this meant that no registration shots could be fired. Range would have to be worked out in theory only. Not only did this pose a problem for the artillery experts, but most of the 1,003 guns allocated to the battle had to be brought up to the front. In addition, the 474 tanks to be used had to be moved forward, as well as the additional infantry divi-sions—and all without giving the Germans any indication that an attack was being prepared. The administrative prob-lems were enormous.

A few days later, on October 29, Elles and Fuller attended a conference at Third Army headquarters to go over the final plans drawn up for the battle. Behind the tanks, which were to be the spearhead of the attack, six infantry divisions were to take part in the first phase—with IV Corps, to the left, the 62nd West Riding Territorials and the 51st Highland Territorials; and with III Corps, on the right, the 20th Light, the 6th, the 12th Eastern and the 29th Divisions. In addition, IV Corps was to be assisted by the 36th Ulster and the 56th London Territorials, and three Army reserve divisions of V Corps, the 40th, 59th and the Guards, were to be held on call. At a later stage in the battle, the five divisions of the Cavalry Corps were to be employed. There were also to be subsidiary attacks in the adjoining sectors of the Front, but these were not part of the Cambrai operation proper.

The main attack was to come from the III Corps, and two tank brigades, the 2nd (Colonel A. Courage) and 3rd (Colonel Hardress-Lloyd) were allocated to this sector. On the right, the 12th Division (Major General A. B. Scott) was to capture the Gonnelieu Ridge and Lateau Wood. The 20th Division (Major General W. D. Smith) in the centre was to carry the attack from La Vacquerie to Welsh Ridge and the Hindenburg Support line beyond. The 6th Division (Major General T. O. Marden) on the left was to capture the village of Ribecourt and the eastern part of the Flesquieres Ridge. The 29th Division (Major General Sir H. de B. de Lisle) was to pass through the 20th and 6th Divisions in order to capture the heights south of Rumilly and the Bois des Neufs. When the first objectives had been won, one company of tanks from each of the first three divisions was to push forward to seize the bridges over the Canal de L'Escaut from Masnieres to Marcoing and hold these until the 29th Division arrived. This was a vital part of the operation for it was over these bridges that the 2nd and 5th Cavalry Divisions were intended to cross in order to advance east of Cambrai. In addition, the 4th Cavalry Division was to send out raiding detachments south-westwards across the Canal towards Evalincourt.

The IV Corps was allocated the 1st Tank Brigade (Colonel Baker-Carr). The 51st Division (Major General G. M. Harper) had as its first objective the capture of Flesquieres Ridge and village, and was then to push forward to capture the German guns to the north and the village of Cantaing. Meanwhile, on the left, the 62nd Division (Major General W. P. Braithwaite) was to clear the Hindenburg Support line up to the Bapaume-Cambrai road, and in particular take the Canal du Nord bridge on that road, then capture Graincourt and Anneux and assist the 1st Cavalry Division (Major General R. L. Mulens) in taking Bourlon Wood and the village beyond. This was considered an essential objective. From there, the cavalry was to advance north-west towards Cambrai and cut off the Germans caught in the salient. The other two divisions, the 36th (Major General O. Nugent) and the 56th (Major General F. A. Dudgeon) were to provide assistance, particularly in holding the canal bridge on the Bapaume-Cambrai road and carrying out mopping up operations west of Flesquieres.

The detailed allocation of tanks was as follows:

IV Corps

Tank Brigade	Tank Battalion	Division	Brigade	Number of tanks and mechanical reserve
1st	D	51st	152nd	42
1st	E	51st	153rd	28
1st	E	62nd	186th	14
1st	G	62nd	185th	42

III Corps

Tank Brigade	Tank Battalion	Division	Brigade	Number of tanks and mechanical reserve
2nd	A	20th	60th	24 (4)
2nd	A	29th	—	12 (2)
2nd	B	6th	16th	36 (6)
2nd	H	6th	71st	36 (4)
3rd	C	12th	35th	24 (4)
3rd	C	12th	37th	12 (2)
3rd	F	12th	36th	36 (6)
3rd	I	20th	61st	30 (5)
3rd	I	20th	62nd	6 (1)

This gave a total of 376 fighting tanks, of which 34 were held in mechanical reserve. But to Fuller's disgust, two of the divisions, the 51st and 62nd, did not allocate any tanks for reserve at all. And as it transpired, when the battle started, all the tanks were thrown in anyway, reserves and all. In addition to the fighting tanks, each tank brigade had 18 supply and gun-carrying tanks and 3 wireless tanks. A further 32 tanks were specially fitted with towing gear and grapnels to clear the wire for the cavalry advance, 2 carried bridging materials and one carried forward telephone cable for the Third Army Signal Service. There was therefore a grand total of 474 Mark IV tanks to take part in the attack on Cambrai.

Fuller had been giving a great deal of thought as to the best method of attack by the tanks. The biggest problem seemed to be the sheer size of the trenches, which were too wide and too deep for the tanks to cross. But fortunately, the Central Workshops at Erin came up with an answer. Bundles of brushwood of the kind used for road repairs were bound together by heavy chains to make huge fascines which could be carried on the nose of the tanks and then released from inside by a special triggering device so that they dropped neatly into the trenches to make a bridge. Sixty to seventy bundles of wood were required for each fascine, and in order to make the 350 fascines required, one for each tank, the Central Workshops had to work day and night for three weeks. Each fascine weighed nearly two tons, and it took twenty men to roll one through the mud. Specially equipped tanks worked in pairs to pull the chains tightly round each one in order to compress the wood. Not only was there a problem in collecting the 21,000 bundles of brushwood, but in order to provide the 2,000 fathoms of heavy steel chain required, sources of supply had to be found quickly. Park railings throughout Britain were stripped, and lengths of chain were also obtained from shipyards and other industrial plant.

Each tank could carry only one fascine, and once it was dropped into a trench, there was no way of picking it up again. But there were three main lines of trenches to be crossed. This led Fuller to devise a special method of attack by which the tanks were formed into sections of three to work together. One of these was an " advance tank " and the remaining two were " main body tanks ". The first tank was to go forward through the enemy's wire, flattening it for the oncoming infantry, and then turn left without crossing the trench, but shooting down at the German infantry inside. This was to keep the enemy down and protect the two main body tanks following behind. These were to make for one selected spot in the trench. The left-hand one dropped its fascine, crossed over, and then turned left to work down that side of the trench. Meanwhile, the right-hand tank crossed over on the same fascine and made for the next line of trenches where it cast its own fascine. Then the advanced guard tank returned to cross over these two trenches and was ready to go forward to the third line with its own fascine still intact. The infantry were also formed into three platoons of 36 men each, one to mark the paths which the tanks had made through the wire, another to clear the trenches and dug-outs, and the last to garrison the trenches when they were captured. They were to follow closely behind the tanks in single file. Finally, the special wire-pulling tanks were to roll up the flattened wire to make broad paths through which the cavalry could advance.

These methods of attack, which were to be used for the first time ever, required combined tank and infantry training. On November 1, Fuller issued brigades with a memorandum on training, together with information compiled by the Reconnaissance Officer, Captain Hotblack, on the enemy defences. There was very little time available for adequate training, but most of the infantry commanders were prepared to co-operate willingly. In order to maintain secrecy, the training areas were split up behind the British lines. The 1st Tank Brigade trained with the 51st and 62nd Divisions at the Wailly tank training school, the 2nd Brigade trained with the 29th Division at Wailly and with the 6th Division at Avesnes-le-Comte, and the 3rd Brigade trained with the 12th Division near Bermicourt and with the 20th Division at the Loop, near Bray.

Fuller's tactics were approved by Third Army Headquarters. But one commander, Major General G. M. Harper of the 51st Division, refused to co-operate. At GHQ he had originally been one of those opposed to the development of machine-guns. Now he had the same lack of faith in the tanks, and proclaimed the idea of the battle to be " fantastic and un-military ". But he went further and devised tactics of his own which were at variance with Fuller's. To begin with, he insisted that the tanks should turn right instead of left after crossing the trenches. It didn't make any difference which way they went, but it was obviously preferable that all the tanks should go in the same direction. Then he divided the tanks up into sections of four instead of three, to move line abreast, and told his infantry to maintain a distance of at least 100 yards behind them. These tactics were not only silly because they were the result of an obstinate intention not to co-operate with the Tank Corps—not that he was known to co-operate with anyone, in fact, being solely concerned with the pride and record of his Highland regiments—but they were to have tragic consequences when the battle started, being mainly responsible for one of the only hold-ups during the first attack. Fuller complained about Harper's attitude to the Third Army staff, but the doctrine of delegation of command was so deep rooted that Harper was allowed to go his own way.

It was not only the tank and infantry tactics that were new. In order for a surprise attack to be possible, the artillery had to devise a method of shooting effectively without previous registration, so that when the barrage opened on the Hindenburg Front Line, the advance could begin immediately. As it was so necessary to ensure an accurate range, the artillery consulted the Royal Flying Corps for weather forecasts so that the effects of wind and air temperature could be taken into consideration, a technique started earlier in the year but to come to fruition at Cambrai. It was planned for the 1,000 guns to open fire all at once at zero hour with a barrage of smoke, shrapnel and high explosive shells on the front-line system, and then lifting to bombard the lines further back as the tanks advanced. And again, in the air, new tactics were devised. Fourteen squadrons of the Royal Flying Corps were to be employed, not only to carry out normal observation work and to bomb German aerodromes and headquarters at Caudry and Escaudoeuvres, but to move forward with the infantry on the first attack, flying low to fire into the enemy trenches.

On November 8, Elles and Fuller attended a full-dress conference at Third Army headquarters at Albert at which General Byng explained his plan to Corps and Divisional commanders. General Kiggell, the gloomy pessimist, and General

Davidson were there from GHQ. Fuller wrote of this conference: " To me, the conference was of intense psychological interest for it showed that very few of the generals attending it had any understanding of and consequently confidence in the powers of the tank. The two Corps commanders seemed to be completely out of their depth and in spite of the obvious necessity for a free hand, the Cavalry Corps commander, strange to say, tied his command down in such a way that in any conceivable set of circumstances, it would have been impossible for it to develop its mobility." Most of the discussion centred on what the cavalry would do, for it was realised that at Cambrai, there was a genuine chance for the cavalry to take advantage of the breakthrough which it was hoped the tanks would make. It was the opportunity that the cavalry had been seeking since the war started, and one that was always in the mind of military leaders like Haig who were themselves cavalrymen. The plan was for the cavalry to be ready to move forward at zero plus two-and-a-half hours, by which time it was hoped that the infantry divisions would have occupied the ground up to a line from Flesquieres, through Marcoing, to Masnieres. Then the 5th and 2nd Cavalry Divisions were to advance south of Cambrai, and the 1st to isolate Cambrai from the Bourlon position. From then on, there was a broad, if rather vague plan, for the cavalry to exploit the area to the north, securing the passages over the Sensée River, breaking up the railways, rounding up the various German headquarters in the rear, and generally to drive north-east towards Valénciennes in preparation for rolling up the German front.

" In themselves," Fuller later wrote, " these movements may have been sound enough, though the first depended very largely on whether the bridge at Masnieres would be found intact. What was wrong was not the dispositions, but the leadership. In place of moving as close up to the front as possible, the Cavalry Corps headquarters remained at Fins, six miles in rear of the nearest point on the front-line and some twelve miles from Masnieres, and as no action was to be taken except by order of these headquarters, this meant that opportunity would be lost as all information would have to go back to headquarters and from there be transmitted to cavalry divisions and by them to brigades and thence to regiments and squadrons. Yet at the time, General Byng never once criticised the Cavalry Corps commanders' proposals, neither did General Kiggell, who throughout this conference scarcely uttered a word but sat pensively silent, wrapped in the profoundest gloom. The truth is that, possibly for the last time in the history of war, the cavalry were offered a chance of operating as a mounted arm."

This chance, as the battle was to prove, was missed, not because of lack of courage, but because the Corps commander, Lieutenant General Sir C. T. McM. Kavanagh, who should have led his men remained miles in the rear, and was too much out of touch with what was going on to get orders through in time for them to take advantage of any situation. And he prevented his divisional and brigade commanders from doing so by insisting that no one moved until orders had been received from Corps headquarters.

By this time, the Tank Corps had established advance headquarters in the town of Albert. In order to maintain secrecy, it was known simply as "Tank Training Office". The "office" was in fact the ruins of what had once been a small cabaret in the main street. Not only were the windows broken and the walls in danger of collapsing, but there were still large posters on the hoardings, revealing the physical talents of the dancing girls who had once occupied the building. Fuller wrote a nostalgic account of those early November days while he was planning tactics for the coming battle:

" My original staff had been increased by the appointment of Major H. Boyd-Rochfort and Captain the Hon. Evan Charteris, who Elles had got out from Tank Corps command in London to compile our records and write up our history . . . Charteris was older than most of us. He was somewhat of a sybarite, an electic and an epicurean. In London he lived in an equisite maisonette in Mount Street, surrounded by exquisite pictures and exquisite furniture, and all in exquisite taste. He was so obviously fashioned by his Creator to rule our mess that his presidency over it was one of those gravitational processes which have no fixed origin. No sooner was he one of us than strange little packets began to arrive from Paris and London, containing beach-nut bacon, rose-leaf honey, and rare, exotic condiments. In the cabaret, " Des Hommes Mort " or whatever its true name was, often he must have dreamed of Mount Street. Now he sat in a room, one of the outer walls of which had been badly holed, and over the gaps a former occupant had fixed a hoarding which in more peaceful days must have contained a gigantic poster of a dancing girl. All that was now left of this charmer was a wreath of white frilling, out of which protruded a well-shaped leg. Facing this severed limb, Evan Charteris would sit in a fur-lined British warm by an oil-drum stove, the smoke of which went anywhere but up the chimney, descending upon him in flakes of soot."

The final approval for the attack was given by General Headquarters on November 13. But Haig still insisted that he would stop the offensive after 48 hours unless the situation justified a continuation. He thought that the Germans would not be able to bring up reinforcements within this time, and it would still be possible to withdraw if necessary before a counter-attack could be mounted. Also, Haig stressed the importance of the early capture of Bourlon Ridge, over-looking as it did the approaches to Cambrai. With a week to go before Z day on November 20, Fuller began issuing tactical notes to the battalion commanders. They showed an insight into the nature of tank fighting that was many years ahead of its time, and was still valid long after the war was over. A new method of modern warfare was being evolved.

Meanwhile, a complex operation was under way to bring the 474 tanks up to the front for the attack. They came from workshops, Army supply bases and ports, the biggest concentration of tanks ever seen. Some were fresh from the manufacturers in England, where Stern and his Tank Supply Department had been pulling out all the stops to get them ready in time. Others had been sent from the training establishment at Bovington Camp, Dorset, where the personnel realised that something big was up which might well decide the future of the Tank Corps. A few of the tanks had already been blooded, survivors of the disastrous battles in Flanders, and now, repaired but still carrying their scars, they were ready to vindicate themselves.

In addition to the tanks, 670 field-guns had to be brought up, making a grand total of 1,003 for the operation and ranging in size from 4-5 inch howitzers to 60-pounders. Five or six artillery field brigades were allocated to each infantry division. Then there was the great mass of supplies and equipment required, which all had to be transported by lorry. The tanks alone needed 165,000 gallons of petrol and 75,000 lbs. of grease; 500,000 rounds of 6-pounder shell and five million rounds of machine-gun ammunition. The artillery bombardment was to be far more limited than for any previous battle, but even so, 5,000 tons of shell were required. This was a trifle, however, compared with Flanders, where during the campaign, 465,000 tons of shell were expended, costing £84,000,000.

All this created not only a huge problem of transportation, but the utmost secrecy was essential. This was in fact the prime purpose of the plan. If the Germans found out about it, the attack would become a massacre, especially as there was to be no softening-up artillery bombardment beforehand. Orders were issued that all officers carrying out reconnaissance should remove their unit badges, so that if they were captured the Germans would not realise that additional divisions had been brought up to the Front, and for the same reason, on the 51st Division front they had to wear trousers instead of Highland dress. All moves up to and in the forward area were carried out at night, and of the thousands of trucks employed, only those moving away from the front were allowed to use their lights, in order to confuse the enemy. The guns were hidden in the woods and orchards, and in open fields under camouflage netting. The tanks were the most difficult problem. They could not move for long distances under their own power and so they were brought up, under canvas cover, by train. All such movement was carried out at night, and 36 trains were used. The tanks were de-trained at various points along the front, the main staging area being Le Plateau. Major Watson, who was in command of a company of D Battalion, described seeing his tanks successfully loaded on to the trains at Beaumetz station:

" I watched the trains pull out from the ramps. The lorries had already started for our next halting-place. We were clear of Wailly. I motored down to the neighbourhood of Albert, and at dusk my car was feeling its way through a bank of fog along the road from Bray to the great railhead at Le Plateau, at the edge of the old Somme battlefield. It was a vast confusing place, and one felt insignificant among the multitudinous rails, the slow dark trains, the sudden lights. Tanks, which had just detrained, came rumbling round the corners of odd huts. Lorries bumped through the mist with food and kit. Quiet railwaymen, mostly American, went steadily about their business. Just after midnight, word came that our train was expected. We walked to the ramp and at last, after an interminable wait, our train glided out of the darkness. There was a slight miscalculation and the train hit the ramp with a bump, carrying away the lower timbers so that it could not bear the weight of the tanks. Wearily we tramped a mile or so to another ramp. This time the train behaved with more discretion. The tanks were driven off into a wood, where they were carefully camouflaged. The cooks set to work and produced steaming tea . . ."

Not all the tanks were brought up without accident. At a level-crossing near Ypres, a train collided with a lorry and the last truck was derailed. The tank it was carrying toppled over and crushed the lorry, with two men inside, against the embankment.

From Le Plateau, the tanks were driven, still under cover of darkness, to various lying-up areas near the front. They were guided by their tank commanders, walking in front and following white tapes which had been laid on the ground. The noise of the engines was drowned by machine-gun fire. Luckily, from November 10 onwards, there was a good deal of ground mist to hide all these activities, and also, the rain held off so that the ground remained firm.

Mr. F. R. J. Jefford, M.B.E., who was one of the tank commanders, has given this account of the preparations : "The tank commanders went out on foot under cover of darkness and laid white tapes through the maze of trenches to the points behind the front lines. The tanks reduced speed so that the engines were just ticking over by the time the starting point was reached. It was a dangerous operation for the commanders, who had to walk in front of their tanks to guide the drivers. The greatest hazard was barbed wire, for if a commander got caught up in this the chances were that he would be crushed down by his own tank. In fact, we lost several officers in this way before the battle started."

These operations took place between the nights of November 15-18. The tanks were hidden under trees and in the ruins of shelled houses. The 1st Brigade was hidden in the western edge of Havrincourt Wood, of which the Germans actually held the eastern extremity, 3,000 yards away. The 2nd Brigade was in Dessart Wood, two miles south of Havrincourt. And 3rd Brigade, having no convenient wood in which to hide, was concealed under camouflage netting in and about Gouzeaucourt and Villers-Guislan. When all the tanks were in position and tied down under camouflage netting, the crews were sent out with brooms to obliterate any track marks, and during the day, planes of the Royal Flying Corps were sent up to photograph the area, to make sure no signs of the tanks could be seen by enemy reconnaissance aircraft. The whole operation was highly successful. Movements had been carried out so secretly and the tanks and petrol dumps so well concealed that even most of the British troops in the area didn't know they were there.

But on the night of November 18, thirty-six hours before the attack was to start, the secret leaked out.

CHAPTER SIX

Dawn Attack

RESERVE Lieutenant Hegermann of the 84th Infantry Regiment was one of a new elite of the German Army, and proud of it. Together with others, he had been seconded into a special commando force, known as "Stosstrupps", which operated as a tough and resourceful team outside the framework of the normal infantry regiments to carry out individual raids on the Western Front. They were the German answer to the rigid immobility of trench warfare and had already caused considerable havoc by penetrating the British lines at various sectors of the Front, and carrying out daring raids in the rear. On the evening of November 18, Hegermann was ordered by his commanding officer, Captain Soltau, to carry out a sortie near the village of Trescault for the purpose of bringing back prisoners.

This was a fairly routine operation to try and find out if the Allies were planning any attacks. It was felt by the German High Command that the heavy defeat of the Italians at Caporetto would prompt the British and French to become more aggressive on the Western Front, particularly now that the campaign in Flanders had ended. They were not to know just how much that campaign had depleted the British forces. Accordingly, German units were instructed to make constant armed sorties to capture prisoners for interrogation. General von der Marwitz's Second Army had complied with these instructions, but knowing how the British had elaborately strengthened their defences on the Cambrai front, Marwitz was much less apprehensive of an attack there. On November 16, he had reported: " The distribution of the enemy's forces has been again explored through patrol fighting which took place in many parts of the Army's front. Wherever it has not been possible to bring back prisoners, the hostile divisions deployed in the front line have been confirmed in the same sections which they have held for some time by intercepting telephone messages."

"Major attacks of the enemy against the front of the Second Army are not to be expected in the foreseeable future," concluded Marwitz.

A raid on the morning of November 18, when Captain Soldan of the 184th Infantry Regiment captured forty British prisoners near Gillemont Farm, to the south of the VII Corps sector, seemed to confirm this. The prisoners were all of the British 55th Division, which had been holding the front for some time, and they gave no hint of the attack being planned. Later that night, Lieutenant Hegermann carried out his own raid near Trescault and captured a sergeant and five men of the 1st Battalion, Royal Irish Fusiliers. He took them back to Captain Soltau's headquarters in Havrincourt village. The prisoners all belonged to 36th Division which was known to be holding the line, and when Captain Soltau began to question them, he did not expect to discover anything new. But to his surprise, two of the men volunteered the information that a large attack was being prepared in the region of Havrincourt, and one of them even gave the correct date of the attack—November 20. Another man spoke of seeing camouflaged tanks in the wood.

Captain Soltau was perplexed. He couldn't believe that the British would attack such a heavily defended position without a considerable artillery bombardment beforehand to cut down at least some of the wire. And as yet, there had been no signs of such bombardment. He came to the conclusion that the men were mistaken, certainly about the date, and if there was anything in the story it was probably only a small raid that was being planned. As far as the tanks were concerned, he attached no importance to these. His own feelings, after seeing the British tanks in action in Flanders, were that such vehicles were virtually useless anyway.

So he sent the prisoners back to Caudry Group headquarters, together with a report of his conclusions.

Here, the information was received more seriously. Aircraft observers had already reported a build-up of traffic behind the British lines, and there seemed to be a large number of British aircraft in the vicinity. Also, the fragment of a telephone message saying "Tuesday, Flanders . . ." had been picked up at Riencourt. It was felt that these facts, together with the prisoners' statements, were worth forwarding to General von der Marwitz at Second Army headquarters. Marwitz decided that an attack was unlikely, and that in any case it would not take place as early as November 20. But to be on the safe side, he ordered the number of reserves around Havrincourt to be increased. This, if any, seemed to be the area threatened, and it was regarded as a highly important position to hold if an attack did take place. The defence of the village was given to the 54th Division under the command of Lieutenant General Frieher von Watter, a relative of the Caudry Group commander of the same name. And so matters stood. The Germans possessed, unknown to the British then, sufficient information and hints about the forthcoming attack to enable them to have prepared an extremely unpleasant welcome. But the idea of tanks or anything else being able to cross the wide trenches of the Hindenburg line seemed wildly impossible. The Germans were inclined to treat tanks as lightly as some of their counterparts in the British High Command.

Nevertheless, as the hours wore on, the tension increased. There was still no barrage from the British front, but during November 19, more and more lorries were seen moving along the road between Metz and Gouzeaucourt. Some local commanders were convinced that an attack was about to take place, and ordered their troops to be in a state of readiness. At Caudry Group headquarters, another officer re-examined the British prisoners and decided that there might be something in the story about the tanks after all. The German machine-gunners had only scanty supplies of the special SK ammunition with steel-filled conical bullets that were capable of piercing light armour. An order was rushed through for further supplies to be issued. But it was too late for anything to be done about it before the attack started. From his headquarters in Havrincourt village, Lieutenant General von Watter requested, during the evening of the 19th, artillery fire into Havrincourt Wood and Trescault to try and get an answering fire from the British guns, in order to estimate their numbers. He was told that this could not be done until early on the morning of November 20.

Meanwhile, at the aerodrome at Awoingt where Captain Richard Flashar's No. 5 Flight was the only German fighter group operational at the time, an urgent call from Caudry headquarters told him to stand by the following morning, just in case the British made an attack. " I gave instructions for the pilots to be called at 6 a.m.," Flashar wrote in his diary. " But personally, I feel certain that tomorrow morning we shall do just as little flying as we have done for the last few days and weeks. November in northern France—rain, mist, cloud, and then rain again. For nearly a fortnight, no machine has left its shed. And now the British are supposed to be going to attack tomorrow at Havrincourt. How often have we had such alarming reports before ! "

All through the day and night of November 19—" Y " day —last minute preparations were being made behind the British lines. In the morning, Fuller closed up his office in Albert. But before he did so, Elles walked in and said, " Everyone has worked so splendidly that I think we ought to issue a special order. Will you write one?"

Fuller sat down and began to scribble out a message. Then he looked up. " No—you write it. It should come from you."

So Elles took a sheet of waxed duplicating paper and wrote the following:

SPECIAL ORDER No. 6

1. Tomorrow the Tank Corps will have the chance for which it has been waiting for many months—to operate on good going in the van of the battle.

2. All that hard work and ingenuity can achieve has been done in the way of preparation.

Special Order No 6.

1. To-morrow the Tank Corps will have the chance for which it has been waiting for many months, — to operate on good going in the van of the battle.

2. All that hard work & ingenuity can achieve has been done in the way of preparation

3. It remains for unit commanders and for tank crews to complete the work by judgment & pluck in the battle itself.

4. In the light of past experiences I leave the good name of the Corps with great confidence in their hands

5. I propose leading the attack of the centre division

Hugh Elles.
B.S.

19th Nov. 1917.   Commanding Tank Corps.

Distribution to Tank Commanders

Facsimile of Special Order No. 6 by Hugh Elles.

91

3. It remains for unit commanders and for tank crews to complete the work by judgement and pluck in the battle itself.

4. In the light of past experience I leave the good name of the Corps with great confidence in their hands.

5. I propose leading the attack in the centre division.

> HUGH ELLES, Brig.-Gen.
> Commanding Tank Corps.

This message was to be read out that night by every tank commander to his crew. It was a message that was to become as famous to tank men the world over as Nelson's had been before Trafalgar. But it was the last point that caused Fuller to raise his eyebrows. For a general to lead his Corps into battle was almost unheard of in the First War.

"You can't do that," Fuller argued. "Suppose you're killed or wounded—it would be a disaster for the Corps."

But Elles was adamant. He insisted on the right to lead his men into the first real tank battle in history. And he intended carrying the Corps flag which he and Fuller had devised earlier—the brown, red and green flag which symbolised mud, fighting spirit, and fields for good going. It was a decision, as Fuller was later to admit, which was not only a brave one, but which was the spiritual making of the Tank Corps.

At the advance aerodrome which had been established at Bapaume, near the Bapaume-Cambrai road, pilots of the 3rd Brigade Royal Flying Corps were receiving their briefing for the following day from the brigade major, Captain R. H. Jerman. The brigade had been built up to a strength of fourteen bomber, fighter and reconnaissance squadrons comprising Sopwith Camels and Scouts, Bristol Fighters, and D.H.4's and D.H.5's—a total of 275 serviceable aircraft, as well as six kite balloons. The Germans were known to have only 78 planes at the front at that time, of which only 12 Albatross Scouts were fighters, Captain Flashar's No. 5 Flight at Awoingt. The priority target, given to Nos. 3, 46 and 68 (Australian) Squadrons, was to locate and bomb these planes while still on the ground. Other fighters were to support the first wave of infantry, machine-gunning the German trenches, while the bombers were to attack road and rail targets behind the enemy lines. An important task of the reconnaissance aircraft was to locate German field-gun batteries and give the information to the British artillery gunners so that they could be put out of action before causing too much damage to the tanks. Later in the battle, No. 35 Squadron was to work specially with the Cavalry Corps when it moved into action.

When darkness fell, at about five o'clock in the afternoon, the tanks began to leave the hidden lying-up positions for their starting places on the front line. One of the section commanders was Captain D. E. Hickey of " H " battalion, then 22 years old. He wrote this description of the approach march with his three tanks:

"At about five o'clock we left Dessart Wood on our approach march to Beaucamp. A white tape, about 2 inches wide with a black line along the centre, had been laid over the whole distance. The officer walked in front of his tank to be able to see the tape and direct the driver, guiding him by the glow of a cigarette. A tank was not allowed to go astride the tape for fear of ripping it up. For some considerable distance the tape remained intact and was of great assistance. Then it ended abruptly. It was quite impossible to direct the tanks by the lie of the country for the night was pitch black and no landmarks were visible. There were several breaks like this where the tape had been ripped up. On these occasions I walked ahead trying to pick out the track marks of a preceding tank by the light of a cigarette. During the approach march the front of our sector was ominously quiet.

"About midnight, we reached our jumping-off place, taking up a position behind a hedge. The four miles of approach march had taken seven hours—an average speed of little more than half-a-mile an hour. The rollers of the tanks were greased up, and the men turned in to snatch a few hours sleep inside the tanks."

Another member of a tank crew described the problem of finding the tanks in the darkness:

"We were in the wood, about 2,500 yards away from the Germans. The wind had dropped and the stillness was very little disturbed, with only the occasional sputter of a machine-gun and the roar of a heavy gun. Verey lights cast a pale, unnatural light over wide tracts of country and illuminated the clouds, which were lying low and heavy over our heads. It seemed quite hopeless to try and find any particular tank but Mansfield, with his earthenware keg of rum tucked under his arm, plunged into the darkness like a sprite. Soon he picked up a strip of white tape and we followed across what seemed moorland, taking heavy falls and periodically getting tangled up in the barbed wire. One could hear tanks moving, purring very mildly on their second speed, and one could see pinpoints of light, no bigger than fire-flies, behind their portholes. Presently we came across one in difficulties and from the officer we learned that the tank we were seeking was in front. Another half-a-mile brought us to a group of four, drawn up in a line under some trees. They were filling up with petrol. Some of the men were trying to sleep on tarpaulins spread on the ground. Behind them were sledges laden with drums of telegraph wire and reserves of petrol. We found our tank, and tried to sleep—without success."

One of the most important jobs had been the laying of the tapes for the approach march. This had been done by Captain Hotblack and his reconnaissance team, who had also surveyed No Man's Land for the best paths of attack. Hotblack seemed to be everywhere during the preparations on the night of the 19th; one tank commander recorded an encounter with him as follows: "We crept out of the trench and ran into a tall and sinister looking man who had his head inside my tank. He might have been a spy—we all had a mild attack of spy mania—but he turned out to be the ubiquitous Hotblack, so all was well."

Zero hour was 6.20 on the morning of Tuesday, November 20, when the heavy guns were to commence their barrage after the tanks had started to move forwards. The artillery barrage was mostly designed to provide a smoke screen and was to lift deeper in to the enemy defences as the tanks advanced. By 5.00 a.m. all the tanks were in position and the British infantry began to cut through their own wires, ready for the assault. This was observed by the Germans, and a battery of mortar and rifle fire broke out. This was soon taken up by the German artillery—the fire which had been requested by Lieutenant General von Watter in Havrincourt village the previous evening. For a while it seemed that the Germans themselves were preparing for an attack, or, at the least, they knew of the British attack and were out to prevent it.

" It grew in intensity and spread along the whole front," Fuller wrote afterwards. " It was accompanied by a great display of rockets and Verey lights. We were thoroughly alarmed that something must have happened and the Germans were anticipating our attack. All around us was massed our artillery, and the restraint imposed on them not to fire back was traumatic. The front was now ablaze. It did not seem to be one of those panicky episodes that flare up suddenly in the night and as quickly subside. It was steady and sustained and seemed to have some directing significance behind it. It was disquieting in the extreme."

But the barrage died down suddenly at 5.30 as quickly as it had started, and the Front was once again still and quiet—uncannily so to those who had experienced the bombardment in Flanders.

The dawn came up very slowly, grey and overcast with a fine ground mist. The shapes of the woods and ridges ahead began to emerge out of the darkness. The rolling expanse of matted grass was a kind of greyish-green, broken by brown patches of withered thistles and docks. Coveys of partridges sprang up, and larks and crows took to the sky. There was no sign of the Germans, hidden deep in their trenches and dug-outs. Only the long lines of dense barbed wire.

Captain Dugdale had established his 6th Division observation post on the highest ground he could find in the centre of the Front, from where he had a commanding view over the whole area. To his left, Havrincourt Wood was bustling with activity as the camouflage netting was lifted off the guns and the artillery officers supervised the loading of shells. All along the Front were the grey hulks of the tanks, hidden behind trees, hedges and shelled buildings. Behind these, the infantry battalions were lining up, while from the aerodrome behind, squadrons of biplanes were beginning to appear as dark specks in the grey sky.

" In the distance, we can see a long way over the German lines," he reported, " where the country is flat. Immediately in front of us at a distance of 500 yards is the German wire and the first Hindenburg Line trench system. The ground behind this slopes down to the village of Ribecourt, of which we can only see the tops of the roofs. This lies in a valley, and behind, the ground gradually slopes up to the Flesquieres Ridge, extending along the whole of our immediate front. Behind this in the distance, a few miles away, the ground again slopes up to culminate on the horizon with Bourlon Village and Bourlon Wood. On our right, the ground slopes downwards to a valley in which lies the village of Villers-Plouich, inside our lines. This valley extends through the German Hindenburg lines until it reaches the valley extending from left to right. At the far end of this are the villages of Masnieres and Marcoing, and beyond them, a slope leads for miles up to Cambrai."

It was now 6.00 a.m. and the tank crews were climbing into their vehicles which were formed up some 500 yards behind the British front lines. Once inside, the men were in another world. The driver and gunners wore strange armour-plate face masks with slotted eye-holes and chain mail hanging down to cover the mouth and lower part of the face. This was to protect them from the tiny particles of red-hot metal that would fly around inside of the tank once heavy machine-gun fire began to hit the outer walls. One crew member described the scene:

" Nothing could be seen outside, nothing could be heard, while inside one half-shaded lamp gave an eerie, murky glimmer in the stygian gloom. The walls represented the limits of one's world and the crew of eight—and the three carrier-pigeons—the population. One was completely isolated. Existence depended on the driving skill of the driver and the wits of the officer. Tanks on the left and right might be seen through the tiny peep-holes in the armour-plate walls, but they existed merely as other worlds. Once we started there was no co-operation between tanks, no tactics, no external command—only the objectives we had been given and the method of attack we had been taught during training."

In the centre of the line, opposite the village of Ribecourt, were the tanks of H battalion. One of the company commanders, Major Gerald Huntbach, was standing beside the front row of tanks when a lithe figure, pipe clenched between his teeth and carrying an ash stick with a cloth wrapped round it, strode up past the waiting infantry. It was Brigadier General Elles. " Five minutes to go," he said. " This is the centre of our line, and I'm going over in this tank." And he tapped the side of the front row tank named " Hilda ".

Huntbach opened the door of the tank and informed Lieutenant Leach and his surprised crew that they were to take the commander of the Tank Corps into action with them. Elles shook his ash stick, revealing the brown, red and green flag of the Corps, and squeezed through the opening. The door closed with a clang, and a few minutes later the head and shoulders of Elles appeared through the man-hole at the top. He was to remain in this position, holding the Corps flag, while the tanks rolled into action.

At ten minutes past six, " Hilda " and all the front tanks along the line began to move forwards. Engines which had been purring at idling speed broke into a loud roar. Slowly, the tanks approached the British front line trenches. And then, just as they began to head into No Man's Land at zero hour, 6.20 a.m., there was a devastating blast as the 1,000-gun artillery barrage opened up from behind. At the same time, from out of the sky swept squadrons of the Royal Flying Corps, flying low and spraying the German trenches with machine-gun fire. The battle of Cambrai had begun.

CHAPTER SEVEN

The Big Breakthrough

" SUDDENLY, the air itself seemed to reel under a tremendous blow. A dull and curiously mellow roar broke forth and continued with a peculiar rhythm. The atmosphere became alive with the scream of shells. On the opposite slope we could see them bursting on the German trenches, while behind these there was a huge black curtain, thrown up by our smoke shells. As they landed, they gave the effect of the embers of a burning haystack. Splinters of flame were on every side like exploding stars in the night sky. The Germans were sending up S.O.S. rockets from their trenches all along the line. They shone out vividly against the black curtain beyond."

This is how one tank commander described the opening of the British artillery barrage as the tanks rolled forward, slowly and relentlessy, each carrying its enormous bundle of brushwood on top. They looked like monstrous, pre-historic animals in the half-light of dawn.

"The whole of the enemy's lines were lit up in a tossing, bubbling torrent of multi-coloured flame," reported another tank crew member. "And, best of all, nothing came back in reply. As we lurched along, we expected the most frightful crash to come at any minute. It seemed almost too good to be true, this steady rumbling forward over marvellous going, no craters in the ground, no shelling from the enemy, and our infantry following steadily behind. Emerging out of the gloom, a dark mass came steadily towards us—the German wire. It appeared absolutely impenetrable. It was certainly the thickest and deepest I had ever seen, stretching in front of us in three belts, each about 50 yards deep. It neither stopped our tank nor broke up and wound round the tracks as we had feared, but squashed flat as we moved forward and remained flat. A broad carpet of wire was left behind us, as wide as our tank, over which the infantry were able to pick their way without any difficulty."

The troops in the German front-line trenches had gone down into the dug-outs as soon as the artillery bombardment started. Only the lookout sentries were left on top. One of these was Infantryman Hans Hildemann of the 1st Battalion, 84th Infantry Regiment, holding the front sector near Havrincourt.

"You'll be all right," a sergeant told him cheerily as he descended to the safety of the dug-out below. "The British infantry will never attack while the artillery is still firing."

Soon, Hildemann was left alone in his observation post. The sergeant's words had done little to reassure him. But at least the shells seemed to be falling on the trenches behind him. This was his first experience of battle, and he hardly knew what to expect. He had heard stories of the insane attacks by shouting British soldiers against machine-guns in Flanders, and his hands trembled nervously as he peered into the gloom ahead. He was 19 years old. Suddenly, over the rhythmic sound of the shelling, he heard a new noise. It sounded like an aeroplane engine and he instinctively looked overhead. He had already seen some British aircraft that morning. But there was no sign of any now. He looked down again—and then he saw it. A huge grey shape looming towards him out of the mist. As it came nearer, the sound of its engines becoming louder, it seemed to tower above him, blocking out the sky. He stared at it, unable to move. His only thought was, how did it get there? What about all that wire, which the officers said proudly that nothing could penetrate? And then came the question—what was it? Was he really awake? Was this some kind of terrible nightmare?

By now, the warning had been given and the men came rushing up out of the dug-outs. Many wore gas-masks because at first they had mistaken the smoke shells for a gas attack.

Machine-guns were manned and a hail of fire directed towards the tanks—for there were more of them now. But the bullets simply glanced off the monsters. Nothing seemed to be able to stop their relentless advance. Now the female machine-gun tanks were rolling along the parapets of the trenches, firing continuously at the occupants below. And behind the tanks, British infantrymen were now visible, advancing with fixed bayonets. This was no battle—it was a massacre. Dazed and bewildered, Hildemann and all those around him threw down their guns and raised their arms in surrender.

This scene was repeated all along the front-line trenches, and was later vividly described by another tank commander, Captain D. G. Browne:

"The immediate onset of the tanks inevitably was overwhelming," he wrote. "The German outposts, dazed or annihilated by the sudden deluge of shells, were overrun in an instant. The triple belts of wire were crossed as if they had been beds of nettles, and 350 pathways were sheared through them for the infantry. The defenders of the front trench, scrambling out of the dug-outs and shelters to meet the crash and flame of the barrage, saw the leading tanks almost upon them, their appearance made the more grotesque and terrifying by the huge black bundles they carried on their cabs. As these tanks swung left-handed and fired down into the trench, others, also surmounted by these appalling objects, appeared in multitudes behind them out of the mist. It is small wonder that the front Hindenburg Line, that fabulous excavation which was to be the bulwark of Germany, gave little trouble. The great fascines were loosed and rolled over the parapet to the trench floor; and down the whole line tanks were dipping and rearing up and clawing their way across into the almost unravaged country beyond. The defenders of the line were running panic stricken, casting away arms and equipment."

Frightening though the tanks were to the Germans, it was no joy-ride to be inside one. Apart from the shaking and the vibration, the noise inside was deafening and drowned all sound of the artillery barrage. The rattle of the tracks produced an illusion of tremendous speed, but in fact most of the tanks moved at no more than about two miles an hour, and never more than about 5 m.p.h. Speech was impossible because of the noise, and all commands were given by signals. It took four of the crew, including the commander, to make a turn. First of all, the driver had to bring the tank to a halt. Then a knock on the left side would attract the attention of the left gearsman, working at the back. He would put the track into neutral with an iron lever, and signal with a clenched fist that this had been done. Then the officer, who controlled the brake levers, would pull on the left one, holding the left track. The driver would accelerate and with only the right track moving, the tank would slew round to the left. When it had turned sufficiently, the tank would again be stopped and the same procedure carried out in reverse. It was no easy job to run a zig-zag course if under fire from an enemy field-gun.

All the while the sweating gearsmen were working, the four gunners—two on either side—would be blazing away with the 6-pounders and the Lewis machine-guns. The heat inside was suffocating, generated not only by the guns but also from the engine in the centre of the cabin. And there were other dangers.

" I finished up with only the driver and myself conscious, due to the escape of exhaust gas in the pipe from the engine," recalls Mr. Jefford. " The crew were so badly affected that they were sent straight back to England. The driver and I escaped the gas, having the advantage of fresh air coming through the front flaps. At one stage of the battle I was faced with the rest of my crew unconscious, the engine stopped, and the enemy firing on my tank. It required four men to work the starting handle, so I had to shake three of the crew alive to get the engine started so we could drive back to safety."

Mr. Jefford remembers that it took all one's wits to watch the course of the battle from the enclosed world inside a tank. " Firstly, we used the periscope to judge the effect of our firing. Secondly, by lifting the shutters of the peep holes, we could watch the fate of other tanks next to us, which wasn't pleasant when they were hit. It was also important to watch the visual compass in order to know one's direction if it became necessary to get out of difficulties quickly. It was extremely difficult to concentrate the gunners on the required target when under shell or machine-gun fire. The gunners on the 6-pounders had vertical gaps through which to aim their telescopic sights, but inside the tank, when machine-guns sprayed our armoured plating, it was like the sparks flying around in a blacksmith's forge. When I was using my forward machine-gun, it was impossible to sustain firing for any length of time, as the hot sparks hit my hand and wrist. My skin was mottled for days afterwards."

Before the battle started, the one point which had worried the reconnaissance officers was that area shown on the map as the Grand Ravine, passing in front of Ribecourt village. Ground and air observation had failed to reveal the depth of this dried-up stream bed. But in fact, it proved not to be an obstacle at all, and the tanks took it in their stride. By 8.00 a.m. the whole of the Hindenburg Main line, from Havrincourt to L'Escaut Canal, was in British hands. Everywhere along the front, prisoners were being rounded up in their hundreds, while the tanks were rolling on towards the second objective, the Hindenburg Support Line.

In the centre of the line, General Elles in "Hilda" had reached the outposts in the van of the battle. Nudging his driver in the ribs to indicate direction, he had succeeded in locating a number of targets. Then, as the tide of the battle swept on, Elles reluctantly left the tank and walked back through the British lines to Beaucamp, still pulling at his pipe. Behind him, at a respectful distance, followed several parties of German prisoners. "Hilda" meanwhile pushed on towards Ribecourt, but then became ditched in a trench just outside the village and had to be pulled out by another tank. Within another half-an-hour, tanks had advanced into Ribecourt.

The captured German trenches and dug-outs turned out to be a revelation, certainly far better equipped than those of the British. During a brief pause in the attack after the Hindenburg Main Line had fallen, several tank commanders and crews inspected the famous trenches they had heard so much about. Mr. William T. Dawson, who fought in one of the C Battalion tanks, recalls his first sight of a German dug-out. " It was very deep, probably in the region of 20 feet, and consisted of a number of rooms off a long, wide passage with an entrance down stairs at each end. The roof and sides were all covered with heavy timber and the rooms made comfortable with beds and furniture taken from houses in the vicinity. It must have taken a great amount of labour and a long time to construct. In the trench outside there was even a kind of summerhouse where the officers could sit."

There were signs of confusion everywhere at the suddenness of the attack. Blankets had been flung to the floor, boots and rifles and helmets still stood in corners, and letters from wives and girl friends, trailing along the passages, showed in what haste the owners had fled. One tank commander who stopped for a few minutes to reconnoitre the ground ahead found, on his return, that all his crew except the driver had disappeared. " I searched frantically right and left, and in a few minutes they trickled back in ones and twos, laden with the most amazing collection of loot I have ever seen, chiefly consisting of field-glasses, greatcoats, cigars, spirits, and water-bottles. A particularly tough little Scots lance-corporal had come back with a frying pan of sausages he had found in an officers' dug-out, still cooking on the fire."

Major Watson of G Battalion had crossed the line with the 51st Highland Division, and also left his tank to inspect the trenches. " At first we were unhappy; a machine-gun from the right was enfilading the trench and the enemy gunners were still active. We pushed along to the left, and after a slight delay came to a deep sunken road, which cut through the trench system at right angles. We walked up the road, which in a few yards widened out. On either side were dug-outs, stores and cookhouses. Cauldrons of coffee and soup were still on the fire. This regimental headquarters the enemy had defended desperately. The trench-boards were slippery with

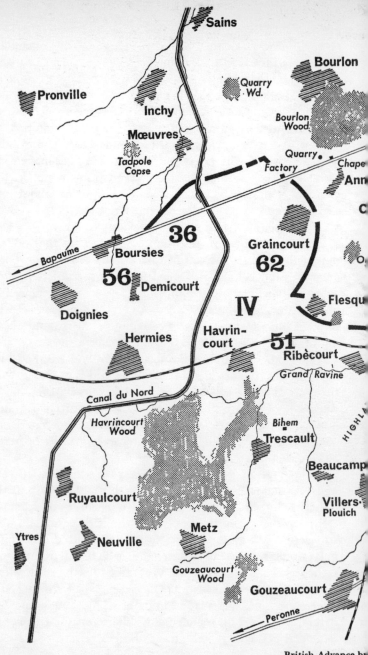

Sains

Bourlon

Pronville

Quarry
Wd.

Inchy

Bourlon
Wood

Mœuvres

Quarry

Tadpole
Copse

Factory

Chape

36

Ann

Bapaume

Boursies

Graincourt

C

56

Demicourt

62

O

IV

Doignies

Flesqu

Hermies

Havrin-
court

51

Ribècourt

Canal du Nord

Grand Ravine

Havrincourt
Wood

Bihem

HIGHLA

Trescault

Beaucamp

Ruyaulcourt

Villers-
Plouich

Ytres

Neuville

Metz

Gouzeaucourt
Wood

Gouzeaucourt

Peronne

British Advance by

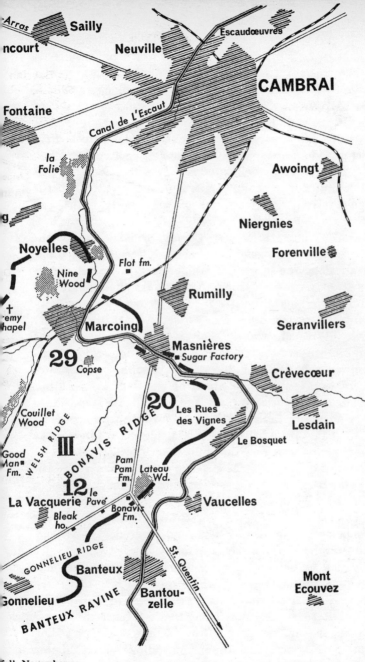

Arras   Sailly

ncourt   Neuville   Escaudœuvres

                                              CAMBRAI

Fontaine   Canal de L'Escaut

        la
        Folie   Awoingt

                                        Niergnies

Noyelles   **Forenville**

        Nine   Flot fm.
        Wood

+   **Rumilly**
emy
hapel   **Marcoing**   **Seranvillers**

29 Copse   **Masnières**
                    ■ Sugar Factory   **Crèvecœur**

        Couillet   **20** Les Rues
        Wood   des Vignes   **Lesdain**

Good   Le Bosquet
Man   **III**
Fm.

12 le   Pam   Lateau
        Pavé Pam   Wd.
La Vacquerie Fm.   **Vaucelles**

    Bleak   Bonavis
    ho.   Fm.

        GONNELIEU RIDGE   **Mont
                                                Ecouvez**
    Banteux

Gonnelieu   **Bantou-
BANTEUX RAVINE   zelle**

fall, November 20.

blood, and fifteen to twenty corpses, all Germans and bayoneted, lay strewn about the road like drunken men. A Highland sergeant who, with a handful of men, was now in charge of the place, came out to greet us, puffing at a long cigar. All his men were smoking cigars, and it was indeed difficult that morning to find a Highlander without one. He invited us into a large chamber cut out of the rock, from which a wide staircase descended into an enormous dug-out. The chamber was panelled deliciously with coloured woods and decorated with choice prints. Our host produced a bottle of good claret, and we drank to the health of the 51st Division."

From his observation post, Captain Dugdale viewed the scene with fast growing excitement. It seemed incredible, but all along the front, the Hindenburg Line, the impenetrable barrier, was falling to the tanks and the British infantry. Nothing quite like it had ever been seen before—during this or any other war. " Behind us there was great activity," Dugdale wrote. " For the first time we saw the magnificent spectacle of our field artillery limbering up and going forward, first at a trot, then at a gallop, battery after battery, to take up new positions on the German front line. Special tanks for clearing the wire trundled up and down the Hindenburg Line, gathering up the wire with hooks and rolling it into huge balls so that it should not get in the way of our cavalry, which was due to come up shortly."

Commanding one of these " wire-pulling " tanks was Mr. J. T. G. Bancroft. " We went forward in pairs," he recalls. " The wire entanglement was terrific. It stretched forward for 200 yards. We dropped our clearing anchor, held back by a belay pin inside the tank, and proceeded to diverge, rolling up the wire to make paths for the cavalry."

Dugdale and the other observation officers sent the news of the capture of the Hindenburg Line back to their divisional headquarters, and from there it went to Third Army H.Q. But so sudden and complete had been the breakthrough, so startling after all the failures of the preceding months, that many of the commanding officers simply couldn't believe it. "General Duncan told me afterwards," wrote Dugdale, "that this message was so incredible that so far as he was concerned, he sent it forward adding a note to say he could hardly believe it. I think that the powers that be waited for this message to be confirmed before ordering the cavalry forward. In fact, it was not until 12.30 p.m. that the cavalry received orders to advance."

The surprise and speed of the attack had not only created havoc among the German infantry in the trenches, but because many telephone lines had been destroyed, there was confusion and bewilderment at 2nd Army headquarters. Roused out of his bed, General von der Marwitz first heard that British tanks had broken through in the areas of Havrincourt and La Vacquerie, but the extent of the attack and the size of the forces involved were unknown.

"What do our reconnaissance planes report?" he asked.

General Baron von Watter, speaking from his Caudry Group headquarters, had more bad news. Captain Flashar's flight had been unable to carry out reconnaissance because of bad weather. The General had himself spoken to Flashar earlier.

"He was very excited and nervous," Flashar wrote, "and demanded to know why I wasn't flying. I tried to explain that it was impossible to reach the Front. There was a dense fog, and the pilots would have lost their way. But my views were not accepted. The English machines were over the Front and I was to get there at once. I was even threatened with a court martial."

Just as Flashar and his flight were preparing to take off, a squadron of British planes arrived and bombed the airfield. In the fog, however, with targets difficult to see, it was not a successful raid. Two of the planes were brought down by anti-aircraft fire, and a third shot down by Sergeant Major Mai, who had managed to take off in one lone Albatross. The pilot of this aircraft was Lieutenant Hall of the 164th Canadian Battalion. Shortly afterwards, Flashar led his flight into the air. But they were unable to reach the front lines, as Flashar had predicted, and six of them had to make forced landings after losing their way, severely damaging their aircraft.

Marwitz received the news in stony silence. " Well, do what you can to send up reinforcements," he ordered at last. " And tell the men to stand fast. We've got to hold those two positions." He did not know then, and neither did von Watter, that the whole of the Cambrai front had been breached.

News of the attack was sent through to Crown Prince Rupprecht, commanding the Northern Group of which the Second Army held the left flank, and so seriously did he take it that shortly after 8.00 a.m. he informed General Erich Ludendorff, commanding the German Armies. Ludendorff's immediate reaction was to accuse the Second Army of not taking sufficient precautions and of being too concerned with watching the situation in Flanders, to the neglect of their own defences. However, he promised to send reserves as soon as he could, and told Rupprecht to make plans for a counter-attack. But as more news came in and the extent of the British attack became known, this possibility seemed more and more remote. Reserves could not possibly arrive before 48 hours, and meanwhile, the tanks were penetrating deeper into the German defences and closer towards Cambrai. Rupprecht and Marwitz were forced to contemplate an extensive withdrawal of the whole Cambrai front.

Nothing had been able to stop the first onslaught of the tanks and the overrunning of the Hindenburg Line trenches by the British infantry. But in several places, pockets of resistance formed. One was at Bleak House, on the Peronne-Cambrai road where, on the extreme right of the front, tanks of C and F Battalions had led the 12th Division attack along the Bonavis Ridge. The 6-pounder guns of C Battalion soon overcame this resistance, but further on, at Lateau Wood, there was a more serious hold-up. The Germans had a battery of guns, including a 5.9 howitzer, concealed in the wood, and they were beginning to take a heavy toll of both troops and tanks. Eventually, it was a tank of C Battalion which settled matters. The tank was approaching the battery when it was hit and severely damaged by the howitzer. The crew scrambled out and ran for cover but, more by accident than intent, they had left the tank in gear. Unmanned, the tank continued relentlessly forward. Nothing could stop it. With a loud crash it hit the gun and crushed it into the undergrowth.

To the left of 12th Division, tanks of I and A Battalions had led the 20th Division into the valley beyond the Gonnelieu spur and Welsh Ridge. Some resistance was coming from La Vacquerie, and it was in fact a section of tanks of F Battalion which solved the problem here. Major Philip Hammond, the battalion commander, described the incident in a letter written home to his wife. "Suddenly I was aware there was a hell of a lot of rifle fire from La Vacquerie and I knew someone was held up and the Germans were firing as hard as they could. I sent a runner across to Maude, my second in command, to carry on and I moved across to my left with four tanks. We turned and came into the village by the back door. The shooting died down and heaps of Germans came running out of the houses. Our people were through by now, so we got on our own line again."

The tanks of I and A Battalions, after an easy start, were meanwhile suffering a considerable number of casualties from direct hits by German artillery. In attacking a building known as Good Old Man Farm, near Marcoing, one of A Battalion's tanks, commanded by Captain R. W. L. Wain, was hit at point-blank range by mortar fire. Wain and another man were severely wounded, and the rest of the crew killed. Nevertheless, Wain picked up a Lewis gun and rushed the stronghold single-handed, taking half the garrison prisoners while the rest of the Germans retreated. Although bleeding profusely from wounds, he continued to fire at the retreating enemy until he was fatally wounded by a bullet in the head. For this action, which enabled the infantry to continue their advance, Wain was posthumously awarded the Victoria Cross—the second ever to be won for the Tank Corps and the only one to be awarded to the Corps during the Cambrai battle.

In the centre, the tanks of B and H Battalions, personally led by General Elles, spearheaded the attack by the 6th Division along Highland Ridge to Ribecourt, which lay behind the Grand Ravine and between the Hindenburg Main and Support Lines. The entry into Ribecourt was made by two companies of the 2nd Battalion Sherwood Foresters and 9th Battalion Norfolk Regiment, who had forged ahead of the tanks, but resistance continued until the arrival of B Battalion tanks. From Ribecourt onwards, heavy artillery fire was encountered from German guns in the direction of Flesquieres, which also held up the advance of 51st Division and the tanks of E and D Battalions.

It was on the extreme left of the front, where 62nd Division was attacking from Havrincourt Wood with G and E Battalion tanks, that the Germans put up the most notable fight. The first main objective was Havrincourt village, an extremely important position as it stood on the Flesquieres Ridge, screening the ground to Cambrai behind. The Hindenburg Main Line here was built on the slopes beyond the village, and had been out of sight of the British artillery observers. There were also a number of German field-gun batteries behind the ridge, which unfortunately had not been spotted by reconnaissance planes. From the ruins of Havrincourt Chateau on the very top of the ridge, there was a commanding view over the entire countryside.

Soon after the attack started, it was this area that the German Second Army had ordered to be defended most strongly. And it was Havrincourt village that was the headquarters of Captain Soltau, commander of the 11 Battalion of the 84th Infantry Regiment who had been the first man to learn of the tank attack from the captured British prisoners 36 hours before and who had discounted the information.

The progress of the tanks from Havrincourt Wood at the start of the battle had been delayed by fallen trees and stumps in the ground. In spite of this, in less than an hour, most of the 84th Infantry Regiment who had been manning the front line trenches were either killed or taken prisoner. Captain Soltau gathered together the remnants of the regiment and prepared to make a stand in the village. For over an hour they successfully held off troops of the 2nd and 6th

Battalions West Yorkshire Regiment, who had entered the village from the east, with concentrated machine-gun fire. It was then that the tanks came up, having been delayed not only by the rough ground, but by the German guns firing from behind the ridge. Six tanks had been put out of action by direct hits before the first male tank, 43, commanded by Lieutenant William McElroy, entered the village. The tank made its way up the main street under heavy fire from the machine-guns, and succeeded in silencing three of these by Lewis gun fire and three more by means of the 6-pounders. A large shell crater full of water stopped the tank's progress, and it was while McElroy was backing it down the street to look for another way through that a bullet hit the reserve petrol tank on the roof and the flaring petrol streamed down inside the tank. The crew tried to extinguish the fire, but the fumes eventually forced them to make a run for it and take cover in a shell-hole. The Germans tried to rush the tank, but McElroy climbed back inside and held them off by firing through the doorway, killing eight with his revolver. He managed to get the fire under control and called back the crew. Just then, a party of British infantry came down the street, and a hundred or more Germans surrendered. For this action, McElroy was awarded the Distinguished Service Order, one of ninety-eight awards for gallantry won for the Tank Corps on the first day of the battle, thirty-eight by officers and sixty by other ranks.

Captain Soltau fell back with his men to a farmhouse on the outskirts of the village which had, in fact, been his battalion headquarters. But ammunition was now running short, and there was heavy bombardment from the tanks which were coming up in increasing numbers. At 8.45 a.m. he established telephone contact with his regimental headquarters, and sent back the message, "We are holding out to the last man." Shortly afterwards, he and the rest of his battalion were all killed. It took another two hours for the troops of 62nd Division finally to clear out the maze of dugouts built under the ruins of the Chateau. And by this time, the tanks and infantry were pressing on towards the next objective at Graincourt, three miles ahead, accompanied now by the 186th Reserve Infantry Brigade which was commanded by Boys Bradford V.C., at twenty-five the youngest brigadier general in the British Army. On the far left, meanwhile, the 36 (Ulster) Division was preparing to assist in the attack by sending forward the 109th Brigade to the west of the Canal du Nord.

By 11.30 a.m., five hours after the attack had started, almost the whole of the Hindenburg Main and Support Line system along the six-mile front had been captured. Heavy losses had been inflicted during the 4,000 yards advance at very little cost in British casualties. Many guns had been captured, and more than 2,000 prisoners. The German divisions holding the front, the 20th Landwehr, the 54th, and 19th Reserve Regiment, had been almost wiped out. The losses of the 20th Landwehr were so great in fact that the division was never reconstituted. Only a few German reserves had been available to be rushed up to the Front, mostly units from the 20th and 111th Divisions and the 107th Division which had just arrived from Russia, but these had been unable to stem the tide. The tanks had re-grouped for the next advance forward. Batteries of field-guns were being brought past the captured trenches to take up forward positions. And everywhere, the arrival of the main bodies of the Cavalry Corps was imminently awaited, to surge through the broken defences and into the open country beyond. The German Second Army was preparing for a wholesale withdrawal of the sector. And in Cambrai itself, where the sounds of the attack and the confusion amongst the Germans had been heard first with bewilderment and then with growing excitement, an early liberation was keenly anticipated. Everywhere, the initial attack had succeeded beyond the highest hopes—to such an extent that some rearward commanders couldn't bring themselves to believe it. At only one point was there a hold-up, at Flesquieres, in the centre of the front. It was to have serious consequences, and lead to one of the strangest incidents of the whole battle.

CHAPTER EIGHT

Legend of Flesquieres Ridge

THE most important objective in the centre of the attack was the village of Flesquieres, behind and slightly to the left of Ribecourt and situated on the high ridge extending from Havrincourt to Marcoing. This ridge held a commanding view over the whole countryside to Cambrai and also shielded the Hindenburg Support Line, which was built on the slopes behind the crest. The village was on the route from Trescault intended for the 1st Cavalry Division, and its capture was essential before the cavalry could pass through and spread out into the open fields beyond. The attack in this sector was made by General Harper's 51st Highland Division. From previous experience in Flanders, this was one of the divisions most feared by the Germans. The Highlanders had a well earned reputation for tough, determined fighting, and their commander, " Uncle " Harper as he was known, was widely respected as a fearless leader. But he was also a narrow-minded soldier of the old school. He disapproved of tanks, and wanted his men to have as little to do with them as possible. Training between his infantry and the tanks before the battle, in what little time there was anyway, had been perfunctory to say the least, and he ignored the tactics recommended by the Tank Corps. The result was that from the very beginning of the attack, there was a marked lack of co-operation between tank crews and infantry.

The attack started smoothly enough at 6.20 a.m. when

forty-two tanks of D Battalion and twenty-eight of E Battalion (less one company) rolled down the slopes of the Trescault spur towards the German outpost zone and the Grand Ravine beyond. Keeping well behind the tanks, as Harper had ordered, came the infantry—the Black Watch and Gordon Highlanders of 153rd Brigade behind D Battalion to the right, and the Seaforth Highlanders and Argyll and Sutherland Highlanders of 152nd Brigade behind E Battalion to the left. The Hindenburg trenches in this centre section of the front were wider and deeper than elsewhere, but the Germans showed little inclination to resist. Both tanks and infantry crossed without much difficulty. And when they came to the Grand Ravine, it proved to be not the obstacle feared. By 8.30, the Hindenburg Main Line had been captured and all was ready for the attack uphill to the crest of Flesquieres Ridge and the Hindenburg Support Line beyond, the second objective. But Harper's time-table read that this assault should not take place until 9.30—another indication of his lack of confidence in the success of the operation because he did not really believe the Main Line would fall so easily, if at all—and it was decided that this should not be changed. There was a needless delay of one hour, when infantry and tank crews went on a looting spree in the trenches. This hour gave the Germans a breathing space in which to muster their scattered forces.

When the attack had started, Major Hofmeister, commanding the 84th Infantry Regiment which held the Hindenburg Line on this sector of the front, had been caught completely off guard. Unlike some other German local commanders, he had not believed the rumours of a British attack. From his headquarters in a blockhouse on the Support Line, east of Flesquieres, he sent Captain Willie with the *1* Battalion forward to "hold the line." Captain Willie reached the Main Line trenches, but then, to his consternation, he saw the extent of the British attack and the unprecedented sight of tanks mowing down the barbed wire. He called urgently for reinforcements and was promised them. Then came the news that *11* Battalion to the right, under Captain Soltau, had been overrun. Willie suggested a withdrawal, but he was ordered to stay put. By now the tanks were rolling past his position, and Willie and a few survivors of his battalion had taken shelter in a dug-out.

" The battalion has been cut off," Willie reported by telephone to his headquarters. " No trace of a counter-attack can be seen. But we hear clearly the shouting and orders being given by the British . . . All documents are being destroyed. Now a tank is rolling over the top of the day common room of battalion headquarters, which is separated from our dug-out by a wooden wall. The tank stops and the crew dismount. They seem to believe they have captured the battalion's command post . . . There are corpses everywhere. Every few minutes we peep through a hole in the wooden planks to see what is happening . . . British infantry are attacking the trenches to our right, passing barely twenty yards away . . . Our own position is desperate . . . we have not even a dozen rifles and hand grenades left . . ."

Frantic requests for a counter-attack were made to Major Hofmeister. And suddenly one of the men whispered to Willie and pointed behind the dug-out. A long line of men in German steel helmets was moving down the hill, marching straight towards them. This must be the counter-attack. But as the troops came nearer, it was seen they carried no rifles. They were prisoners, being led away under escort. And a few minutes later, Captain Willie's own dug-out was surrounded, and he and his men were taken prisoner.

Meanwhile, shortly after 8.00 a.m., some reinforcements had arrived from Cambrai in answer to Hofmeister's appeals for help. They were units of the 27th Reserve Infantry Regiment, accompanied by the regimental commander, Major Krebs. He joined Hofmeister in his command blockhouse, and together they planned for the defence of Flesquieres village and the Support Line behind the ridge. Realising that to be effective against tanks, it was more important for field-guns to be mobile rather than hidden in fortified positions, Hofmeister ordered the guns of 2nd Company 108 Field Artillery Regiment to be pulled out into the open and pointed towards the top of the ridge, from where the attack would come. Four batteries were positioned in this way by Lieutenant Ruppell, while the remainder of that regiment and also 282 Field Artillery Regiment continued what fire they could in the general direction of the British advance. The guns were moved between 9.30 and 10.00, while the British 51st Division was taking an hour's rest, and at a time when, to the relief of the defenders, the British artillery barrage had lifted to attack targets further behind.

The four 77 mm gun batteries, now able to swivel round to either side, were ideally placed to cover the slopes down from the ridge where, to the right and left, tanks were advancing towards Graincourt and Marcoing. The guns had not been spotted by R.F.C. air reconnaissance earlier, when they had been hidden in their original positions, and so, for the first time that morning, the tanks found themselves in the position they most feared—slow-moving targets in open country, vulnerable to accurate gun-fire. Shells burst all around them, and of the 56 tanks of G Battalion and the one company of E Battalion which had left Havrincourt and were heading towards Graincourt, eleven were put out of action. The tanks on the other side, moving towards Marcoing, were luckier as they were further away, but Captain Hickey, leading his section, reported some near misses and he had an uncomfortable half-hour zig-zagging forward to avoid being hit. But the most devastating casualties were yet to be inflicted, on the tanks coming up directly in front of the ridge.

It was 9.30 when the 51st Division commenced their attack again uphill towards Flesquieres. They were completely unaware of the German guns on the other side of the ridge. The tanks went first while the infantry, in accordance with Harper's instructions, hung back. There were now some 400 yards separating the two, and as the tanks began crushing the barriers of wire near the top of the ridge to make pathways through, they were too far ahead for the infantry to see just where these paths were. When the troops eventually reached the wire, they had to waste valuable time searching for the ways through, and while doing so, machine-gun fire suddenly opened up from Flesquieres village to the right, where Major Krebs had been able to place his 27th Reserve Infantry Regiment in defensive positions.

Unaware of what was happening behind, the tanks continued blithely on to the crest of the ridge, in line abreast as instructed. They came to the top, huge, dark shapes silhouetted against the skyline. And there before them were the German field-guns. Had the infantry been close behind the tanks, as Fuller had planned, they could easily have dealt with these guns in a matter of minutes. But the infantry were far behind, not only held up by having to find their way through the wire but, because of the machine-gun fire from the village which was causing heavy casualties, they had been forced to fall back. The tanks were on their own.

With such perfect targets in front of them, the German gunners opened fire. One by one the tanks were hit, while the crews worked desperately at the cumbersome gears to drive a zig-zag course and the gunners tried to return the fire. But taking accurate aim in all the pitching and tossing was virtually impossible. It was some minutes before the German guns had been put out of action, one at a time until eventually only one was firing and then this too, was silenced. But by this time, sixteen tanks had been destroyed, with huge, gaping holes in their sides. Most were on fire, and those crew members who had not been killed outright by the blasting shells were burned to death. There were no survivors.

"The hold-up on Flesquieres Ridge was entirely due to faulty tactics," Fuller wrote later. "It would have been in no way disastrous had the infantry been on the heels of the tanks, for then they could have settled with the German gunners in a few minutes."

Some of the tanks moved forward to cross the Support Line, now virtually deserted, while others turned towards Flesquieres village where heavy fighting was taking place. The battle between guns and tanks on Flesquieres Ridge, in which four German guns had claimed 27 victims—sixteen tanks of D and E Battalions and eleven of G Battalion—was over. But it was to have a strange sequel. Early in the afternoon, Captain Dugdale, the 6th Division observation officer, came up to see for himself where the action had taken place. "I came to a German field battery, every gun out of action with the exception of one," he reported. "By this was lying a single German officer, quite dead. In front of him were five tanks, which he had evidently succeeded in knocking out single-handed with his gun. A brave man."

This report, together with others mentioning the German officer, found its way to 51st Division headquarters. It came as a godsend. Harper and his staff would certainly not admit that they had been at fault in ordering the wrong tactics to be followed, and that the incident would not have occurred if they had followed those laid down by Fuller. But they couldn't help but be aware that the only hold-up in the whole attack had been in their sector. All along the Front, tanks and infantry were advancing according to plan. Only at Flesquieres, first on the Ridge and then in the village, were the Germans holding out. What better than to play up the part played by this one German officer, which would help to deflect criticism from themselves. Admiration for a brave enemy would be sure to win sympathy. Accordingly, with suitable embellishments, the report was passed on to Third Army headquarters and from there to General Headquarters.

Here, it was seized upon for other reasons. Artillery officers at GHQ were becoming concerned that steel and other materials which should have been used to provide them with even more guns and ammunition was being diverted to build these new-fangled tanks. Now there was a case in which one artillery officer, even though a German, had seemingly knocked out many tanks single-handed. It proved how much more effective guns were than tanks. And so, in Haig's Official Despatch on the battle, the following appeared:

"The capture of these two villages (Ribecourt and Havrincourt) secured the flanks of the 51st (Highland) Division (T), advancing on the left centre of our attack up the slopes of Flesquieres Hill against the German trench lines on the southern side of Flesquieres village. Here very heavy fighting took place. The stout brick wall skirting the Chateau grounds opposed a formidable obstacle to our advance, while German machine-guns swept the approaches. A number of tanks were knocked out by direct hits from German field batteries in position beyond the crest of the hill. None the less, with the exception of the village itself, our second objectives in this area (the Hindenburg Support Line) were gained before midday."

"Many of the hits upon our tanks at Flesquieres were obtained by a German artillery officer who, remaining alone at his battery, served a field gun single-handed until killed at his gun. The great bravery of this officer aroused the admiration of all ranks."

Such a tribute to one of the enemy was unprecedented, and would certainly never have been given if it had been cavalry or infantry involved. Appearing as it did in a dry, factual Despatch, it was understandably seized upon by the British Press, and the "Hero of Flesquieres" made the headlines. It was only one incident in the battle, but it had far-reaching consequences. For the rest of the war, and even in the years afterwards, it was often quoted as a reason for dispensing with tanks. After all, if one man could knock out so many, what good were they? The legend grew, and by the time Sir Arthur Conan Doyle wrote his account of the campaign in 1919, it was widely accepted that this one German officer had knocked out all sixteen tanks on his own.

There was only one snag. With all the enthusiasm for this brave German officer, no one apparently had bothered to find out his identity. It was certainly news to the Germans that they had a hero on their hands. After the war, the German High Command asked the Imperial Defence Committee for information about the officer. It was discovered that nothing was known about him. Everyone had been so willing to accept the story that no one had bothered to check it. His identity remained a mystery, and there grew up a feeling within the Tank Corps that he really did not exist at all, that his exploit was either a gross exaggeration or a complete fabrication by those who had reason to denigrate the idea of tanks. It certainly had that effect. Research today amongst

German records reveals that there was such a man, and he continued to operate one gun after the rest of the gunners had been killed and their batteries put out of action. He certainly did not knock out all sixteen tanks. Five would have been the maximum, a considerable exploit even so. German records give his name as Lieutenant Karl Muller of the 108th Field Artillery Regiment, and his battery commander, Captain Lorenzen. Another source, quoted in the British Official History of the Great War, suggests it might have been an under-officer named Kruger.

The fight for Flesquieres was by no means over with the silencing of the German guns. Within the village Major Krebs had taken over full command after Hofmeister had been killed, and with some 600 survivors of the 84th and 27th regiments, he was putting up a strong resistance, although himself wounded. A number of tanks trundled up to the outskirts of the village and the neighbouring chateau, firing at the defenders. Several times the enemy troops were forced to take cover in ruined buildings and cellars, leaving the way open for the British infantry to enter the village. But they failed to take advantage of these opportunities, preferring to keep well out of the way of the tanks. When the tanks tried to enter the village themselves, they found that German sharpshooters had been placed in positions from where they could aim through the lookout slits in the armour-plate and hit the crews inside. Also, the Germans had discovered the most vulnerable part of the tanks—their caterpillar tracks. One hand-grenade was not sufficient to damage these, but by bundling several together and rushing forward to throw them under the tracks, they made a very effective weapon.

"We met and crossed another partially finished trench and, reaching flatter going, we were now in full view of the wood in front of Flesquieres, where the machine-gun fire was intense," reported a tank commander with D Battalion. "We lumbered slowly up to the wood, which was fairly thick, and saw the Chateau through the trees. It was tremendously satisfactory after seeing two years of nothing but ruins to shoot at those wide glass windows, which disappeared as if with-drawn by an invisible hand. Two alternatives now appeared; to go through the wood and risk bellying on the trees, or to try and bring up the infantry. Our tanks had only a very small clearance between the fly wheel and the hull and if one ran on to a stump which could not be cleared, the belly of the tank stuck on it, the hull buckled and fouled the fly wheel, and the tank was a salvage job. We had also been told our job was to see the infantry on to the top of the hill. There were very few of them about, and all lying down, so for an hour or more we cruised up and down looking for machine-guns and shooting into the wood. The hostile fire was intense the whole time. Our masks slipped on the sweat of our faces and had to be removed. Two more of the crew were hit, and every time we skirted the wood a sniper shot at the cracks in the hull. Eventually, three of the Lewis guns were out of action, only the driver remained unwounded, our petrol was getting short, and there was no sign of any other troops coming up, so we broke off the action and went back to the rallying point. There, we found the tank was an extraordinary sight. One unditching rail had been cut right through and was hanging down in front, the front flap was at an angle of 30 degrees, the beam had great grooves cut in it, and the hull had innumerable pitmarks all over it from point-blank machine-gun fire. The front gun was bent and battered in its port, looking rather like a splayed-out, rusty cigarette-end stuck on the ball mounting."

On the eastern outskirts of the village, another tank, com-manded by Lieutenant William R. Bion of E Battalion, was put out of action by a direct hit from a howitzer. Bion left the tank with his crew and, together with ten stray Gordon Highlanders, manned a German communication trench with machine-guns taken from the tank. Finding that one German outpost gave more trouble than the others, he climbed back onto the top of the tank to get a better aim with his Lewis gun. He later took command of a company of Seaforths when its commander had been shot, and kept a German counter-attack at bay, using a German gun when his own had run out of ammunition. He was put in for the V.C., and received the D.S.O.

The fight at Flesquieres continued thoughout the afternoon. The village was now virtually outflanked by 62nd Division on the left and 6th Division on the right. But still the lack of co-operation between the tanks and infantry resulted in deadlock. When six tanks did manage to drive into the village, forcing the Germans to take shelter in dug-outs, the infantry failed to come up in time. They only appeared as the tanks were withdrawing and the Germans were coming up from their shelters again. Fierce house to house fighting broke out, but eventually the Highlanders were forced to withdraw. By the time night fell, the position at Flesquieres was much as it had been at midday. A handful of German snipers and machine-gunners had held up the advance of virtually a whole infantry division and a brigade of tanks. Major Krebs's spirited defence ended during the night when he was ordered to withdraw since no reinforcements were available to send to his aid. But the delay he had caused to the British advance had enabled much of the field artillery and rolling stock to be taken back safely, although twenty guns had to be left in the village and fell into British hands. It also had a serious effect on the advance of the neighbouring 62nd Division.

This Division, under the command of Major General Braithwaite, had also met with strong resistance, at Havrincourt, but this did not stop later waves of infantry from bypassing the village and pressing on deeper into the enemy lines, leaving other units and some of the tanks to clear the village. By 11.00 a.m., Brigadier General Bradford's 186th Infantry Brigade had arrived, well on time after moving forward at 9.00. Together with one company of G Battalion tanks and several squadrons of the 1st King Edward's Horse, they advanced with orders to capture Graincourt, three miles further on, Anneux, the high ground west of Bourlon Wood, and bridges on the Bapaume-Cambrai road over the Canal du Nord. Meanwhile, the 36th (Ulster) Division was moving up on the left of the Canal du Nord towards Moeuvres. Little resistance was met by 186th Brigade, except from the guns firing from behind Flesquieres Ridge, until it arrived at the outskirts of Graincourt. There, two German field-guns on the edge of the village opened fire and six tanks were disabled by direct hits. Three more tanks came up from a different direction and destroyed the guns, then entered the village and opened the way for the infantry. Unlike the situation with 51st Division on the right, there was excellent co-operation between tanks and infantry. Graincourt was speedily taken and Bradford ordered troops and two squadrons of cavalry forward to Anneux and the factory buildings on the Cambrai road, while a patrol of three tanks, under Lieutenant Baker, was sent towards Bourlon Wood to see what conditions there were like.

Lieutenant Baker returned after an hour or so with the information that the Germans were in full retreat towards Cambrai and Bourlon Wood and Ridge were free to be occupied. But while the patrol had been away, Bradford received orders not to advance beyond Graincourt. Learning of the delay at Flesquieres and considering it a risk for his division to push forward alone with an exposed flank on the right, Braithwaite had offered to help 51st Division by attacking Flesquieres from the rear. But Harper turned down this suggestion, and Braithwaite, following the orthodox doctrine of uniformity of advance, felt compelled to order a halt. Later in the day, after the cavalry had been held up in front of Anneux by machine-gun fire, Bradford ordered his forces to withdraw to Graincourt. The opportunity to occupy the all-important Bourlon position was lost. It was not to occur again.

CHAPTER NINE

The Advance Continues

WHILE the advance of the IV Corps had been held up at Flesquieres, the main attack on the III Corps front fared much better. On the extreme right, 12th Division, with the tanks of C and F Battalions, had overcome the centre of resistance in Lateau Wood by 11.00 a.m. and now held the Bonavis Ridge overlooking the Canal de L'Escaut, together with the fork where the roads from Gouzeaucourt and Peronne joined to lead into Cambrai. The Germans had made an effort to hold this position, and the night before the attack, units of the 9th Reserve Division had been brought up to reinforce the 19th Reserve Infantry Regiment, which had been holding the line. The defence had not been as strong as it was at Havrincourt and Flesquieres, but the main factor was the degree of co-operation which existed between the British infantry and the tanks. Faced with this, the Germans had been forced to withdraw, and once started it became a near rout. Only at le Quennet Farm was there a further, purely local attempt to make a stand and this was quickly overcome by companies of the Queen's and Royal West Kent's. When the tanks rallied at midday on the Hindenburg Support Line, 55 of the original 76 which had started the attack that morning were still operating. Twelve had been hit by artillery fire, and the rest had become ditched.

The next move forward was a vital one, to capture intact if possible the crossings over the canal at Masnieres in order to make a way for the main body of cavalry. Twelve tanks of F Battalion set off to make this attack. Meanwhile, the follow-up 88th Brigade of 29th Division, which had left at 10.15 behind four tanks of A Battalion, came up by way of La Vacquerie and Welsh Ridge towards the same objective, with the intention of securing the bridgehead at Masnieres and clearing that section of the Masnieres-Beaurevoir line which lay to the east of the village. In fact, they arrived at about the same time as F Battalion, which had held back until the artillery barrage had been lifted.

Major Philip Hammond, the officer commanding F Battalion, argued against this delay, but he was overruled. So he decided to go forward himself to Masnieres, on foot. " I asked for a volunteer to go with me," he wrote afterwards, " and Private Roberts, a ship's fireman from Musselburgh, jumped out of one of the tanks. A stout-hearted bloke, because he knew I must be looking for trouble."

The two men set off across country. " I had to keep stopping to cough because the gas from Ypres was choking me," wrote Hammond, " and all at once I noticed that Roberts was armed only with a water bottle. He said he had forgotten his revolver and only grabbed up a water bottle—which was Paton's I believe and full of whisky. We came on a German, lying dead. Roberts took his rifle and some cartridges and we ran on. When we started on the last slope down to the village and river, the place was full of Germans running, the large majority unarmed. I was looking out for a rifle too because I thought that if only we could get to the bridge before the Germans blew it up, two determined men with rifles might be a bit awkward for the German sappers, and in view of the general stampede we might possibly bring it off till our people came up. We got down to the outskirts of the village. I took a look around, but our troops were not yet visible. Everyone was on the run, so we ran too, down the road into the street leading to the bridge. I just had time to see a German standing there, waving his arms, when there was a heavy thump, a cloud of dirty white dust, and the bridge was gone. We were beaten by only a few minutes and a few yards. No one took any interest in us or offered any interference, except that we were kissed and hugged by the French populace. We went on to the bridge and found that the near end had fallen at a slope into the canal."

Soon afterwards the tanks arrived, with the infantry following. Captain G. le Q. Martel, the Tank Corps staff officer who together with Fuller had done much to plan the battle, also came up on foot, and as senior officer, took charge. He saw that the bridge was only partially destroyed, and as the cavalry were due at any minute and could still have gone across, he stopped the leading tank from trying to make the crossing itself. But the cavalry didn't arrive, and by 12.40 the Germans on the other side of the canal bank, seeing that the British weren't following up their advance, had positioned machine-guns to cover the bridge. As these would have stopped the cavalry anyway, Martel gave the go-ahead for the first tank, which was commanded by Lieutenant Edmundson, to make the attempt to cross over.

" The engine had been running for some time," reported a member of one of the other tank crews who witnessed the incident, " and the silencer which was situated on top of the tank was almost red-hot. The doors were kept ready to open at a moment's notice in case the tank should drop through into the canal. The tank advanced slowly up the street, while we watched from the houses. It was a tense moment. The tank slowly tipped on the edge of the canal bank and slithered down on to the remains of the bridge. But as the full weight of the tank came on to the roadway there was a tearing sound and the whole tank descended into the canal, taking the remains of the damaged bridge with it. The fall caused the water to sweep back in a wave which then returned and rushed over the top on to the red-hot silencer. A great cloud of steam came up. At that moment the crew scrambled out through the manhole on top of the tank, and were fortunately screened by the cloud of steam. They climbed up the remains of the broken girders and gained the near bank of the canal, rushing to the cover of the houses on our side. The last to leave the tank was Lieutenant Edmundson. He was quite bald and always wore a wig—a most expensive one. As he climbed the girders, this wig fell into the water and drifted slowly away. He was quite a strange sight without his wig and the effect was increased by the fact that he and his crew were all wearing chain masks. The enemy did not fire at all while all this was going on. It is impossible to say whether this was due to the screening effect of the steam or to stupefaction at the strangeness of the whole spectacle. None of the crew was wounded."

Edmundson's wig had an amusing sequel. On return to the rest billets several weeks later, he put in a claim for the price of a new wig. This led to an endless correspondence. Would an Ordnance wig be all right instead? Why not go back and recover the original wig? Edmundson pointed out that the yellow Ordnance tow was the wrong colour, and that he could not recover the lost wig as the enemy were shooting at it. Eventually, he recovered most if not all the money he had claimed for a new wig.

Although there were a number of other bridges on either side of Masnieres, these were not strong enough to support tanks. Efforts by the infantry to get across were checked by heavy machine-gun fire from the Germans. And then, early in the afternoon, the first squadrons of the Cavalry Corps clattered into the village and up to the bridge. In describing their arrival, Major Hammond revealed something of what the soldier in the field felt about the cavalry.

"Then a most ludicrous thing happened," he said. "There was a great deal of clattering, galloping and shouting, and a lot of our medieval horse soldiers came charging down the street. I yelled to them that the bridge was gone, but they took no notice of me and went right up to it. One machine-gun would have wiped out the lot. They turned about and came trotting back with a very piano air."

No attempt was made by the main column of cavalry to cross by the other bridges, despite the fact that one was hidden from enemy fire and quite suitable for horses. But at 3.30 p.m., a squadron of the Fort Garry Horse from the Canadian Cavalry Brigade arrived, and, becoming impatient with the needless delay and the endless conferences that were taking place on the Masnieres road between Captain Martel of the Tank Corps, Brigadier General H. Nelson commanding the 88th Brigade, and Major General W. H. Greenly commanding the 2nd Cavalry Division, they decided to cross the canal by a footbridge over which units of the Hampshires were trickling forward. Within half-an-hour, they had assembled on the other side of the canal. By now a drizzling rain had started, but B Squadron the Fort Garry Horse, commanded by Captain Duncan Campbell, galloped up the slope and pressed on towards Rumilly, over-running a German field-gun battery and several parties of infantry. By now, a long column of horsemen, guns and vehicles stretched all the way back to La Vacquerie. But because no orders for cavalry movement had been received from Cavalry Corps headquarters, it was decided that nothing more could be done before dark and the advance was halted. Messengers were sent to recall the squadron of the Fort Garry Horse, but they failed to overtake it. The Canadians had reached a sunken road near Rumilly, but their commander had been killed and only 50 of the original 150 troopers remained. Lieutenant Harcus Strachan took over the command and kept a keen look-out for the main body of cavalry. But they never appeared. Finally, as the Germans were preparing to attack, the Canadians drove off their horses to create a diversion and began to straggle back to Masnieres. The last men did not arrive until 3 a.m. the next morning, by which time they had been fighting without support for twelve hours with sword, rifle and bayonet. They had made the only worthwhile contribution by the cavalry throughout the day, although this was slight because of their limited number. Meanwhile, infantry troops of 29th Division completed occupation of the village, while the 11th Battalion Rifle Brigade of 12th Division managed to fight their way into les Rues Vertes.

A similar situation had occurred on the 20th Division front, to the left. Here, the 61st and 60th Brigades, led by tanks of I and A Battalions, had advanced rapidly along the north-western slopes of the Gonnelieu spur and Welsh Ridge into the valley beyond, leaving the 7th Battalion Somerset Light Infantry to clear Le Vacquerie, with the help of two companies of the 8th Battalion Royal Fusiliers of 12th Division. The Hindenburg Support Line was taken by about 9.00 a.m. Meanwhile, the 1st Company of A Battalion had been ordered forward to clear the canal bank between Masnieres and Marcoing, and particularly the canal locks and the railway bridge at Marcoing. The company commander, Major J. C. Tilly, rallied eight of his tanks, and leaving Captain Maskin to bring these forward, he went on ahead by mule, accompanied by two orderlies, a company reconnaissance officer, and two German prisoners carrying a pot of stew on a pole.

" We passed several batteries of field-guns abandoned except for odd individuals, who ran away as they saw us coming," reported Tilly. " There were a few shots fired at us from the outskirts of Marcoing, but these ceased on our taking cover and firing back. On reaching Marcoing, we found French people in the streets, all very excited and wanting to kiss us. We made for the bridge and there saw Captain W. Bayley, our battalion reconnaissance officer, who had run all the way from the Hindenburg Support Line and come up just in time to prevent a party of Germans blowing up the bridge. He had fired his revolver at them and they ran. He then cut the electric leads to the charge. When I saw him, he was crossing the bridge with a French woman hanging round his neck. He had one arm round her which held his revolver and in the other he was waving the leads. They were both laughing and shouting. My orderly and a tank crew from B Battalion on the left were ordered to guard the bridge."

Shortly afterwards, Tilly's eight tanks arrived. It was now 10.50 a.m. and there was no sign of resistance anywhere. So Tilly and Major M. L. Lakin, the 3rd Company Commander, went forward on mule and horse respectively to reconnoitre the area towards Cambrai.

" We kept in the low ground near the canal to start with," said Tilly, " and then gradually climbed the slope to the east.

We went very cautiously, stopping to have a good look round at frequent intervals. We were fired on once at longish range from the direction of Cantaing by machine-gun or light automatic, and crossed to the other side of the ridge, after which we were unmolested. We reached the outskirts of the southern suburb of Cambrai, where we saw some British wounded lying on stretchers outside a house and two or three German medical orderlies, who saluted. I have often wondered since where these wounded men came from. They could not have been taken that day. Lakin wanted to go into Cambrai, but I dissuaded him from this and we returned to Marcoing. On the way back we could hear fighting going on to the east, probably in Rumilly or Masnieres."

By the time they arrived back in Marcoing, at about 2.30 p.m., the village had been cleared of snipers by a company of Suffolks from 29th Division, and 14 tanks of B Battalion, allocated to 6th Division, had also arrived. The 387th Landwehr Regiment had hurriedly departed, leaving behind important papers which were secured. Outside the village a cavalry brigade had also arrived and dismounted, but lacking specific orders, they had no inclination to push forward to Cambrai.

The 6th Division, on the right flank of Flesquieres, had met with virtually no opposition at all and with the tanks of B and H Battalions, the 16th and 71st Brigades had captured their section of the Hindenburg Support Line by 11.00 a.m., leaving a company of the Buffs to clear Couiller Wood. Fourteen tanks of B Battalion then moved forward towards Marcoing, but found that the job of capturing the bridges had already been undertaken by A Battalion. Meanwhile, seventeen tanks of H Battalion swung round past the edge of the village and headed for Nine Wood. This was an important objective, for from its position at the end of the Premy Chapel ridge, it commanded the village of Noyelles, half-a-mile away in the valley below. Three of the tanks were knocked out by artillery fire from the Flesquieres Ridge, but the remainder cleared the wood and the slopes between there and Marcoing of machine-gun posts and then handed over to the 16th Battalion Middlesex Regiment of 86th Brigade, after "obtaining a receipt for the wood from the local infantry commander". Shortly afterwards, a squadron of the 7th Dragoon Guards of the 5th Cavalry Division, which had reached Marcoing, was sent across to Noyelles. Little fire was met, and the squadron galloped into the village and rounded up a number of prisoners without suffering any casualties. The village was later occupied by a patrol of Royal Fusiliers.

By three o'clock in the afternoon, the British line of attack extended, right to left, from Gonnelieu—Lateau Wood—Masnieres (south of the canal)—Marcoing—Nine Wood—Noyelles—Flesquieres—Graincourt to west of the Canal du Nord, where some parties of the 36th (Ulster) Division had even reached Moeuvres, but without any tank support to help them, had been driven back by a counter-attack. In the villages and hamlets within the salient, French citizens were liberated after three years of occupation. They streamed out into the streets, old men, women and children, many of them weak and half starved. "We lived in a nightmare," said the Mayor of Masnieres, "and now we seem to be in a dream too good to be true." The Germans had requisitioned all the available food, and the civilians were only kept alive by supplies provided by the American, Spanish and Dutch Relief Committees. In one village, a Frenchman of military age was liberated after he had hidden in the attic of his own house for three years. He had been fed daily by his wife from the surplus rations of a baby born just before the beginning of the war. Every two or three months, the house was searched according to a regular routine and discovery would have meant immediate death for both husband and wife. For several nerve-racking months, a number of German officers had even billeted in the same house. On such rations, the leavings of a baby, and from long confinement in the dark, the man was feeble and emaciated. He looked like a man of 60, although his actual age was 35.

Within eight hours, the British had advanced up to four-and-a-half miles on a six-mile front, an achievement virtually unprecedented in the three years of war. The tanks had more than proved themselves, and now that they were operating for the first time in suitable conditions, they ably justified the faith which Churchill, Swinton, Stern and the rest of the little band of enthusiasts had in them. They had sliced through the Hindenburg lines and everywhere, except for small pockets of resistance, the Germans were in full retreat, taken completely by surprise. A great opportunity awaited. The Germans were still holding out at Flesquieres, and the canal bridge at Masnieres had been destroyed. But other bridges were still intact, particularly the one at Marcoing, and the way was open through Graincourt to occupy Bourlon Wood and push on to Cambrai from the left. It was true that the tanks were over-heated and both the tank crews and the infantry were tired, especially as each man had to carry 72 lbs. of " fighting order " equipment. There were few infantry reserves available to move forward and continue the attack, taking advantage of the enemy's confusion. But there were still five cavalry divisions, thousands of fresh horsemen now presented with the opportunity for which they said they had always been waiting. The trenches had been crossed, the wire rolled up, the machine-gun posts destroyed and many of the roads and bridges cleared. But where were the cavalry?

The main body, the 1st, 2nd and 5th Cavalry Divisions, had assembled at Fins at 6.20 a.m. When the battle started, the 3rd and 4th Divisions were further back, at Bray and Athies, and ready to concentrate at Fins when the 1st and 5th Divisions moved forward. Apart from a few individual squadrons assigned to the infantry brigades for specific tasks, they waited at their assembly points for further orders. The news of the first breakthrough was frankly doubted, so successful did it seem after years of failure, and it wasn't until 8.25 a.m. that the 1st Cavalry Division was ordered forward. By 10.30, it was at Metz while the leading brigade of the 5th Division had arrived south-west of Gouzeaucourt. At 11.7 a.m., the IV Corps received a message from the Royal Flying Corps that a pilot had observed British troops in Flesquieres and that the road from Trescault-Flesquieres was now open. The pilot had made a mistake, in fact, for Flesquieres was still in German hands. But the 1st Division was ordered forward.

" What a wonderful sight they were," recalled Captain Dugdale, who saw them cross the original British lines at about 12.30 p.m. " Regiment after regiment passed by, going down the valley to our right. When they got behind the line occupied by our troops, they dismounted, waiting under cover for orders."

For now it had been discovered that the road to Flesquieres was not open, as they had been led to expect. " Masses of them assembled in and along the Grand Ravine, which runs south of Ribecourt and Havrincourt, and there they waited," Fuller wrote later. "All they had to do was wheel right and left, spur their horses, and the open country was theirs. But they did nothing but wait, because they were commanded not from the front but from the rear. Had they moved forward round the flanks of Flesquieres and then dismounted, they could have cleared the village within half-an-hour. Had they gone forward north of Havrincourt, they might have pushed on beyond the leading troops of the valiant 62nd Division and occupied Bourlon. Instead, they did nothing but wait. It was not their fault, but the fault of their command, which was handling a pursuit on trench-warfare lines."

Meanwhile, at 12.5 p.m. the 5th Cavalry Division had moved forward from Fins. The Canadian Brigade took the route to Masnieres by way of La Vacquerie valley, whilst the Secunderabad and Ambala Brigades went via Villers-Plouich and Couillet Wood to Marcoing. The 2nd Cavalry Division didn't move off from their assembly area at Villers-Faucon until 2.8 p.m. While the 4th Brigade followed the main body of the 5th Division to Marcoing, the 5th and 3rd Brigades, followed later by the Lucknow Brigade, made for Masnieres.

In every sector of the Front where opportunities occurred for exploitation by the cavalry, these were delayed until the necessary orders had been received from Corps headquarters, and by then it was usually too late. The village of Cantaing was reported empty at 1.40 p.m. for instance, but when the 4th Dragoon Guards of the 1st Cavalry Division eventually received orders to advance towards the objective at 4.00 p.m., the Germans had re-occupied their positions with troops of the 107th Division which had luckily been available as reserves. The Dragoons lost two officers, 13 other ranks and 30 horses before they were forced to retire to Nine Wood and Noyelles. The 2nd Brigade of the same division was ordered at 2.45 p.m. to move over the Premy Chapel ridge and capture Orival Wood, but the message was not received until 4.30 p.m., by which time it was too late to be acted upon. The division also had under its command the tanks of B Battalion, and sixteen of these had been waiting in the Grand Ravine since midday to help the cavalry advance on Fontaine. But, like the majority of the cavalry brigades, they were not used.

By the time night fell, it was recorded at Cavalry Corps headquarters that, "the situation is such that the cavalry are unable to carry out their original task. Owing to the shortage of water and the congestion, the advisability of withdrawing the 2nd and 5th Cavalry Divisions to the area about Villers-Faucon and Fins should be considered." This was carried out, in addition to the withdrawal of the bulk of the 1st Cavalry Division which had been uselessly waiting at Ribecourt all day. There was no doubt that opportunities had occurred of which the cavalry could have taken advantage. It was not until later in the afternoon that the Germans, seeing the British advance falter, had turned to hold their positions. For a period of two or three hours, it would have been possible for the attack to drive straight into Cambrai, as originally planned. But it required a flexibility of movement and an understanding that local commanders could make decisions of their own, according to the situation, that had been such an impossibility throughout the three years of immobile trench-warfare that such tactics had been forgotten. The old doctrine of delegation of command, which kept incompetent generals at the top and prevented freedom of action in lower commands, still operated.

The kind of campaign at Cambrai made possible by the tanks was too new, and although a few such as Fuller understood this, the majority could not make the mental adjustment to it. But over and above all this, the operations on November 20 proved once and for all just what little scope there was for the cavalry in modern warfare. All along the cavalry had said, with some justification, that they had never been given a real chance on the Western Front. At Cambrai, they had that chance, created for them by the tanks. But it didn't work and not only because of the opportunities that had been bungled by an inept command. Even if they had been taken, it had still been made painfully obvious just how vulnerable the cavalry were, even in open country.

Nevertheless, by the end of the first day of the attack, it was apparent that a considerable victory had been achieved, more than anything on a relative scale since the war started. The number of prisoners taken amounted to more than 8,000 and in addition, 123 guns, 79 trench mortars, and 281 machine-guns had been captured. German casualties, in dead and wounded, totalled many more, and two divisions of infantry had been virtually wiped out. British casualties hardly exceeded 4,000. But when the tanks rallied that night, 1st Brigade at Havrincourt, 2nd Brigade at Ribecourt, and 3rd Brigade at La Vacquerie, it was found that 179 of the 374 which had taken part in the day's fighting were out of action—65 by direct hits, 71 by mechanical troubles, and 43 by ditching. Of those remaining, many had been in action almost continually for 16 hours and required maintenance services.

The news was received with great jubilation in London, and the church·bells were ordered to be rung the next day. The tanks had at last proved their worth. Churchill especially was delighted. In his history of the Great War, *The World Crisis,* he later wrote: "Accusing as I do without exception all the great Allied offensives of 1915, 1916 and 1917, as needless and wrongly conceived operations of infinite cost, I am bound to reply to the question—what else could be done? And I answer it, pointing to the Battle of Cambrai, ' this could have been done.' This in many variants, this in larger and better forms ought to have been done, and would have been done if only the generals had not been content to fight machine-gun bullets with the breasts of gallant men, and think that that was waging war."

The night after the attack was one of feverish activity in the newly established British lines. The tanks had to be overhauled and refuelled. Infantry companies and battalions needed reorganization as they dug themselves into the captured German trenches. Guns and supplies and equipment had to be brought up by wagon and mule, and now that it was raining, the ground was being churned up into the kind of mud which was so familiar on the Western Front. At General Headquarters, Haig had been delighted with the success of the attack, but he was concerned that the Bourlon ridge position had not been taken. Previously, he had agreed to accept the offer of French reserves, made by General Petain, if the situation warranted this. Haig hesitated. He knew how short the British Army was of reserves, although he had already asked the Chief of the Imperial General Staff for the two divisions now on their way to join the four already in Italy. But he still retained doubts about the French, following the widespread mutinies some months earlier. At 4.30 p.m., he visited Byng at Third Army headquarters in Albert, and after discussing the situation, sent a message to the French Commander-in-Chief turning down the offer. The French troops who had already detrained at Peronne in preparation to take part in the battle were ordered to stay there.

At 8.00 p.m., Third Army issued orders for the next day. The III Corps was to " make every effort " to gain the Masnieres-Beaurevoir line east of Marcoing and Masnieres, and to capture Crevecoeur in order that the cavalry could pass through. The IV Corps was ordered to take Bourlon, " the capture of which at an early hour tomorrow is of paramount importance ". The Royal Flying Corps was to help in these operations by making low-flying attacks on Rumilly and Bourlon. At the same time, a decision was made to re-allocate some of the tanks. Those which had been engaged on wire-pulling were to revert to their brigades as fighting tanks. A Battalion with the 29th Division and those of B Battalion which had been put at the disposal of the Cavalry Corps and had not taken part in the battle, were to be withdrawn as soon as possible. In order to give IV Corps all the assistance possible for the attack on Bourlon, the 2nd Brigade was transferred over from III Corps, leaving the " minimum number considered necessary to ensure success " in the capture of Crevecouer and the Masnieres-Beaurevoir line. Unfortunately, the cross-country driving necessary to get the tanks into their new positions resulted in the cutting of many of the telephone wires which had just been laid, and communications, never very reliable, became even more difficult.

On the German side, the confusion of the morning had given way to a feeling of helplessness as the fragmented reports coming in gradually built up a picture of the extent of the tank onslaught. The 54th Division, together with its artillery, was virtually destroyed—5,785 officers and men were reported missing at the end of the first day. The 20th Landwehr Division and 19th Reserve Regiment had suffered almost as badly. While an extensive withdrawal was contemplated, the town commandant of Cambrai was ordered by Caudry Group headquarters to put up whatever barricades he could across the streets leading into the town—anything to slow up the British advance while guns and troops were evacuated. And then, surprisingly, the British attack had slackened during the afternoon, and following the evacuation of Flesquieres, an emergency front-line had been established between Moeuvres - Anneux - Cantaing - Rumilly - Revelon, manned by a " piebald mixture of various infantry units ". Luckily, the 107th Division had arrived that morning from the Russian Front, intended to relieve the 20th Landwehr Division on November 25. Battalions of this division were hurried forward, but they had no knowledge of this section of the front, and General Baron von Watter, the Caudry Group commander, requested three more divisions, artillery, and two or three divisions for emergency reserves to be rushed up. The 119th Division from Flanders, the 30th Division from the Aisne, and the 214th Division from Douai were all ordered to entrain at once, but it was impossible for them to arrive and assemble until November 23. Meanwhile, during the afternoon, such reserves as were available were ordered forward. One battalion of the 52nd Reserve Regiment occupied Cantaing, and two battalions of the 232nd Reserve Regiment strengthened the line between Cantaing and the canal. Three battalions of the 227th Reserve Regiment arrived to help man the Masnieres-Beaurevoir line and Crevecoeur. During the evening, the German line between Moeuvres and Bourlon Wood was considerably strengthened by the arrival of units from the 20th Division of the Arras Group, as well as a battalion from the 183rd Division of the Caudry Group and a number of others who were resting behind other parts of the front at St. Quentin, Lens and Loos.

However, despite these reinforcements, von Watter viewed the situation with great alarm. Everywhere there was a shortage of field-guns and armour-piercing ammunition, and a general fear of the tanks. " We must not hush up the fact that any renewed tank attack before the arrival of strong artillery forces would lead to further breaches in the lines," he wrote in an analysis of the position, " and a true breakthrough may then become inevitable. Even if we master the present crisis, the situation remains serious."

Everything depended on what would happen the following day, November 21, the second day of the battle.

CHAPTER TEN

The Second Day

" IT was an extraordinary sight as we went over the ridge. We could see the whole valley and the attack coming down. Battalion headquarters was a flag stuck in the middle of a field, with a row of officers watching through field-glasses. The infantry was advancing in lines and columns everywhere. Battalions in reserve were streaming up behind and cavalry patrols going along the ridges. All the old " shock troops " were there, and quite apart from that there was the astonishing sight of tanks advancing in waves and cavalry galloping across fields with drawn sabres."

This is how Lieutenant A. Macdonnell, an artillery liaison officer with the 4th Battalion Seaforth Highlanders described the scene on the morning of November 21 when the 51st Division moved over Flesquieres Ridge and advanced towards Cantaing. The rain which had started the previous evening was still falling—it was to continue non-stop for 36 hours, and together with the poor visibility seriously hamper flying operations. But one major obstacle was out of the way. During the early hours of the morning, Major Krebs and his little group of defenders who had been holding out in the village of Flesquieres had withdrawn, after being told by Caudry Group headquarters that they could not be given any support. An advance patrol of 153rd Brigade had found the village empty, and at 6.00 a.m. it was occupied by the Highlanders. Very little resistance was met after this, and by 9.00 a.m. the road from Premy Chapel to Graincourt was in the hands of the 5th Battalion Seaforth Highlanders and the 8th Battalion Argyll and Sutherland of 152nd Brigade. An attempt was made by the Seaforths to push into Cantaing, but they were driven back by heavy machine-gun fire.

The main objective of the 51st Division was the town of Fontaine-Notre Dame, close to the western suburbs of Cambrai on the main road leading into the city. But the Germans held a position extending from just behind Nine Wood, past Cantaing, to the dominating mass of Bourlon Wood overlooking Fontaine. This position, the Cantaing Line, joined the Masnieres-Beaurevoir Line at Nine Wood. It consisted of barbed wire and machine-gun posts, but the trenches were not deep or particularly well prepared—the Germans had thought the Hindenburg Line would give enough protection. The Cantaing Line could have been taken during the initial drive forward the morning before, when the tanks and infantry of 62nd Division had reached Graincourt and reported Bourlon Wood to be empty. But during the night, the Germans had brought up battalions from other sectors of the Front, particularly from the Arras Group to the west, and now the line was well defended and effectively blocked the advance to Fontaine. In spite of the bad weather, the whole area was open to observation from the German gunners on Bourlon Ridge.

Because of a delay in receiving their orders that morning, the tanks of 2nd Brigade were late in starting out and were not up with the leading infantry battalions. While the tanks made their way slowly across country towards Cantaing, Brigadier General K. G. Buchanan, commanding 154th Brigade which had moved up to make the attack, decided not to wait for them. At 10.30, he ordered the 4th Battalion Gordon Highlanders and 7th Battalion Argyll and Sutherland to advance on the Cantaing Line. Fierce fighting broke out when they reached the German trenches, and a hail of machine-gun fire checked the whole movement. It was back to the usual impasse again. The cavalry were also in difficulties. Earlier in the morning, the 1st Cavalry Brigade had set out from Trescault to work forward east of

Cantaing by way of Premy Chapel and Nine Wood. The bulk of the brigade was held up by fighting in Nine Wood and Noyelles, but patrols of the Queen's Bays did manage to push through in the direction of Cantaing.

The situation was getting desperate when, shortly after midday, thirteen tanks of B Battalion came thundering over the top of Premy Chapel ridge, making directly for Cantaing. The Gordons had managed to reach the outskirts of the village by this time, but were held up by machine-gun fire. A squadron of the Bays lined up behind the tanks during the charge into the village. Although three tanks were knocked out by direct hits, the rest got through and fierce fighting broke out in the streets. One tank, in a section commanded by Captain T. D. Raikes, which had defective armour plates, was penetrated by 43 bullets, of which several went through both sides. But the only casualty among the crew, apart from metal " splash ", was one man wounded in the finger.

This account of the attack on Cantaing was written by a German observation officer who was present in the village and later taken prisoner: " The British artillery is bombarding us and their aeroplanes are continually diving low over the houses. Everywhere on the enemy side movement can be seen. Cavalry are in Nine Wood and the infantry are assembling on the road from Marcoing to Graincourt. It seems impossible but we think we hear sounds of music in the middle of a great battle. The sounds become clearer and then we realise they are made by bagpipes. In company columns, the Highlanders are advancing. The commanders are mounted and can easily be identified through field-glasses. The British must indeed feel sure of their victory. These beautiful targets remain unengaged. Can't our artillery observers see them? But nothing is being done on our side. The British deploy and advance their companies at about 700 metres. Our 52nd and 232nd Divisions open rapid fire. The company commander telephones to the battalion: ' It is an absolute shooting match. We are shooting standing as fast as we can.' The British advance stops and the numerous waves take cover. Small grey-black points appear here and there and continue their movements forward. They are becoming larger and clearer. They must be the tanks. Our machine-guns fire incessantly and rifle and grenade fire is added, but as with the regiments of the 54th Division yesterday, so our 52nd and 232 regiments must admit that all our efforts to stop these tanks are ineffective. We can do nothing against them. They come steadily forward and are not bound to roads or tracks. With horror we see that our wire entanglements are crushed down and that fences and even garden walls do not stop them."

By 1.30 p.m. the tanks had cleared the village, destroying the machine-gun posts and leaving the infantry to round up 400 prisoners. The tanks then withdrew, and the village was occupied by the Gordon Highlanders and the Bays. The commanding officer of the Gordons, Lieutenant Colonel Rowbotham, who was only 26, had ridden in on horseback at the head of his battalion. For his work that day he was awarded a bar to his D.S.O.

Later in the afternoon eight tanks of H Battalion under the command of Major A. G. Pearson appeared with orders to push on to Fontaine and hold it until the infantry took over. On the way past Cantaing, they came to that part of the Line where the Highlanders were being held up 300 yards from the German trenches by fire from Cantaing mill. The tanks forced their way across the trenches, followed by the infantry, and quickly overcame the resistance in the mill. Then the tanks turned towards Fontaine. Two infantry battalions, the 4th Seaforth and 7th Argyll and Sutherland, lined up behind them to follow. They did not know that their divisional commander, General Harper, had issued new orders that the advance was to be halted, and no further movement was to take place until the 62nd Division had taken Bourlon.

The advance lay along a narrow ridge between Cantaing and Fontaine. On the left towered Bourlon Wood. On the right, beyond Cantaing, was La Folie Wood. Both were in German occupation, and the 4,000 yards to Fontaine was over ground exposed to fire, not only from the front, but from both sides as well. Nevertheless, Pearson decided to run the gauntlet. Three of the tanks, "Hadrian", "Havoc" and "Hong Kong", were in Captain Hickey's section.

"Shells were bursting all round us, and fragments were striking the sides of the tank," Hickey wrote. "While the four gunners blazed away, the rest of the perspiring crew kept the tank zig-zagging to upset the enemy's aim."

Miraculously, the tanks were not hit, although one became a stationary target for a while after its engine failed. They entered the village at "top" speed—about five m.p.h.—with guns blazing. The 6-pounders silenced the machine-gun posts and also knocked out two German field-guns to the south of the village and another near Bourlon Wood. "Twilight was falling and there was a mist rising from the ground as we reached the village," said Hickey. "We scoured the streets for half-an-hour without seeing any enemy. Cambrai was only two miles away—and the gate to it was ours. The tanks commanders all told of shortage of petrol and ammunition. The male tanks had practically come to the end of their 200 rounds each of 6-pounder shells; the engines of the tanks were running hot because of their oil; and the crews were exhausted."

The infantry arrived about half-an-hour later. They had suffered considerable casualties, particularly in passing by the hamlet of La Justice. Of the 375 men of the Seaforths, only 120 arrived in Fontaine, and the Argyll and Sutherlands had suffered nearly as badly. But they had reached Fontaine, and like the tank-crews, they found that the enemy, troops of the 52nd Reserve Regiment of the 107th Division, had fled towards Cambrai and left the village deserted. Now was the time for the cavalry to move up and consolidate the gain. In the dusk light, they could have done so without suffering the casualties of the two infantry battalions. But because of General Harper's halt order, no more troops came up to Fontaine. At 5.15 p.m. the tanks returned to Cantaing, leaving the village in the hands of the weakened infantry units.

The capture of Fontaine, so near to Cambrai, marked the high point of the whole British advance and the one which most worried the Germans. The loss of the village was regarded as a disaster and it was from here that the break-through to Cambrai and beyond was expected. But again, the opportunity was missed. As a German military commentator wrote shortly afterwards: " On the afternoon of November 21, the British missed the chance to continue their attack towards Cambrai. Their leaders failed to recognise the advantage of piercing through the German lines at Fontaine. They did not even send out cavalry or reconnaissance scouts."

To the left of the fighting at Cantaing and Fontaine, the 62nd Division was moving up from Graincourt, with the object of capturing Bourlon Ridge and the village of Bourlon behind. The attack was made by Brigadier General Bradford's 186th Brigade, supported by several squadrons of the 1st Cavalry Brigade and eighteen tanks of G Battalion. Here again the tanks were late in arriving because of delayed orders, and one reason for this is explained by the experiences of a liaison officer, typical of many, who spent hours the night before trying to locate the infantry commanders to see what requirements they had for the tanks. " I was due to take some officers up during the night to put them in touch with their respective infantry brigadiers. It was raining and we were all cold and very weary. When we reached the vicinity of the first Brigade HQ we could find no flag or light, neither did any of the sleeping men seem to know. We stumbled in and out of various dug-outs, making ourselves very unpopular and seeing the precious time slipping away. At last we found the HQ, but the Brigadier did not seem very pleased to see us either. He pressed the tank commanders for ' guarantees ' as to what the tanks could do and indicated that they and their machines were useless if the guarantees were not forthcoming. They were not. Eventually we trudged on to Graincourt where another Brigade HQ was in a large crypt under the ruins of the church."

Here they found the young and well-liked Boys Bradford. " He looked hard at each of the officers and said that they were to have something to eat before anything was discussed. I looked at them too and saw that they were of the curious grey colour that comes as a result of prolonged fatigue, following excitement. The brigadier them told them very clearly the outline of his plan and explained where and when he most wanted the tanks. He realised their difficulties but his brigade was satisfied that the crews would do all that was possible to do. He added that if there was time he would like to speak to the crews himself on their way forward. If not, they were to be given that message from him. His quiet confidence put new life into us. I was childishly pleased to hear after we left the HQ that the tank officers were making ' adjustments ' to the allotment of tanks whereby this brigade would have more and better tanks."

It was not surprising that the co-operation between the tanks and the infantry of Bradford's brigade was excellent, unlike that of some other brigades and divisions. It remained so until Boys Bradford, V.C., M.C., at 25 the youngest Brigadier General in the British Army, was killed by a shell at Graincourt on November 30.

Three battalions of the Duke of Wellington's Regiment made the attack. On the right, the 4th Battalion advanced on Anneux and Anneux Chapel, on the Bapaume-Cambrai road just north of the village. Anneux was captured with the help of six tanks after heavy fighting, but further advance was stopped by machine-gun fire. The attack on Anneux Chapel took place down an open valley, and severe casualties were suffered before the German resistance was crushed, mainly by shell-fire from the tanks and the efforts of one infantry platoon which rushed a building and put out of action a machine-gun post firing on the road. After the Chapel and the adjacent buildings had been captured, a further advance was made to the edge of Bourlon Wood. But it was found that the trenches of the Cantaing Line there had not been dug, and without shelter from the fire coming from the Wood, the battalion withdrew to a sunken road near Anneux Chapel.

The centre 7th Battalion reached this sunken road as well,

after moving forward at 10.00 a.m. without waiting for the tanks, but were also unable to reach the wood. On the left, the 5th Battalion met the fiercest resistance, but with the help of a bombing attack by the Royal Flying Corps, managed to reach a point on the Hindenburg Support Line some 700 yards east of the Canal du Nord. Meanwhile, the 6th Battalion was brought up to fill the gap between here and Anneux. Some of the tanks managed to enter Bourlon Wood, but the infantry, exhausted after a long day's fighting and with little help in the way of reserves against a growing opposition, were unable to follow. Nevertheless, during the first two days of the battle, the 186th Brigade had done extremely well, covering 5,000 yards of ground and capturing 1,200 prisoners and 38 guns of all sizes.

To the west of the canal, the 36th (Ulster) Division pushed forward slowly against increasing resistance and forced an entry into the ouskirts of Moeuvres. But the 10th Battalion Royal Inniskilling Fusiliers and the 14th Battalion Royal Irish Rifles, who were engaged in the advance, were unable to hold the village because of machine-gun fire and heavy bombardment from the German trenches to the west, and eventually withdrew to a point only half-a-mile from where they started. Troops of the 56th Division further to the left kept up with the advance by moving northward along the German outpost line.

On the III Corps front, the main effort during the night and early hours of the morning was centred on Masnieres, where the eastern end of the village was held by units of the 29th Division. Battalions of the Hampshire and Worcestershire regiments worked their way through the village in the darkness, clearing the Germans from the houses, and except for a small party of the enemy who held out in the catacombs of a church until noon, this task was completed by 4.30 a.m. As dawn came up, patrols of 88th Brigade pushed forward to the Masnieres-Beaurevoir line, and despite heavy machine-gun fire from the high ground in front of Rumilly, they succeeded in occupying a short section of these trenches up to the Rumilly road. Meanwhile, at 6.30 a.m., the 20th

ABOVE: "Little Willie", built in September, 1915. Its first trials were witnessed by King George V. This photograph was taken during a demonstration after the war; in the background is a Mark IX tank. BELOW: The first of the tanks— "Big Willie"—during trials at Hatfield Park in January, 1916. Later called the "Wilson" and "H.M.L.S. Centipede", it eventually became universally known as "Mother". It was the prototype of a series of nine marks of tanks, totalling over 2,300 machines, which bore the brunt of tank fighting in the Great War.

ABOVE: The first official photograph of a tank going into action, at the Battle of Flers-Courcellette on September 15, 1916, after the new weapon was taken off the secret list. The crew member is wearing a leather tank helmet. BELOW: Troops marching behind a Mark I tank, going into action at the Battle of the Somme.

The mud of Passchendaele—typical of the fate of many tanks in the Flanders campaigns.

An artist's impression of tanks in battle.

The new Mark IV tanks, complete with fascines, on their way by rail to take part in the Cambrai offensive.

Tanks in training just before the Battle of Cambrai.

The evening before the battle. Equipment check by a tank crew.

The great breakthrough—tanks slicing through the barbed wire at the start of the Battle of Cambrai on November 20, 1917.

German view of a tank as it mounts the parapet of a trench. Not for nothing were tanks known to the Germans as "devil's coaches".

A tank of F Battalion smashes through the German defences.

A captured 5.9 inch German gun, east of Ribecourt. The tank is preparing to tow it away.

The face of the wicked Hun—a prisoner captured near Havrincourt on November 20.

Men of the 11th Leicester Regiment of 6th Division take over a captured trench near Ribecourt, complete with machine-guns.

The cavalry wait to take advantage of the breakthrough at Cambrai.

"Hyacinth" of H Battalion, ditched on Flesquieres Ridge.

This was the fate of many tanks on Flesquieres Ridge.

And men and horses too paid the price of success.

A tank and troops enter a liberated village.

ABOVE: Inhabitants leaving the
village of Noyelles on November 22.
BELOW: An urgent message for headquarters.

RIGHT: The German counter-attack
before dawn on November 30.

ABOVE: Men of the 11th Engineers (Railway), U.S.A., caught at Gouzeaucourt during the counter-attack but later escaped. *From left to right*: Captain C. Raymond Hulsart, Lt. Paul McLeod and 2nd Lt. E. N. Holstrom. The former two were decorated for gallantry. BELOW: It was nearly a year before Cambrai was eventually liberated. Men of the 19th Division hear Mass in the ruins of Cambrai Cathedral on October 13, 1918.

Division launched an attack from Bonavis Ridge against les Rues des Vignes. Three companies of the 10th Battalion Rifle Brigade managed to reach the canal-lock crossing, but they were unable to drive the Germans from the northern end of the village.

Now was to come the main assault of the day, to capture the 2,000-yard section of the Masnieres-Beaurevoir Line from the main Cambrai road to Crevecouer. It was intended to be a combined operation, starting at 11.00 a.m., with the 88th Brigade of 29th Division and 59th Brigade of 20th Division taking part. But again the tanks were late in arriving—they did not receive orders at their rallying place until zero hour itself. After waiting several hours, the infantry began to move forward without tank support. But the 88th Brigade was held up from the very start by concentrated fire from Rumilly, and when the 11th Battalion King's Royal Rifle Corps of 59th Brigade began to move eastwards towards Crevecoeur, they soon came under cross-fire from the Germans holding the line. A halt was ordered before the canal had been crossed, and then the advance was directed towards Revelon Chateau. Soon after 3.00 p.m., four tanks of F Battalion arrived, but although several parties of Germans were put to flight, it remained impossible to cross the canal bridges. The tank commanders doubted whether they could take the weight of the tanks, and the infantry felt disinclined to cross the canal without them.

Further to the left, in the bend of the canal east of Marcoing, the 87th Brigade of 29th Division was also attempting to gain possession of the Masnieres-Beaurevoir Line, but was just as unsuccessful. This brigade had much better tank support—eighteen tanks in fact of A and F Battalions, which was more than expected. But although they managed to reach the trenches, and patrolled up and down for two hours, directing fire into them, they could not subdue the German machine-gunners. For by now, the Germans were becoming used to the lumbering monsters. They found that by diving down into the dug-outs when the tanks passed, they only had to wait a while and then come out again to fire at the rear of the tanks and on the British infantry trying to move forward. It was also becoming apparent just how vulnerable the tanks were to armour-piercing bullets. In this action, the tanks were in fact badly mauled. Two were knocked out by direct hits from German field-guns, one was stranded after reaching Rumilly and fell into enemy hands, and many others were holed and set on fire.

The growing zeal of the Germans after the first shock of the attack resulted in their first determined effort at a counter-attack, to retake the village of Noyelles which was in the hands of units of the 86th Brigade. The attack was made by the 232nd Reserve Regiment of 107th Division at 10.30 a.m. and for several hours the units of the Royal Fusiliers, the Middlesex and the 18th Hussars holding the village were hard pressed. Mounted operations by the cavalry were not possible, and the fighting became a slogging match on foot, from street to street and house to house. Several parts of the village changed hands a number of times until eventually at 4.00 p.m., the British troops succeeded in clearing out the Germans completely. They were later relieved by the 16th Brigade of 6th Division, and withdrew into billets at Marcoing. An effort by the Germans to re-take Nine Wood was also repulsed by a battalion of the Royal Guernsey Light Infantry.

By the afternoon, it was apparent at III Corps headquarters that far from being able to push the advance forward to the objectives laid down, there was difficulty in holding the ground already gained in the face of counter-attacks. So the Corps went on the defensive. Orders were issued for the divisions to consolidate their positions. The 6th Division was to establish a well-wired line of resistance from Nine Wood to the canal south of Noyelles and join up with the 51st Division at a point mid-way between Noyelles and Cantaing. The 29th Division was to strengthen its position north and east of Masnieres and across the canal bend north of Marcoing, preparing the bridges over the canal for demolition. The 20th and 12th Divisions were to prepare defences along their Bonavis Ridge line, west of the canal. These positions were to remain static while the main area of attack reverted to the IV Corps front.

It had been a disappointing day for Byng's Third Army. To begin with, delays in communications had held up the receipt of orders so that attacks had started later than planned and the impetus forward of the previous day had been lost. The tanks in particular had been affected by this, and they were additionally delayed by having to cross several miles of country from their rallying places to the front line, not arriving until the afternoon. The infantry either moved forward without them or waited until they arrived. In either case, it gave the Germans a breathing space to continue the rallying of their forces, and they took full advantage of it. Also, team-work and co-operation between the tanks and the infantry was not as efficient as it had been the day before— although at least the units of Harper's 51st Division had altered their previous views and come to appreciate the value of tank support. The III Corps had made virtually no headway during the day, and the IV Corps had really only achieved what it should have done during the first day of the attack. The cavalry had again found no opportunity for effective action, beyond sending forward a few patrols. Only at one place, Fontaine, had there been a real chance, created by the tanks, where a gap of three miles existed between Moser's Arras Group to the west and von Watter's Caudry Group to the east. The extent of this gap could not have been known to the British at the time, but even so, it was an opportunity lost.

By the morning of November 21, Rupprecht and Marwitz had a good idea of the strength of the British forces. In spite of the fall of Fontaine and Marwitz's fears of a breakthrough to Cambrai, it seemed that the British were not pressing their initial advantage to the hilt, either because they were unable to do so from lack of sufficient reserves, or because they did not understand how to make the best of their gains. In any event, the German reserves were being built up—by the evening of the 21st Rupprecht estimated that he had the equivalent of four divisions holding the line between Moeuvres and les Rue des Vignes on the L'Escaut Canal. The 214th Division had arrived from the Aisne, and the 119th and the 3rd Guard Divisions from Flanders were beginning to assemble north and south-east of Cambrai, bringing support to the regiments of the 107th Division and what remained of the 20th Landwehr and 54th divisions. Battalions of the 50th and 363rd regiments of the 214th Division had immediately been moved to the front from Bourlon Wood to Moeuvres together with a large number of field-gun batteries. In addition, the 5th Guard Division from the Aisne and several field artillery regiments were on the move towards Cambrai, and six more divisions had been warned to stand by. When Ludendorff demanded on the telephone that evening that the Fourth Army in Flanders should be combed for reinforcements, Rupprecht was able to tell him that this had been done and the troops were already on the way. Rupprecht realised that he wouldn't have sufficient forces for major counter-attacks until November 23. Everything depended on holding out for one more day.

Meanwhile, the 48-hour limit which Haig had set on the attack before it should be reconsidered was fast expiring. On the evening of November 21, Byng was able to give GHQ a clear idea of the situation. Fontaine had been captured, but Bourlon Ridge and Moeuvres were still in enemy hands. Little progress had been made on the III Corps front against the L'Escaut Canal. It was up to Haig to make the big decision, whether to continue the battle or, as Fuller had originally wanted, to regard the whole operation as a raid and withdraw to the original lines, being content to have inflicted a severe blow against the Germans and captured a large number of prisoners and guns. One point was in no doubt. The advance on the III Corps front was so unpromising that Haig showed no hesitation in closing it down, confirming the decision already made by Byng to stand the Corps on the defensive. It was on the position of Bourlon Ridge that the whole decision depended. Possession of this would seriously menace the German defences and communications northward as far as the Sensee river, and command the western approaches to Cambrai. But what were the chances of taking it?

Although the British troops were already showing signs of fatigue and a good proportion of the tanks were out of action, either from enemy fire or mechanical breakdown, the cavalry divisions were still, in the main, unused. The Third Army had not yet called on the three V Corps divisions on reserve, the 40th, 59th and the Guards. And in reply to his request to Sir William Robertson, Chief of the Imperial General Staff, Haig had been told that he might retain the two divisions under orders for Italy. As opposed to this, it was felt at GHQ that the Germans were still showing an inclination to retire, and that the reserves that had been brought up had done no more than replace casualties. Haig suspected that the Germans were bringing up more reserves, although he did not realise just how many. But in making his decision, he faced pressure from another source—public opinion at home. News of the initial breakthrough had been received with tremendous jubilation, and as the reports continued to speak of advances, first to Cantaing and then Fontaine, it really seemed that a major victory was in sight. No one knew on what slender threads these were supported. It would have seemed incomprehensible to withdraw now, especially after the failures of the spring and summer. Haig did not normally take any account of public opinion, but at this point he knew that his reputation was at its lowest ebb. If he could sustain the success at Cambrai, this would be greatly restored. And so, shortly after 9.00 p.m., he made the decision to continue the offensive.

What had been a general attack on a six-mile front now became a fight for one main objective, Bourlon Ridge. The slopes of this ridge rose from the western side of the Bapaume-Cambrai road to a height of 150 feet. At the crown of the ridge was Bourlon Wood, 600 acres of thick woodland giving great advantages to the defence. Behind the wood, on the lower slopes on the other side, was Bourlon village.

An assault on such a position required a great deal of planning to prepare adequate artillery bombardment, bring

British Advance Durin

Arras
Sailly
Mencourt
Neuville
Escaudœuvres
CAMBRAI
Fontaine
Canal de L'Escaut
la Folie
51
Awoingt
ng
Noyelles
Niergnies
Flot fm.
Forenville
Nine Wood
6
Rumilly
remy hapel
Marcoing
Seranvillers
29
Masnières
Sugar Factory
Copse
Crèvecœur
Couillet Wood
20
Les Rues des Vignes
Lesdain
ood an Fm.
WELSH RIDGE
III
BONAVIS RIDGE
Le Bosquet
Pam Pam Fm.
Lateau Wd.
12
le Pavé
La Vacquerie
Vaucelles
Bleak ho.
Bonavis Fm.
GONNELIEU RIDGE
St. Quentin
Banteux
Mont Ecouvez
onnelieu
BANTEUX RAVINE
Bantou-zelle

nd Day, November 21.

up fresh infantry battalions, and make the tanks ready for further battle. Accordingly, the day of November 22 was devoted to making these preparations. While the field artillery of the 51st Division began the bombardment, the reserve 40th Division was moved up in readiness to lead the attack on the 23rd. And the tanks that were still in working order were overhauled and replenished with fuel and ammunition. Meanwhile, without tank support for there was none available, the IV Corps divisions did their best to consolidate their positions and to gain ground wherever they could, except towards Bourlon Ridge. The Highland battalions of 51st Division were to establish a defensive line from Cantaing to Fontaine, to consolidate the Cantaing Line, and to occupy the high ground north of Fontaine. The 62nd Division was to consolidate its forward positions below Bourlon Wood and gain ground where possible. The 36th Division was to take over the Hindenburg Support Line from the 62nd and continue its advance on either side of the Canal du Nord. And the 56th Division was to take over the Hindenburg front system and capture Tadpole Copse, west of Moeuvres.

But, in fact, very little was accomplished. In the face of determined German resistance, most of the battalions which made any ground at all were pushed back by the end of the day to where they had started from. The only significant success was the capture of Tadpole Copse by units of the London Scottish Regiment of 168th Brigade. Against this there was a much more serious loss. Fontaine, which had been taken at such risk the day before by the tanks, fell back into German hands. The village had been left in the occupation of little more than a hundred battle-weary men of the 4th Battalion Seaforth Highlanders. During the morning, the Argyll and Sutherland companies had been withdrawn to a position facing Bourlon Wood between Fontaine and Anneux, and nothing had been done to support this very vulnerable forward position. At 9.00 a.m., German aircraft flew over the village, observing the situation and occasionally firing at the defenders. Then, an hour later, parties of German infantry began advancing on the village from Cambrai and Bourlon, under covering machine-gun fire. The Seaforths fought stubbornly to defend the village, but they were greatly outnumbered. An S O S was sent for more support. But this was ignored. With a disregard for individual human life that was so typical of the Great War, the divisional command felt it was not worth retaining the village since it could easily be recaptured once Bourlon was taken. After fighting for several hours until ammunition was running short and there was a danger of being encircled, the Highlanders were forced to retreat. The last company left at 2.30 p.m. and Fontaine was re-occupied by the Germans. In spite of the optimism that it could be re-taken again, it never was, and later fighting in Fontaine was the fiercest and most wasteful of the whole battle.

During November 22, the Germans had not only prevented any significant advances, but they had even taken back some ground. But most important of all, while Byng and his Third Army staff were preparing for the following day's attack on Bourlon, Rupprecht had obtained the one day of grace he so desperately needed. He now had sufficient reinforcements to be able to discount any idea of a general withdrawal. And so, with fresh troops entering the battle on both sides, the lines were now drawn up for a life and death struggle for the vital Bourlon Ridge.

CHAPTER ELEVEN

Fight For Bourlon Ridge

A COLD wind was blowing over the flat countryside, bringing
fitful showers of rain, when on the morning of November 23,
eighty-eight tanks and twenty-two infantry battalions prepared for the IV Corps assault on the Bourlon position. The
line of attack extended 10,000 yards from Cantaing on the
right to Tadpole Copse. Zero hour was 10.30 a.m., but the
leading battalions were in position well before daylight in
order to escape observation from the German positions on
Bourlon Ridge. On the right, one battalion each of the
Gordons and Seaforths of 51st Division lined up with 36
tanks of B, H and C Battalions in the sunken Premy Chapel-
Graincourt road to lead the attack to recapture Fontaine. A
support battalion of the Argyll and Sutherland Highlanders
sheltered further back in Orival Wood. In reserve were four
battalions of the Seaforth, Royal Scots, Gordon and Black
Watch regiments, and waiting at Ribecourt to come up later
were twelve tanks of I Battalion.

During the night, the fresh troops of 40th Division had
replaced the 62nd Division and eight battalions moved into
position with sixteen tanks of G Battalion and thirteen of
D Battalion to make the main attack on Bourlon Wood and
Bourlon village. Four battalions of Welch Fusiliers, South
Wales Borderers and the Welch Regiment lined up with the
tanks of G Battalion on the slopes below Bourlon Wood,
near Anneux Chapel. To the left, four battalions of the
Middlesex, Green Howards and Suffolk regiments with D

The Fight For Bourlon, November 23.

line in morning ▬▬▬▬ gains during day ●●●●●● Corps boundaries —··—··—··—

Battalion tanks prepared to swing round the wood to attack the village from south and west. The 36th Division to the left was to clear the Hindenburg Support Line as far as the canal and capture Moeuvres and Quarry Wood to the west of Bourlon village, employing four battalions of the Royal Irish Rifles and one battalion of the Royal Irish Fusiliers, together with eleven tanks of E Battalion. And on the extreme left, companies of the London Scottish and 4th London Battalion Royal Fusiliers of 56th Division were to extend their hold on the Hindenburg front system and advance towards Inchy.

Despite the unfavourable weather, German air attacks during the past two days had increased as a result of squadrons being brought up from other sectors of the front, and fifty fighters of the Royal Flying Corps were allocated to provide infantry support during the attack. But unknown to the R.F.C., Richthofen's famous fighting squadron was on its way. Richthofen himself arrived during the night of November 22 and took over command of air operations from Captain Flashar, his former pupil. His squadron arrived on the afternoon of November 23. This build-up of German aircraft was to play a very important part at a later stage in the battle.

From reports brought in from captured British prisoners, and particularly the information that the Guards Division was being held in readiness, the Germans expected that further attacks were coming. Preparations were made to meet these. Now that the main area of attack had moved over to the left of the sector, defence was in the hands of the Arras Group under the command of General von Moser. He now had the 20th Division holding the front from Inchy to Moeuvres, the 214th Division from Moeuvres to Bourlon Wood, and the 119th and 107th Divisions from Bourlon Wood to la Folie Wood, including Fontaine. In addition, the 21st Reserve and the 3rd Guard Divisions were arriving from Flanders. The Lehr Regiment of the 3rd Guard Division was in fact already in position in Bourlon Wood and village, supporting the 50th Regiment of 214th Division.

Fontaine particularly had been reinforced by troops of the 46th Infantry Regiment of 119th Division. These had already seen tanks operating on the soggy ground of Flanders, but they were under no illusions as to the effectiveness of the tanks under the kind of conditions which existed around Cambrai. Several companies had been specially trained for repelling tank attacks. In a Regimental Bulletin, Colonel Zunehmer had laid down that, " The first line should seek cover, or take evasive action towards the sides, letting the tanks pass through. The enemy infantry, believing that its opponents had been flattened by the tanks, could then be taken by surprise. Meanwhile, the fighting of the tanks should be left to units in the rear." These tactics, of separating the armour from the infantry, were later to become the classic means of anti-tank defence. But on the morning of November 23, Colonel Zunehmer's troops were waiting to try them for the first time.

The attack started at 10.30 a.m., following half-an-hour of artillery bombardment which had also laid down a smoke screen. Three tanks of C Battalion made for la Folie Wood, while thirteen tanks of B Battalion and six of C Battalion set off towards Fontaine, followed by the 6th Battalion Gordon Highlanders. Although the male tank of the three attacking la Folie Wood was immediately put out of action by a direct shell hit, the other two reached the wood and dispersed many groups of German infantry. But without the 6-pounders of the male tank, they were unable to deal with the accurate machine-gun fire coming from la Folie chateau in the middle of the wood. Meanwhile, the main body of tanks swept on towards Fontaine.

" In front of us was perfect going," wrote Captain C. W. G. Grimley, a section commander of B Battalion. " Occasional shells were bursting, but one heard only a very muffled explosion. Then I opened fire with the 6-pounder, and our five Lewis guns opened up on a battery to the south-east side of the village. We were doing a good 4 m.p.h. when on nearing the village, German infantry ran out of a shallow fire trench. First a few, then about two companies got up and

legged it for the village. There was great excitement in the
tank. Those who were handy to the Lewis guns took turns in
firing at the fleeing infantry. We bowled over quite a few,
and I heard an awful shriek of fear and pain as we ran over
one. We dare not stop at our slow speed of 3-4 m.p.h. Sergeant Stewart, the layer, seemed exceptionally excited as he
was laughing and gesticulating wildly, trying to tell me something. Afterwards, I found he had seen one round of
6-pounder cut a lone German clean in half. This was a wrong
use of the gun, of course, but there was little fire direction
or control in those days. I, as an odd number, observed with
the periscope half the time; for the rest I hopped about between the tank commander and driver in front and the
6-pounders, giving orders. Occasionally, I had a shot with a
6-pounder or Lewis gun.

" We now swung right and came up along the garden walls
at the back of the houses. Then as we rounded the corner
going through a garden wall there were three field-guns alone
in the open—I only saw a horse and a German hurrying away
with it. Our tank ran over the first gun and just crumpled
it up, and we fired shells into the breach of the second. The
third tank of the section ran over the last gun. So far it was
all our luck—all smiles, laughter, excitement and thrills—
but at this moment hell was let loose as we turned into the
street. We were being fired at from the roofs—front, back
and sides. A combination of splash and armour flaking made
it most difficult to see anything when handling a gun. We
tried the vizor-chain masks, but took them off as we couldn't
see properly. The gun ports were all lit up with sparks. We
could see only through these ports, some pin-holes, and one
small periscope. In order to put sufficient elevation on the
gun, we had to get the tank on the other side of the street.
Bateman and Chappel on the port-side 6-pounder put three
out of action in one house, the shells going below the sills
and taking gun and crew I should imagine most successfully.
Then the next picture was a Lance Corporal grovelling on
the floor, a bullet through the forearm; the poor fellow was
in a blue funk, even when threatened with a revolver he only

grovelled more, so we used him as a mat. Private Westwater was wounded by three bullets in the fleshy part of the thigh, from fire coming through the 6-pounder gun port, but he gallantly worked the secondary gears and fired a Lewis gun alternately.

" By this time, every Lewis gun in the section was riddled like pepper pots. They were unfortunately unarmoured and obviously useless to tank personnel; with Vickers machine-guns we could have given them hell." The atmosphere in the tank by this time was very bad, with fumes from both the engine and the back-flash from the 6-pounders. Two men were wounded and the rest were covered in blood. The Lewis guns were out of action. Then the tank caught fire in the batteries at the back.

" I pointed to the door to Sergeant Stewart and he stood by with his hand ready to open it," wrote the commander. " I thought, ' death by fire or bullets—well, bullets for my own choice.' They were banging away on the door like large hail stones on plate glass. I took the pyrenes to the fire, how-ever, and we managed to put it out. On we went, firing away at likely machine-gun hiding places. Then I saw two tanks of another section on fire in the centre of Fontaine, obviously hit by a field-gun firing up the street. I looked round for the infantry—but none had followed. So I turned about and led my section out to find the Gordons. I found them some 400 yards short of Fontaine, held up by enfilade fire from la Folie Wood. I went over to within range and fired my remaining 6-pounder rounds. I then led my three tanks away as we were useless, first putting up the tank and infantry co-operation flag, ' coming out of action for supplies.' At this juncture I met Captain Hotblack. (No matter where one was, one could always meet Captain Hotblack.) I told him what we had done, and then went back."

It was during this attack on Fontaine that Hotblack was awarded a bar to D.S.O. for his example and initiative in re-organising the infantry whose officers had become casual-ties and in collecting the tanks, all the time while under heavy barrage and continuous machine-gun fire.

All the thirteen tanks of B Battalion and six of C Battalion managed to reach the village, but reverting to the practice of 51st Division once more, the infantry stayed well behind and were therefore halted outside by fire from the houses and la Folie Chateau. The tanks went on alone into a hail of machine-gun fire and grenades thrown from the upper storeys of the houses. Those that weren't put out of action were forced to withdraw. Only three tanks of B Battalion managed to get back to base at the end of the day, together with the crews of four others. Meanwhile, the twelve tanks of H Battalion and three of C Battalion had swung past the left of the village and led the 6th Battalion Seaforth Highlanders without check towards Bourlon Wood. Some of the tanks and infantry became involved in fighting on the western end of the village, but the remainder pushed on up the slope and reached the north-eastern extremity of the wood. Here, the infantry were checked, but the tanks patrolled the edge of the wood and successfully held back German units who were trying to move southward over the shoulder of the ridge. Two of the tanks actually entered the wood and fought all day with the 40th Division, who were having more success than the 51st.

Later in the afternoon, the twelve tanks of I Battalion came up and it was decided to renew the attack on Fontaine. Nine tanks succeeded in entering the village, but again they were left without infantry support. After fighting for several hours, seven managed to return as darkness fell. One had been hit by a trench mortar shell and abandoned. The fate of the other was never known. It was reported by one tank commander that parties of Germans had tried to prevent him from firing his guns by hanging on to them. Despite the fact that German resistance in and around Fontaine was much greater than expected—there were in fact at least ten battalions—only two battalions of 51st Division with the one in support were used. The remaining four battalions in reserve were not called into action at all. This over-cautious attitude—although it did not extend to the tanks who were sent forward regardless of support and suffered severely at

Flesquieres and Fontaine—was fairly typical of the standard of leadership shown during the battle, particularly by the 51st Division. It raises doubts as to the adequacy of the reason afterwards given that the failure of the overall plan was due to a lack of reserves. Often, the reserves were there; they were just not used to replace the battle-weary men in the leading formations, which is the essence of re-vitalising an attack.

The main attack on Bourlon Wood and Bourlon village by the 40th Division was preceded by an artillery barrage which came down on the edge of the wood and then lifted 200 yards at ten-minute intervals. Sixteen tanks of G Battalion had the task of helping the 119th Brigade to clear the wood, while thirteen tanks of D Battalion were to lead the 121st Brigade in securing the village and the western shoulder of the ridge. At the last minute, the tanks of G Battalion failed to arrive as heavy traffic on the roads had prevented their supplies of petrol and ammunition from being brought up to the Front. And so four tanks of D Battalion were switched to lead the right-hand attack by the 19th Battalion Royal Welch Fusiliers and the 12th Battalion South Wales Borderers, with the 17th Battalion Welch Regiment in support. They were in fact part of Major Watson's company of tanks, and he described the opening moves of the attack.

"Across the foreground ran the great highroad from Bapaume to Cambrai. It was wide, perfectly straight, and fringed with orderly trees. Beyond it and to my left was a low hill, which the enemy still held. Our line ran diagonally up the slope of it, and away to the west we were on the ridge. Immediately in front of me on the hillside was the great dark mass of Bourlon Wood, square and impenetrable, covering the highest point of the hill and stretching over the skyline to the farther slope, which we could not see. The wood dominated the whole countryside, and beyond it there was nothing but low open country, extending to the marshes of the Scarpe. We could not live north of Havrincourt while the enemy held the wood, and if we captured the wood there was nothing to prevent us from sweeping northwards to the Scarpe or westwards into Cambrai. At the moment our line ran along the southern outskirts of the wood and to the south of Fontaine, which the enemy held in force.

" At 10.30 a.m. the barrage fell and we could see it climb, like a living thing, through the wood and up the hillside, a rough line of smoke and flame. On the hillside to the left of the wood we could mark the course of the battle—the tanks with tiny flashes darting from their flanks—clumps of infantry following in little rushes—an officer running in front of his men until suddenly he crumpled up and fell, as though some unseen hammer had struck him on the head—the men wavering in the face of machine-gun fire and then spreading out to surround the gun—the wounded staggering painfully down the hill, and the stretcher-bearers moving backwards and forwards in the wake of the attack—the aeroplanes skimming low along the hillside and side-slipping to rake the enemy trenches with their guns.

" We watched one tank hesitate before it crossed the sky-line and our hearts went out to the driver in sympathy. He made his decision, and the tank, brown against the sky, was instantly encircled by little puffs of white smoke, shells from the guns on the reverse slope. The man was brave, for he followed the course of a trench along the crest of the hill. My companion uttered a low exclamation of horror. Flames were coming from the rear of the tank, but its guns continued to fire and the tank continued to move. Suddenly the driver must have realised what was happening. The tank swung towards home. It was too late. Flames burst from the roof and the tank stopped. But the sponson doors never opened and the crew never came out . . ."

By 11.40 a.m., the tanks and the Royal Welch Fusiliers had advanced through the trees, overrun the German machine-gun posts, and reached the road from Fontaine to Bourlon which ran through the centre of the wood. While the battalion was re-organising, thirteen of the tanks of G Battalion came up, two having been knocked out by direct hits and one broken down by mechanical trouble. The advance was continued, and by 12.45 p.m. the tanks and infantry had reached the northern edge of the wood. Further to the left, the South Wales Borderers had met stronger opposition while making their way up the wooded slopes, and in spite of the invaluable work done by two D Battalion tanks in patrolling the western edge of the wood, they suffered heavy losses. However, one company managed to reach the eastern end of Bourlon village while the rest of the battalion, reinforced now by the 17th Battalion Welch Regiment, extended the line along the Fontaine-Bourlon road.

The attack by 121st Brigade was made by the 20th Battalion Middlesex Regiment on the right and the 13th Battalion Green Howards on the left, with the 21st Battalion Middlesex in support and the 12th Battalion Suffolk Regiment in reserve. Following the remaining tanks of D Battalion, they attacked Bourlon village from south and west. Seven tanks managed to enter the village, after three others had received direct hits, but they experienced similar conditions to those which had entered Fontaine. The infantry fought fiercely on the outskirts of the village, but it didn't seem likely that the strongly entrenched Germans could be driven out. Eventually, a withdrawal was made to a line extending from just south of the village to the point on the left from where the attack had started. This was made necessary by the failure of the 36th Division attack east of the Canal du Nord, which was expected to clear the Hindenburg Support Line and capture Quarry Wood, a mile further on. Despite the support of the eleven E Battalion tanks, little headway was made by the 8th and 15th Battalions Royal Irish Rifles against heavy opposition. By the end of the day, five of the tanks had been knocked out by direct hits, one was badly ditched behind the German lines, and one had lost direction and was never seen again.

West of the canal, the 9th Battalion Royal Irish Fusiliers and 2nd and 12th Battalions Royal Irish Rifles made better progress, without tank support. They slowly pushed the Germans back towards Moeuvres, and by dusk, three-quarters of the village was in the hands of the Ulstermen. But they couldn't maintain the position, owing to intense machine-gun fire from both flanks. The worst fire came from a German strong-point to the south-west of Bourlon Wood. This was noticed by a patrolling fighter of the Royal Flying Corps, who dived down to the attack. The Germans returned his fire; the plane was brought down and the pilot killed. Some days later, the following appeared in the " In Memoriam " column of *The Times*: " To an Unknown Airman, shot down on 23rd November, 1917, whilst attacking a German strong-point south-west of Bourlon Wood, in an effort to help out a company of the Royal Irish Fusiliers when other help had failed." In fact, the pilot was Lieutenant A. Griggs, an American volunteer who was flying with No. 68 (Australian) Squadron.

Air activity generally was increasing, particularly over Bourlon Wood. During the afternoon, Richthofen's squadron took off for the first time since its arrival from Flanders, and Richthofen himself claimed his 62nd victim, Lieutenant J. A. V. Boddy of No. 64 Squadron, whose D.H.5 aircraft was brought down while flying north of Fontaine. He was wounded in the head and crashed in the south-east corner of Bourlon Wood. He was later rescued by another pilot who had crash-landed in the same area. As a result of Richthofen's appearance, such was the awe in which he was held, the R.F.C. doubled the strength of its patrols from then on. Losses on both sides were heavy during the 23rd, between 30 per cent. and 35 per cent., but despite the many individual battles that took place in the air, most of these were caused by bad weather and visibility.

On the extreme left of the front, the London Scottish and London (Royal Fusiliers) of 56th Division had slightly extended their hold on the Hindenburg Front system beyond Tadpole Copse. But during the afternoon, the Germans began an artillery barrage of the wood. As it happened, Elles and Fuller were driving forward at that time to inspect the front and witnessed the incident. " We looked down from our position on the Bapaume-Cambrai road on to a veritable inferno," Fuller wrote. " How men could live and remain sane in such shell-fire I do not know. It was one incessant, unceasing tornado. It was getting late and night was approaching when away to the right at Bourlon Wood a barrage of smoke shells sent millions of sparks cascading through the gloom."

This was the prelude to the first German counter-attack on Bourlon Wood. The bombardment started at about 3.00 p.m., and half-an-hour later, German battalions of the 175th and Grenadier Regiments of the 3rd Guard Division came up the slopes from the north. The men of the South Wales Borderers and Welch Regiment fought desperately against being surrounded and were saved just in time by the arrival of the reserve battalion. After fierce fighting, the Germans began to fall back. As dusk fell, the Welshmen pushed on until they had won the crest of Bourlon Ridge. Most of the wood was now in their hands; only the slope on the northern side remained in German possession. Later, contact was made with the 14th Battalion Argyll and Sutherland Highlanders and after more reinforcements from the Welsh regiments had been brought up, a continuous line was formed from the top of Bourlon Ridge down to the 51st Division position south of Fontaine.

The effort of the 40th Division, despite the fact that the troops had never fought with tanks before, was the most successful of the day. But although this had gone a long way towards meeting Haig's insistence that Bourlon Ridge should be taken if the battle was to continue, the failure to take Fontaine on the right and Moeuvres on the left made it a difficult position to hold. This was fully realised at IV Corps headquarters, and every effort was made to bring up reserves. The Guards Division, which had arrived from the Bapaume area, was put under the command of IV Corps and arrangements made for it to relieve the forward positions of the 51st Division during the night. The two divisions originally intended for Italy, the 2nd and the 47th, were on their way from Flanders and were expected to arrive within a day or so. And there was still the cavalry. Earlier in the day, Byng had suggested to the IV Corps that dismounted cavalry could be

...d if an "extra push with fresh troops" was required, but ...hat he really wanted was to retain the cavalry for such a time as they could make a move towards Cambrai from the west. During the evening, however, Haig was so concerned that Bourlon Ridge should be fully secured and held that he sent a special message to Byng to emphasise that dismounted cavalry "in any numbers" should be used for this purpose. Accordingly, the 1st and 2nd Cavalry Divisions were put at the disposal of IV Corps. Two dismounted battalions of the 9th Cavalry Brigade were formed and took up part of the line held by 40th Division near Bourlon village.

During the night, the first snow fell, making communications even more difficult. Then came the incessant rain. It was in these conditions that all the tanks which had been in action were ordered back for re-fitting, leaving only twelve of I Battalion available for the following day. These were to attack Bourlon village at noon with the 121st Brigade of 40th Division. During the morning, this time was changed to 3.00 p.m. Then the IV Corps commander, Lieutenant General Woollcombe, visited the divisional headquarters at Havrincourt and stated that as he thought there were not enough tanks to ensure success, the operation should be postponed until the next day. These orders were sent to all the various brigade headquarters in the Graincourt area, but due to the destruction of telephone lines by enemy shelling, they did not reach 121st Brigade until it was too late. The attack had started.

For the second time, the tanks forced an entry into the village, destroying many machine-gun posts. But the leading companies of the Highland Light Infantry and the Suffolk regiments which had started out behind them failed to appear. Once again, the tanks were compelled to withdraw. Only four managed to reach their rallying point later. Five had mechanical break-downs, one was burnt out by a direct hit, one was ditched, and one was abandoned after its petrol tank was holed. Later, units of the Highland Light Infantry did manage to force their way into the village, but without sufficient numbers to carry out a "mopping up" operation.

The Suffolks were held up outside the village by fire from the Marcoing line, and there was no more support coming from behind because of the order to postpone the attack. Reaching the railway line to the north of the village, the three leading companies of the Highland Light Infantry battalion became completely cut off from the fourth company and battalion headquarters. With most of Bourlon between them still occupied by Germans, the troops did what they could to set up defensive positions in what was an extremely perilous situation.

In Bourlon Wood, meanwhile, the battalions of the Welsh regiments, now reinforced by two companies of the Argyll and Sutherland Highlanders, one company of dismounted Hussars, and eight guns of the 204th Machine-Gun Company, were facing fierce counter-attacks by the Germans. It started at 8.45 a.m. On both flanks, from the direction of Fontaine and Bourlon, fresh units of the 3rd Guard Division and 214th Division made a determined attack on the wood. They were beaten off with heavy losses, but had no intention of giving up so easily. For two hours, the wood was shelled incessantly with high explosive and gas without let-up. It became a hell of torn trees, blazing undergrowth and broken bodies. Then at 11.00 a.m. came another attack, this time concentrated against the right. Again this was repelled, but the Germans managed to establish a forward position on the eastern edge of the wood. British casualties were mounting now. The troops were outnumbered and battle-weary. But more attacks followed, particularly from the north-east, and on the right the line began to give way before the fury of the German assault. The remnants of the 17th Battalion Welch Regiment became cut off in the north-east corner of the wood. And then, dredging up the energy from somewhere, the line of Welshmen, Highlanders and Hussars fought back and succeeded in pushing the Germans down the northern slope of the wood, where they became caught in the British artillery barrage. It was a superhuman effort against superior forces, and although the Germans managed to retain possession of the north-east corner of the wood, after the cut-off Welch companies had fought their way out, most of the wood and the highest ground was still in British hands at the end of the day.

This action should have given warning of the extent to which the German Second Army was bringing up fresh reserves. But Haig, who had visited Byng at Third Army headquarters in Albert that morning, was still yearning for the great cavalry breakthrough. He insisted that no effort should be spared in maintaining and extending the Bourlon position. Disregarding the real facts, he viewed the presence of a few British troops in Bourlon village as a triumph, despite the fact that they were completely isolated and surrounded by the enemy. In a special Order of the Day, congratulating everyone on the success achieved, he stated, "The capture of the important Bourlon position yesterday crowns a most successful operation and opens the way to a further exploitation of the advantages already gained." The exploitation he foresaw was to be the cavalry breakthrough into the open country behind Bourlon Ridge. Apart from the few dismounted troops, the bulk of the five cavalry divisions were still waiting in the Fins area to make their move. Haig gave special orders to Lieutenant General Kavanagh, commanding the Cavalry Corps, to take command of all operations north of Bourlon if and when the cavalry could get through. This was to include the supporting infantry, who were to operate under the Cavalry Corps.

While all this was being discussed, the tanks had virtually been forgotten. When 40th Division asked for twelve tanks to support their renewed attack on Bourlon village the next day, IV Corps promised these, forgetting that all the tanks had now been withdrawn from the front for re-fitting and none could possibly be available for a day or so. A number of tank companies, in fact, were already on their way back to winter headquarters at Bray. And so, from November 25-26, the fight for Bourlon Ridge continued without tank support. On the morning of the 25th, an attempt was made to reach the men of the Highland Light Infantry cut off in Bourlon and at the same time, clear the Germans out of the village.

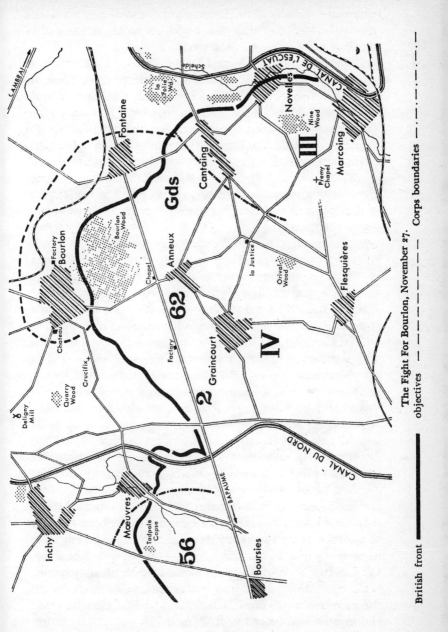

The Fight For Bourlon, November 27.

British front ▬▬▬   objectives – – – –   Corps boundaries –·–·–·–

Both were unsuccessful. Although the 13th Battalion East Surrey Regiment making the attack managed to reach the battalion headquarters, they could not make any headway through the strongly defended houses. In fact, it was all they could do to repel the attacks being made on every side of them. Meanwhile, the forward companies of the Highland Light Infantry had found by morning that they were surrounded by even stronger enemy forces, as a result of reinforcements brought up during the night. They fought until all their ammunition was spent; then at 9.30 a.m. they were forced to surrender. There were 80 men left. Total casualties of the battalion had been 17 officers and 426 other ranks.

In Bourlon Wood, where the 2nd Battalion Scots Guards and two companies of the 11th Battalion King's Own had been sent forward to reinforce the very tired troops of 119th Brigade, a slight advance was made in clearing the Germans out of the north-east corner of the wood, but most of the day was spent in fighting off renewed German counter-attacks. When darkness fell, the general position was much as it had been the night before. The Guards had completed their relief of 51st Division, and now the troops of 62nd were returning to relieve the 40th Division. In just over two days' fighting, the 40th Division had lost 172 officers and 4,017 other ranks. This division had borne the brunt of the struggle for Bourlon, but for all that, the Germans were still in possession of the shoulder of the ridge above Fontaine as well as part of the high ground west of Bourlon Wood. By the evening of November 25, Haig felt there was something seriously wrong with the way in which the operations of IV Corps had been conducted. He estimated that sufficient troops had been made available for the task, and recommended that General Byng should take over personal control himself. He was to have at his temporary disposal the 2nd and 47th Divisions in order to ensure the security of the Bourlon position, and also the Cavalry Corps who were to be used wherever exploitation by mounted troops could be seized.

In a telegram to the Chief of the Imperial General Staff, Haig stated: " My orders to Byng are to complete capture of Bourlon position and such tactical points on its flanks as are necessary to secure it. The positions gained are to be held and troops to be ready to exploit any local advantage and follow up any retirement of enemy. Nothing beyond above to be attempted. For purposes stated 2nd and 47th Divisions and cavalry remain at his disposal for present. Bourlon Hill is a feature of great importance because it overlooks Cambrai and the approaches to the town as well as the country north-wards to the Sensee marshes."

Urged on by Haig, Byng ordered the IV Corps to capture the villages of Fontaine and Bourlon " not later than Tues-day, 27th November," and consolidate a line along the northern slopes of the Bourlon Ridge beyond the two villages and the wood. The attack was to be made by the 62nd and Guards divisions, with as many tanks as could be made available in the time.

The day of November 26 was one of recuperation on both sides, the only direct fighting being spasmodic machine-gun fire and sniping. The 2nd Division came up to relieve the 36th, and the 47th Division was ordered up into the neigh-bourhood of Graincourt. A heavy artillery bombardment in preparation for the following day's attack was laid down on Fontaine, Quarry Wood, Moeuvres, Inchy and Sains (not Bourlon because the East Surreys were still holding out in one corner of the village), and the Royal Flying Corps bombed a number of crossings over the Sensee river. At 9.30, a.m., a conference took place at 62nd Division headquarters at Havrincourt to go over the Third Army plans for the final attempt to win Bourlon Ridge. Lieutenant General Wooll-combe and the divisional commanders, Major General Feild-ing (Guards) and Major General Braithwaite (62nd Division), were the first to arrive. Then came General Byng, and last of all, the Commander-in-Chief himself.

Byng went over his plan. The attack on Fontaine was to be made eastwards by the 2nd Guards Brigade with twelve tanks; that on Bourlon village and the northern part of the wood was to be made by the 186th and 187th Brigades of 62nd Division, with the help of twenty tanks and also three dismounted battalions of the 2nd Cavalry Division. Haig expressed his approval of the plan, realising that with limited resources it was useless to attempt anything other than " to capture and hold the best line for the winter." Then he rode off to view the battlefield from the top of Flesquieres Ridge. When he had gone, a considerable argument broke out. The Guards commander had already voiced his objections to the plan, now he put them forward in a written statement. He considered that he had insufficient troops to make the attack, only six fresh battalions in fact; he thought that a corresponding attack on Rumilly to the west was vital to any attempt to secure Bourlon Ridge because of German artillery fire from the high ground there; and as this was not possible anyway, the best policy would be to withdraw from the low ground held at present to a main line of defence on Flesquieres Ridge. Byng listened to these objections, but he was adamant. The attack would go forward as planned—and as the Commander-in-Chief wanted.

Orders were sent out for the tanks to be made ready. As dusk fell, they set out from the supply dumps east of Ribecourt, twenty-six from F Battalion, four from I, and three from C. During the night, the rain turned to a continuous fall of snow, making it extremely difficult for the routes to be clearly marked as the tanks trundled up to the front. Once again they were preparing for battle at dawn, just as they had done exactly seven days before. Even the zero hour, 6.20 a.m., was the same. But there the parallel ended. This time the tanks were few in number and their crews battle-weary. There was none of the enthusiasm so much in evidence before the initial attack on the 20th; during the long week of bitter fighting, the men of the Tank Corps had seen too many opportunities thrown away, opportunities that they themselves had created at such great cost. This time there was no opportunity for even the slightest degree of co-operation between tanks and infantry to be planned beforehand. And most important of all, this time there would be none of that element of surprise that had helped to make the initial attack such a success. The Germans were waiting for them, and they knew it.

But just to what extent, they could not know. For by now, on the Bourlon front alone, General von Moser had seven divisions stretching from Quéant to Bourlon Wood. A new command, the Lewarde Group under General Albrecht, had been formed to take over the northern half of the Arras Group line to enable Moser to concentrate on the Bourlon position. And further to the east, and south of the Caudry Group, yet another new command had been formed, the Busigny Group, under General von Kathen. All these Groups were reinforced with fresh divisions from Flanders and Russia, to such an extent in fact that Rupprecht now decided he had sufficient forces not only to repel any British attack but to launch a major counter-offensive himself. While Byng was putting forward his plans at Havrincourt on the morning of November 26 for the following day's attack, a meeting was also taking place between Rupprecht and Marwitz at the German Second Army headquarters at le Cateau. With Byng's vulnerable forward positions as their target, they were planning the first major offensive to be launched against the British on the Western Front since " Second Ypres " in 1915.

CHAPTER TWELVE

End of The Attack

"I THINK no man may look into it now and live after his view—neither an English soldier nor a German soldier—because the little narrow streets which go between its burnt and broken houses are swept by bullets from our machine-guns in the south and from the enemy's in the north, and no human being could stay alive there for a second after showing himself in the village . . . Men fought in the streets and in the broken houses and behind the walls and round the ruins of the little church of Notre Dame."

So Philip Gibbs, a *Daily Telegraph* war correspondent at the time, described the fight on November 27 to take Fontaine, the village which had been captured once and allowed to fall back into German hands because it was thought it would be an easy objective to take again. In fact, this last fight for it was the most intense of the whole offensive. As the two armies battled it out in the shell-torn ruins, the village became an inferno of shell and machine-gun fire, grenades, and the cold steel of bayonets. It was street fighting of a kind rare during the Great War, and for which the tanks had no previously prepared tactics. As Fuller wrote afterwards: "There was horrible slaughter in Fontaine, and I, who had spent weeks before the battle in thinking out its probabilities had never tackled the subject of village fighting. I could have kicked myself again and again for this lack of foresight, but it never occurred to me that our infantry commanders would thrust tanks into such places."

The attack had started at 6.20 a.m., just as dawn was coming up and the snow-storm of the night before was turning once again to a drizzling rain. The British barrage opened up and crept forward at five-minute intervals while the machine-gun companies poured fire over the ground east of the village. At 6.45 a.m. the advance towards Fontaine began, from the east in order to avoid German fire from la Folie Wood. On the right, from their position on the Bapaume-Cambrai road, came the 3rd Battalion Grenadier Guards, led by eight tanks of F Battalion. Next to them was the 1st Battalion Coldstream Guards, and to their left, attacking the north-east corner of Bourlon Wood, was the 2nd Battalion Irish Guards. Heavy machine-gun and artillery fire from Fontaine brought casualties almost immediately, particularly on the right which despite the efforts to avoid it, suffered from fire from la Folie Wood as well. Two companies of the Grenadiers were almost wiped out immediately; only one sergeant and six men managed to fight their way through to the outskirts of the village. Here they linked up with the rest of the battalion, also much depleted by now. With the help of the tanks which had all got through, they forced their way into the centre of the village by 7.15 a.m. But the houses and cellars were still full of Germans, and fire was also coming from the sunken road leading to Cantaing. It was along this road that the 1st Battalion Scots Guards were supposed to link up with the Grenadiers to hold the right of the divisional front. But they were unable to do so under the intense fire; one company suffered so badly that after all the officers had been killed or wounded the command passed to a sergeant. When the order came to withdraw, after beating off several counter-attacks, he brought back to safety a number of wounded, including the company commander. The sergeant, John McAulay, D.C.M., was awarded the Victoria Cross for this action.

The Coldstream Guards managed to enter the village after meeting obstinate resistance, but again, they had suffered heavily. Despite this, the two battalions pushed on through the village, but there were serious gaps between the companies and the Germans had by no means been subdued. Meanwhile, the Irish Guards had bayoneted their way through the north-eastern part of Bourlon Wood, taking many prisoners as well, and by 8.00 a.m. they had linked up with the Coldstream.

By now, the eight tanks of F Battalion had been joined by three of I Battalion—one had been lost by " bellying " on a tree-stump in Bourlon Wood. They did valuable work in knocking out machine-gun posts, but they could not help in clearing the village. The Germans were becoming used to the tanks at close quarters and had devised ways of fighting them. A report by a German officer of the 46th Infantry Regiment stated: " Armoured vehicles have entered the village. It is found that they are able to conquer ground but not hold it. In the narrow streets and alleyways they have no free field for their fire, and their movements are hemmed in on all sides. The terror they have spread amongst us disappears. We get to know their weak spots. A ferocious passion for hunting them down is growing . . . As individual hand grenades, thrown on top of the tanks or against their sides are ineffective, we tie several grenades together and make them explode beneath the tanks."

In spite of this, and the use of anti-tank guns, only one tank of F Battalion was actually knocked out. Lieutenant Spremberg of the 52nd Reserve Infantry Regiment, which was helping to hold the village at the time, describes the incident. " At first we tried to throw hand grenades under the tracks of the tanks, but their explosive power was too weak. So I ordered empty sandbags to be brought up. In each bag we placed four grenades . . . Musketeers Buttenberg and Schroeder, both members of our assault group, ran towards one of the firing monsters and put two of the bags under the tracks. A violent explosion followed and the left-hand track was blown completely off its wheels . . ."

Within two hours of the start of the attack, the Guards had succeeded in fighting their way to the far side of the village. But they had paid a heavy price in casualties, and with many Germans still in the village, their position was precarious.

At 8.30 a.m. the brigade commander, Brigadier General Sergison-Brooke, ordered up reserve companies of the Grenadiers and Welsh Guards. At the same time, however, the Germans were also bringing up heavy reinforcements from the direction of la Folie. What was left of the three Guards battalions were to find themselves facing an onslaught of no less than nine German battalions.

The 62nd Division attack meanwhile, which had begun with an artillery barrage at the same time, was pressing forward through Bourlon Wood, led by the tanks. More troops were employed—two brigades in fact, the 186th on the right and 187th on the left—and a total of nineteen tanks went into action; one had developed mechanical trouble and was unable to start. Because of the trees and undergrowth, it was difficult for the infantry to keep pace with the creeping barrage, but good progress was made. Then the 5th Battalion Duke of Wellington's on the right was checked by heavy machine-gun fire from the north-east part of the wood and was unable to make contact with the left of the Guards. The 6th and 7th Battalions of the same regiment swung to the left and managed to enter Bourlon village from the east, where they were greatly assisted by four of the tanks in capturing a factory building and silencing a battery of howitzers. But heavy fire from a strong German emplacement by the railway line prevented any further advance into the village.

On the left, eleven tanks of F Battalion led the 5th Battalion York and Lancaster and the 5th Battalion King's Own Yorkshire Light Infantry into the village from the south, while the remaining four tanks protected the flank by attacking the machine-gun posts in the Marcoing line. On reaching the village, it was found that the shell-fire had done little to damage the German barricades. Hidden field-guns and machine-guns opened fire from every side. The tanks suffered badly, and of the fifteen that entered the village from east and south, ten were destroyed. The fighting raged ceaselessly for two hours; then at 9.30 a.m. a withdrawal became inevitable. Measures were taken to maintain possession of the western crest of Bourlon Ridge by bringing up a West Yorkshire battalion from 185th Brigade, and the attack on Bourlon village came to an end.

Half-an-hour later, the attack on Fontaine was also called off. The weakened Guards battalions had been unable to meet the fierce German counter-attack with greatly larger forces which had also brought other Germans out of the houses and cellars. The fighting reached a greater intensity than at any time during the whole battle, as from street to street, from one ruined building to another, the Guards fought desperately against being surrounded. By the time the order to withdraw came through, so many had fallen that only isolated groups were left. They retreated under covering fire, taking with them as many prisoners as they could, while another battalion of the Grenadiers was brought up to prevent any German advance out of Fontaine. Of the three battalions that had made the attack, under 500 men returned to their lines. The casualties of the 2nd Guards Brigade totalled 38 officers and 1,043 other ranks.

As those tanks which had reached the far side of the village turned to head for home, the crews had their last glimpse along the Fontaine-Cambrai road to the city they had come so near to capturing. They were not to see it again for nearly another year, when during the big advance by tanks and Canadian infantry divisions on September 27 the following year they finally succeeded in driving the Germans out of Cambrai. For by midday on the 27th, it was apparent that the battle for Cambrai had come to an end. When news of the failures at Bourlon and Fontaine was received at General Headquarters, Haig had no alternative but to end the offensive. There were just not enough fresh reserves to keep it going. The week of fighting had by no means justified the hopes following the brilliant success of the first day. Little had been achieved; and much in the way of men and materials had been lost. But on the credit side, apart from the ground that had been captured, over 10,500 prisoners had been taken, together with 142 guns, 350 machine-guns, 70 trench mortars, and great quantities of ammunition and stores of all kinds.

It was agreed that the existing positions should be consolidated while a defensive line on the Flesquieres Ridge was prepared, to which the Third Army would fall back for the winter. The 47th and 59th Divisions would relieve the 62nd and the Guards, although these would be retained in reserve for the time being. The tanks were ordered to be withdrawn. The Tank Corps issued instructions for the three brigades to concentrate around Bray, from where they would be entrained for their winter quarters. Some of the tank crews went home on leave. For them, and for everyone else on the British side, the Battle of Cambrai was over. Or so they thought. For they had reckoned without German intentions. It was now their turn to launch an attack, in every way as sudden and surprising as that of the original British attack on November 20.

On the afternoon of November 27, a highly important conference took place at the le Cateau headquarters of the German Second Army. Crown Prince Rupprecht of Bavaria was there with Lieutenant General von Kuhl, his Chief of Staff, together with General von der Marwitz commanding the Second Army and the Caudry, Arras, and Busigny Group commanders. Shortly afterwards, Ludendorff himself arrived. It was a strained meeting. Marwitz was fully aware that he was under criticism for being taken unawares by the first British surprise attack, and said very little. Ludendorff, a soldier of the old school who was gruff at the best of times, was heavily involved in the tangle of German politics and the set-back at Cambrai which was being acclaimed as a victory by the British didn't help him. Holding the curious title of Quartermaster General, which was by no means an adequate description of his authority, Ludendorff had virtually shared with Hindenburg command of the German armies since Falkenhayn's fall from grace. They were both now suffering from the same lack of confidence towards them by the politicians and public at home that also beset Haig and his commanders. The campaigns in Flanders had done little to help the Allied cause, but they had also cost the Germans heavy casualties. And now there had occurred a breakthrough at Cambrai, where the Hindenburg defences had been proclaimed " impregnable "—and to add to the bitterness, it had been achieved by tanks.

For Ludendorff had made no secret of his indifference towards this new element of warfare. " The best weapons against the tanks are coolness, discipline and courage," he had stated when they first appeared on the Somme in September 1916. A month later, he slightly altered his opinion when he wrote, " without over-estimating their value, one cannot deny that they have met with some success. In any case, an improved model would be an effective weapon. Accordingly, I consider it desirable that the construction of tanks be entered upon forthwith." This started a flurry of activity and the search for Mr. Steiner, the Holt salesman who had tried to interest the German High Command in tractor designs before the war. But the effort was delayed by an even more obstinate military bureaucracy than that which had held up the British tank development. The first German experiments with Holt tracks were not held until May 1917. They were not a success. But by then, the failure of the tanks in Flanders had caused Ludendorff to revise his opinion once again, and the tank programme took a very low place on the list of military priorities, to such an extent that by the beginning of 1918, only five of a crude, early design were available, and during that year, while the Allies were numbering their tanks in thousands, the Germans made use of only fifteen of their own and seventy-five captured ones.

It was against this climate of opinion that the meeting at le Cateau took place.

" We've beaten off the British attacks at Bourlon and Fontaine," Rupprecht began, hoping to lighten the atmosphere with an announcement of good news. Ludendorff merely grunted. Fanatical courage and tenacity was the least he expected of his troops.

"And we destroyed many of their tanks as well," Marwitz interposed hesitantly.

" It's what I told you," Ludendorff grunted, looking at

Rupprecht. "The only reason they got through in the first place was because of tank panic."

That disposed of both the tanks and Marwitz, and Ludendorff turned his attention towards the problem of the counter-offensive against the British. Rupprecht announced that in addition to the reserves that had already arrived, he was expecting the 185th Division and the 9th Bavarian Reserve Division from the Fourth Army in Flanders. But they wouldn't be ready for an attack to be launched until the 30th; meanwhile, he hoped the British would continue to concentrate their attacks on the Bourlon position and not make any drive south of Crevecouer, where the defences were more vulnerable. He did not know, of course, that Haig had discontinued the whole offensive. Ludendorff considered the situation.

"We could roll up the whole British salient," he said at last. "There has never been such an opportunity."

And so the first major offensive against the British in two years was formulated. While Ludendorff drove to Tournai to confer with the Chief of Staff of the Fourth Army, Rupprecht and his Group commanders made detailed plans. The main attack would be made from the south-east by the Caudry and Busigny Groups, taking the British in flank and rear and moving in the general direction of Metz to recapture Flesquieres and Havrincourt Wood. Seven divisions would be used, the 34th, 28th, 208th, 183rd, 220th, 30th, and the 9th Reserve. Meanwhile, the Arras Group would move southwards from west of Bourlon Wood to connect up at Flesquieres and Havrincourt, using three divisions, the 221st, 214th and the 49th Reserve. In this way, it was hoped that all the British forces in the Cambrai salient, nine miles wide and four miles deep, would be cut off, and as a minimum achievement, the Hindenburg Front system would be recaptured. In the event of a great success, further reserve divisions were to be moved up to attack north of St. Quentin. In every way, the offensive was as ambitious as the British had been.

On November 28, Moser's Arras Group began an intense bombardment of Bourlon Wood with gas and high explosive in which 16,000 rounds of field-gun ammunition were used. At this time, the 47th Division was taking over the wood from the 62nd, and the shelling caused heavy casualties. West of Bourlon Wood, the British front was held by the 2nd Division, and in front of Fontaine, the Guards had been relieved by the 59th Division, the last of the V Corps reserve divisions. Thus the IV Corps front, although it did not have the security of possessing the whole of the Bourlon Ridge, was held by three fresh divisions with a majority of the Third Army heavy guns in support. The III Corps, which for some days had been mainly inactive during the fighting for Bourlon, was more vulnerable. The four divisions which had made the original attack still held the right front without having received any relief—the 6th Division from Cantaing and Noyelles to Marcoing, the 29th Division along the Canal de L'Escaut to Masnieres, the 20th Division facing east along the Bonavis Ridge from the canal to Lateau Wood, and the 12th Division holding the remainder of the salient to a point on the northern edge of the Banteux ravine where it joined the VII Corps front.

Throughout the planning of the initial British attack on November 20, Lieutenant General Sir T. D'O. Snow, commanding the VII Corps, had been kept fully informed and at one time it had even been suggested that his Corps might take part in the advance forward with French troops, had these been used. When the French offer of reserves was turned down, Snow's contribution had been limited to helping with the artillery bombardment at zero hour on the 20th. He had closely followed the events of the next few days and kept his divisions in a state of preparedness, particularly the 55th (1st West Lancashire) Division which held the Banteux ravine at the junction with the III Corps. From his own observations, he was aware of greatly increased German activity both in and behind their trenches and this, combined with growing artillery registration, convinced him that the Germans were preparing a counter-attack. On November 25, he had forwarded to General Byng at Third Army headquarters a warning that such an attack might take place on the 29th or 30th, and be aimed primarily at the Banteux ravine. At the same time, he told the commanders of the 55th and 24th Divisions to be on the alert.

This warning of a German attack was corroborated by reports from R.F.C. reconnaissance aircraft that the Germans were massing troops behind their lines and had brought up large numbers of aircraft. And similar indications came from various observation officers. One of these, Captain Dugdale of 6th Division, wrote of the position after the last attack on Bourlon: "The next few days we spent the time in consolidating our line as best we could. The general and staff made many visits to our Front, and under the unpleasant circumstances we did our best to make the men comfortable. It was the end of November, and the weather was wet and cold. The trenches were newly dug, and the men had no dug-outs to sleep in. The difficulty of supplying them with hot food became a serious matter, and I am afraid in consequence the morale of the troops was badly shaken. My particular duty these days was to get my brigade observers into positions from which they could see behind the German lines. I therefore constructed one observation post on top of the ridge overlooking Crevecoeur and another on the ridge behind us. Both were in communication with our Brigade HQ in the sunken road by telephone. During these days, up to November 29, there were many signs of German activity behind their lines. The observers sent messages that they had seen German troops being brought up in motor buses. Also, one afternoon, the Germans opened up a barrage on our right, near Lateau Wood. This looked very much like a practise barrage for an attack."

But despite all these warning signs, they were ignored by General Byng and his staff. They preferred to believe the GHQ intelligence reports which concluded that because of the enemy's losses in Flanders and during the Cambrai battle, he was too exhausted to mount a heavy counter-offensive. As stated in the British Official History of the Great War: "The Third Army issued no warning order, ordered no movement of reserves, took no steps to ensure that troops in the rear areas should be readily available."

During the afternoon of November 29, completely unaware of the gathering storm, the men of the three tank brigades lined up in Havrincourt for an inspection by General Elles. Their ranks were greatly depleted for the battle had cost, in dead, wounded and missing, 188 officers and 965 other ranks. Nearly half of the tanks had been destroyed and many others were disabled, requiring a great deal of mechanical attention. Nevertheless, from the point of view of the Tank Corps, the battle had been a major success. The tanks had shown themselves capable of breaking through the most heavily defended positions, and if the attack had not achieved all that was expected, it had changed the whole climate of warfare. Elles thanked the weary men, goodbyes were exchanged, and the 1st and 3rd Brigades left immediately to follow their tanks which were already being entrained at Fins for their winter quarters in Meaulte and Bray. The 2nd Brigade was to follow a few days later. As far as the Tank Corps was concerned, the Battle of Cambrai was over.

Meanwhile, five miles away to the south-east, a very different kind of meeting was taking place. Aware of the threat of a German attack, in spite of Byng's seeming determination to ignore it, the commanders of 55th Division (Major General H. S. Jeudwine) and 12th Division (Major General A. B. Scott), met at Villers Guislan to consider the situation. Since the village they were in seemed an obvious danger spot, because of the long front held by the 55th Division, machine-gun posts were erected on the outskirts. Battalions of the Queen's and Middlesex regiments were sent forward to reconnoitre the ground from Vaucellette Farm to Gonnelieu, and four 18-pounder batteries, one of which Jeudwine had previously borrowed from 24th Division on the understanding that they might not get it back—and they did not—were ordered to carry out harassing fire on Honnecourt from 5.00 to 7.00 the next morning. Later in the afternoon, even more certain from the reports he had received that the Germans would attack the following day, Jeudwine asked the III Corps to supplement this fire by putting down a heavy artillery barrage on the Banteux ravine at the same time. The request was refused, III Corps headquarters seeing no reason for alarm since they had received no word of warning from Third Army H.Q. And so virtually nothing was done to disturb the German preparations, to the surprise of Rupprecht and his commanders who knew they had not been able completely to disguise their intentions.

The night of November 29 passed quietly. In Bourlon Wood, much of which had been shattered by two days of incessant bombardment, the men of the 47th Division gustily breathed clean air after the gas clouds of the afternoon had drifted away. The troops manning the front trenches to the right of the III Corps front were keeping an alert watch for a possible attack, but behind them there was a general atmosphere of relaxation, particularly amongst the battalions of the Guards and the 62nd Division which had been relieved after their gallant efforts and were now in reserve around Havrincourt Wood and Beaumetz. At Third Army headquarters, Byng, just promoted to General from the acting rank he had previously held, dined with his staff chiefs and discussed the leisurely preparations being made to withdraw to the Flesquieres Ridge, which Haig had suggested. And on the German side, the final assembly of troops was taking place for the great attack on the morning of the next day.

CHAPTER THIRTEEN

Counter-Stroke

HAVRINCOURT Wood on the morning of November 30 was strangely quiet after all the activity of the previous ten days. Most of the tanks of 2nd Brigade that had been lying up in the shelter of the trees had already departed for the railway sidings at Fins, where they were being prepared for entrainment to the winter camp at Meaulte. Nearly all the officers and crews had gone on ahead by road. As soon as it had become light that morning, the remainder of the brigade headquarters staff left in lorries and motor cars, eager to get back to the relative comfort of a permanent camp. Only a few of the tank crews remained with vehicles that required repairs before attempting the cross-country drive to Fins. And only the litter of empty ammunition boxes and spent cartridge cases and the occasional open clearing of shell-torn tree stumps showed that a battle had taken place here.

At 9.30 a.m. Colonel Courage, the brigade commander, was packing the last of his maps and papers before leaving to drive to Meaulte. At the same time, Major Watson and several officers of the 1st Tank Brigade sat down to an improvised breakfast in the deserted camp. They had slept late after working hard the day before to prepare the last few tanks of their battalions for the journey to Fins.

"We had barely sat down when we noticed that strange things were happening," wrote Watson. "We walked out of the wood into the open to investigate. We could hear distinctly bursts of machine-gun fire, although the line should have been six miles away at least. German shells—we could not be mistaken—were falling on the crest of a hill not three-quarters of a mile from our camp. On our left, that is to the north, there was heavy gun-fire. On our right, in the direction of Gouzeaucourt, shells were falling and there were continuous bursts of machine-gun fire."

Colonel Courage heard the firing just as he was about to leave camp. He stopped his car and got out. Something was definitely wrong. But what? Then a number of wounded infantrymen came straggling past. Courage questioned them. They told him that the enemy seemed to be attacking everywhere, that they had broken through at Gouzeaucourt, capturing many guns, and were still advancing. Courage hesitated. He didn't know how accurate the reports were. He had received no order to bring up his tanks, and in any case, many of them weren't in a condition to be moved. Then he made a decision. The entrainment of the tanks was to be stopped immediately, and all the vehicles that could possibly be made available were to prepare for battle. But with the tanks so widely dispersed between Havrincourt and Fins, it looked a hopeless task. Telephone lines had already been taken up and it would take time for his staff to get round to all the camps. Everything depended on the decisions made by the local tank commanders.

Fuller heard the news while sitting in his office at Albert, making final arrangements for the withdrawal of the remaining tanks. At 10.00 a.m. the telephone rang. "The information came over the wire that the Germans had attacked and taken Gouzeaucourt and were advancing on Gouzeaucourt Wood," he wrote later. "Was this a joke or an actual fact? The question was at once answered by the arrival of a telegram. It was true. At HQ, we could do nothing except send staff officers forward. The 2nd Brigade was out of the line at Fins, machines dismantled and the men cleaning up, preparatory to entraining. Everything depended upon the man on the spot."

One such man was Major Algernon Pearson, commander of 23 Company of H Battalion, who had won the D.S.O.

during the attack on Fontaine on November 21 and who was now supervising the despatch of the tanks at Fins. With him was Captain Hickey who had also been one of the few to enter Fontaine on that day. "An SOS reached us for tanks to be rushed into action," Hickey wrote. "As neither Gerrard nor Grounds had been in a second time, Pearson selected them for the attack. In Spray's absence, he made me his second-in-command. We went round to see what tanks could be pushed in. Bown, one of Gerrard's tank commanders, was working hard on his machine, but could not get the sponsons out. They had jammed. He offered to take another tank in. 'Hermosa' was without an officer since Keay's departure and was ready for action, since being a female tank its sponsons had not had to be pushed in for entrainment. Bown with his crew took over this tank. Seven others were comparatively ready, and were hastily got into fighting trim."

The two men, Captain George Grounds and Captain Walter Gerrard, left for Gouzeaucourt, each with a composite section of four tanks of H Battalion. Pearson and Hickey collected another nineteen tanks of H, A and B Battalions which were in reasonable fighting order, and started off after them.

Major Watson, meanwhile, had found a number of G and E Battalion tanks in various parts of Havrincourt Wood, and as the company commanders had already left for Meaulte, he assumed command of them. " In Metz, we discovered the headquarters of the Guards Division. I reported to the Divisional Commander that I was the proud possessor of an odd collection of second-hand tanks. He was not much impressed, but wired the news to his Corps and told me to wait for orders."

As a result of efforts such as these by individual company commanders and section leaders, an assortment of sixty-three tanks, mostly of the 2nd Brigade but including some of the 1st Brigade, were got ready for battle by soon after midday and headed for Gouzeaucourt from Fins and Havrincourt Wood. It was an achievement recognised by Haig, whose Despatch on the counter-attack stated: " Great credit is due to the officers and men of the Tank Brigade concerned for the speed with which they brought their tanks into action." And Fuller later commented that, "they accomplished what I have always felt to be one of the most remarkable tank achievements of the war."

The German attack had started at 6.00 a.m., while it was still dark, with a bombardment against the 55th Division front which opened so gradually that for a time the British observers doubted that it was in fact the prelude to an assault. Then the barrage grew heavier and spread along the whole of the VII Corps front. Gas shells were mixed with high explosive, and by 7.5 a.m. when the first SOS signals were fired by the British units in the front line, many casualties had been caused and all rearward communications were cut. The VII Corps batteries returned what fire they could, but there were too few guns to hold back the attack. When it came, shortly after 7.00 a.m., the full weight of General von Kathen's Busigny Group, a total of three divisions, was launched against just one British division, the 55th, holding Banteux ravine. It was still dark and there was a heavy mist when the first patrols came forward with light machine-guns and flame-throwers. At the same time, a large number of German aircraft flew low overhead, machine-gunning and bombing the British defenders.

As the Busigny Group moved forward, the Caudry and Arras Groups were opening artillery bombardment against the III and IV Corps sectors, in preparation for attacks that were to follow an hour or so later.

Because of the nature of the line thinly held by the 55th Division, the Germans were able to sweep in through weak points in the flanks and take the defences from the rear. Where frontal assaults were made, the British infantry managed to maintain pockets of resistance. The 5th Battalion Kings in the centre of the 165th Brigade held out at Fleece-all Post, and at Little Priel Farm, a battery of heavy guns, firing at point-blank range, effectively held up the German advance for a while. Sergeant C. E. Gourley, who was in charge of this post and who succeeded in withdrawing his section to safety later that evening, was awarded the Victoria Cross. But elsewhere, the sheer weight of the attack broke through the defences, and as more German troops came up, the stream became a torrent. On the extreme left of the division, the 5th Battalion South Lancashire Regiment was completely overwhelmed; hardly a man survived. The onrush of the German 34th Division took them almost unopposed to Villers Guislan, which had suffered from heavy shelling since 6.45 a.m. By 8.00 a.m. the defenders were forced to retire, leaving behind many guns, from 6-inch howitzers to 60-pounders. From here, the Germans could attack the rest of the 166th Brigade from the rear, and at the same time threatened to sweep right across the base of the British salient, as planned.

At 9.00 a.m. Lieutenant General Snow, realising that not only had the expected attack taken place but that the whole of the 55th Division front was in a critical condition, urgently requested reinforcements. Third Army headquarters agreed to let him have cavalry assistance, and the 4th and 5th Cavalry Divisions were ordered to Villers Faucon, where the Cavalry Corps commander, Lieutenant General Kavanagh, established his headquarters later in the morning. Snow also asked for the Guards Division, which was in reserve in the region of Metz and Trescault. But the Guards had already been placed under the orders of the III Corps, which by now was itself in difficulties. For once the Germans had driven through the Banteux ravine, the way was clear for them to drive deep into the flank and rear of the III Corps, and this they did while at the same time, from 8.00 a.m. onwards, the Caudry Group launched its attack on the front of III Corps from Masnieres to Banteux.

One of the groups cut off by the German sweep into Villers Guislan was the headquarters staff of Brigadier General B. Vincent's 35th Brigade, the right brigade of 12th Division. Gathering together as many men and guns as he could, Vincent withdrew from the village, keeping up heavy machine-gun fire on the advancing Germans. But low-flying German aircraft caused so many casualties that Vincent was

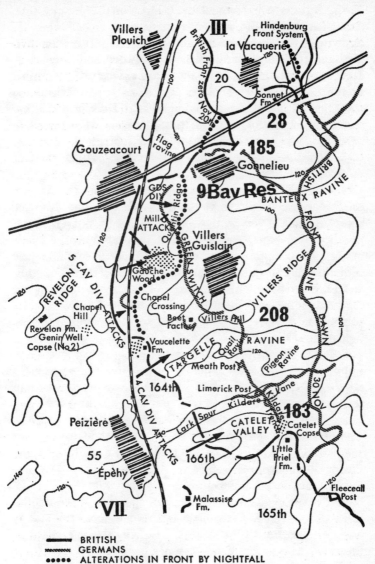

German Counter-Offensive, November 30. Banteux Ravine.

forced to fall back with the few survivors to Gauche Wood. The wood was now being shelled, but Vincent found a protected position along a railway embankment. From here, with no more than a hundred men, he successfully prevented the Germans from advancing through the wood and only withdrew to Revelon Ridge, half-a-mile back, when the ammunition ran out. On the ridge, he was joined by two Middlesex and Queen's battalions of the other 12th Division brigades, and taking over command, he established a defensive position. This was later reinforced by other companies straggling back from the Villiers Guislan area and the British trenches south of Gonnelieu.

One of the men who saw and described the German counter-attack here was Captain Dugdale. "The German aeroplanes were very active, flying over our lines in large numbers, very low," he wrote. "They were shooting with machine-guns at the troops on the ground, and I am quite sure this did more to demoralise our men than anything else . . . In my search for reinforcements, I went further down the valley north of Villers Plouich and there I found a large party of men under an officer who were building a railway line in the direction of Marcoing. They had with them a complete train of open trucks and the engine had steam up. I approached the officer in charge, asking him to immediately fall in his men, so that I could guide them up the line to reinforce our front. Also I told him this was urgent as our line had been broken through. As soon as I said this, the whole crowd bolted for the train and without any delay jumped into the trucks and the train started off in the direction of Gouzeaucourt."

The train arrived in Gouzeaucourt, but to the consternation of the men aboard, they found themselves in the middle of an enemy camp. For shortly before 9.00 a.m., the village had fallen to the Germans. All those that weren't killed as the train came in were taken prisoner.

The fall of Gouzeaucourt was a serious blow, and it was this which woke Third Army headquarters to the alarming weight of the German attack. No defences had been prepared outside the village, and although the assorted units of gunners and pioneers of the 20th and 6th Divisions, as well as the headquarters staff of 29th Division who were there had heard the sound of firing when the attack started, they had no idea that the British front had been broken. Only when a stream of retreating infantry and carts and wagons began coming through did they realise the situation, and by then it was too late. The Germans, who had already taken Gonnelieu, a mile east of Gouzeaucourt on the Quentin Ridge, came sweeping down the slopes of the ridge, overwhelming what little defence the 29th Division units could put up, and poured into the village. Amongst those taken prisoner were a number of American engineers of the 11th Engineer (Railway) Regiment, U.S.A., who were helping with railway construction in Gouzeaucourt.

Under the command of Lieutenant Colonel G. Hayes, contingents of the Durham Light Infantry, the West Yorkshire and Essex regiments withdrew to the main road about a thousand yards west of Gouzeaucourt. Their position might have been precarious, but the Germans did little more than send forward patrols, which were easily stopped. It was an excellent chance for the Germans to have continued their advance, but as the British had found during the first day of the battle, the sheer speed of the thrust had caused a breakdown in the German communications, and opportunities like this were lost.

Meanwhile, the Caudry Group had begun its attack on the III Corps front north of the Banteux ravine. Also under fire from low-flying aircraft, the British infantry were forced back and many heavy batteries were overrun. On the right, part of the 35th Brigade of 12th Division had already fallen back to Gauche Wood. The remaining battalions, after the fall of Gonnelieu, withdrew to Gonnelieu Ridge, and when the German attack was later concentrated on la Vacquerie, they fell back even further to help in the defence of that village. The centre 36th Brigade was pushed steadily back over Bonavis Ridge, and it was here, while leading a counter-attack which temporarily held up the German advance, that the commander of the 8th Battalion Royal Fusiliers, Lieutenant Colonel N. B. Elliot-Cooper, was severely wounded. After ordering a withdrawal to the reserve line south-east of la Vacquerie, he was captured. He later received the Victoria Cross for his leadership; he died as a prisoner-of-war in February of the following year. On the left, the 37th Brigade held the strong-points at Bleak House and Pam Pam Farm which the Germans had so stoutly defended during the original attack on November 20. After fierce fighting, the Germans recaptured these, and the brigade was pushed back to the Hindenburg support line. The Germans then took le Quennet Farm, and penetrated Lateau Wood. Here, where the 12th Division front joined that of the 20th Division, occurred one of the worst disasters of the day.

The 20th Division held a difficult position on the north-eastern slopes of Bonavis Ridge, overlooked from the high ground beyond Crevecoeur. Trenches were in the course of construction along the two-mile divisional line from Lateau Wood to the edge of the Canal de L'Escaut south of les Rues Vertes, but they had not been completed. In view of German artillery fire on la Vacquerie valley which started in the early hours of the morning, hasty preparations were made to meet an attack but there was little time to do very much. And when the attack came, it seemed to begin with to be directed further to the south, the result of the Busigny Group moving forward an hour before the Caudry Group. The first that the 59th Brigade knew of the attack, holding the right of the 20th Division front north of Lateau Wood, was when the Germans appeared from the rear, having broken through at Banteux. Then from the front came the Caudry Group assault. With the Germans appearing from every direction, a desperate struggle began. Companies and even battalions were completely enveloped, and in some cases virtually wiped out. Very few survivors managed to struggle back to la Vacquerie; of the 10th Battalion King's Royal Rifle Corps, all but four officers and 16 men were either killed or taken prisoner, and the 11th Battalion and the 10th Battalion Rifle Brigade suffered equally. To the left, the 61st Brigade fared just as badly. Small pockets of resistance held out for as long as they could, or until their ammunition ran out—and then were heard of no more. The whole division was thrown back to the lower slopes of Welsh Ridge. A description of the utter confusion that prevailed was written by J. H. Everest, an infantryman whose company had already suffered casualties amounting to 60 per cent. while being pushed back before the advancing Germans.

" We had retreated only about two miles when an officer suddenly appeared, shouting, " it's not British to run away like this, boys—let us make a stand." If ever I felt like changing my citizenship, it was at this particular moment, for such an order stunned myself and the others he attempted to rally . . . We were on undulating territory, in a very exposed position devoid of all cover, our ammunition completely exhausted, not the slightest chance of support for at least 24 hours, completely exhausted and under-nourished. Furthermore, on our heels were two fresh divisions of German troops, fully armed. We were in scattered groups of threes and fours, sometimes singly. These scattered groups the officer stopped and attempted to reorganize for a counter-attack. At this time, approximately sixty surrounded the officer. We very quickly took in the precarious position we would be placed in if we stayed where we were until the enemy caught sight of us. At the best they might give us a chance to surrender, but with such an officer in command, surrender was not his intention. We could not protect ourselves with our rifles for the simple reason our ammunition pouches had already emptied themselves through attempting to stem the enemy counter-attack a few hours earlier. Therefore the only order the officer could command was, " fix bayonets and charge." Defenceless as we were without ammunition, ridiculously outnumbered, isolated, unsupported, completely exhausted and without the slightest cover, we would have been annihilated to a man. Neither would the slightest military advantage have been obtained after such slaughter. A rear-guard action of this sort would be nothing short of madness . . . Therefore we wisely decided to disobey this officer and continued to retreat to a more ensconced position . . . After the battle, I began to ask myself: Could this officer who held us up have been a spy, dressed up as a British officer? He certainly could, for taking advantage of our badly broken front line he could easily have penetrated into our lines with the precise object of holding up the retreat, finally delivering us into the hands of the enemy. No British officer would have expected sixty unarmed men to stem the advance of thousands of well-armed troops, unless some important military advantage could be obtained by their sacrifice."

In fact, later that same day, a German spy was found in the British trenches, dressed as a British officer. He was executed.

Eventually, a line of resistance was formed in front of la Vacquerie which managed to hold up the German advance. Instead of fighting their way through, which they could have done quite easily, the Germans decided to turn northwards. This move immediately threatened the rear of the 29th Division and the safety of all the British forces along and beyond the Canal de L'Escaut.

The 29th Division was already engaged in a desperate fight to save Masnieres, held by battalions of the Middlesex, Lancashire Fusiliers, Royal Fusiliers, and Royal Guernsey Light Infantry of 86th Brigade. Despite heavy shelling, bombing by enemy aircraft, and infantry attacks, the defenders managed to hold on, and prevented the Germans driving straight through to Flesquieres and Ribecourt. On the right, the breakthrough against the 20th Division enabled the Germans to pour troops through and spread out towards les Rues Vertes and Marcoing. While an urgent warning was sent through to the 88th Brigade holding Marcoing, Captain R. Gee, a staff officer of the 86th Brigade who was at rear brigade headquarters near the main canal bridge at les Rues Vertes, was ordered to establish a defensive flank. The Germans had already entered the village from the south, and there followed furious street fighting until reinforcements arrived from Masnieres. The Germans were prevented from capturing the village; for his defence, in which "Captain

Gee certainly saved the 86th Brigade," he was awarded the Victoria Cross.

Marcoing was also successfully held by the 87th and 88th Brigades, in spite of fierce attacks. The spirited defence by the 29th Division undoubtedly saved a major disaster and prevented the Germans breaking through to the rear of the IV Corps front at Bourlon. The 6th Division, which held the extreme left of III Corps, repulsed an attack on Cantaing, but was otherwise little engaged.

In attacking the Bourlon position, now held by the 2nd, 47th, and 59th Divisions, General Moser's Arras Group could not rely on surprise since they were not to move forward until about 9.00 a.m., and in the daylight it was easy for British observers to see the troops gathering in the open country between Bourlon and Inchy. Therefore a fierce and concentrated artillery bombardment was launched against the British front positions and Bourlon Wood, and after this, Moser hoped he could achieve a breakthrough by the sheer weight of his attack.

The German infantry came forward as planned, in great numbers. But, protected on their flank by the courageous stand of the 29th Division so that they could concentrate their forces on the frontal attack, the IV Corps divisions fought back with great determination. To the right, the 176th Brigade of 59th Division successfully pushed back an attack on Cantaing. In Bourlon Wood, the biggest section of the front was held by the 47th Division, and it was this diversion which suffered the brunt of the attack. One battalion of the London Regiment was severely gassed, to the extent that only nine officers and 61 other ranks were fit to continue fighting. Reinforced by other battalions, they fought grimly to hold the wood, and although a flanking move by the Germans drove them from the crest of the ridge, they prevented the advance from penetrating right through to the southern slopes.

The 2nd Division to the left faced an advance by large numbers of German troops from Quarry Wood, while others moved towards Moeuvres. The British artillery and machine-guns inflicted tremendous losses on the Germans. But the

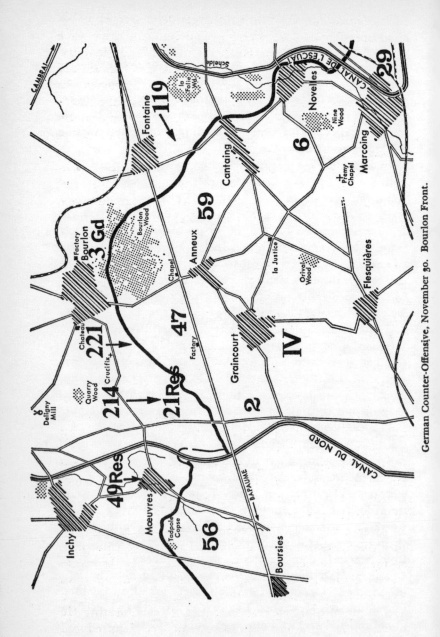

German Counter-Offensive, November 30. Bourlon Front.

advance pressed forward with great persistence and a number of advanced posts were overrun. The Germans made some headway against the Royal Fusiliers and Berkshire battalions, but could not get beyond the trenches of the Hindenburg Support Line. From the shell-torn houses of Moeuvres, the Germans pushed deeply into the defences held by the King's Regiment, but they were pushed back as a result of counter-attacks by units of the Middlesex, Staffordshire, and Duke of Cornwall's Light Infantry.

To the west of Moeuvres, the 56th Division faced a different kind of attack. The front line ran across the Hindenburg Front Line system, and the Germans could attack along the trenches from their own positions. Specially trained storm-troops were used for this purpose. The commander of one such company was Lieutenant Ernst Junger of the 73rd Hanoverian Fusilier Regiment, brought forward several days before to take part in the attack. When zero hour arrived, they moved quietly along the trenches until they came near that part held by the British, and could even hear English being spoken from round the corner ahead.

" Now the technique of the storm-troops came into play," he wrote. " A chain of bombs went from hand to hand along the trench. Snipers took up positions behind traverses, ready to draw a bead on the British bombers; the platoon commanders kept an eye out over the top to watch for any counter-attack; and the light machine-gun section mounted their guns where there was a good field of fire."

When the signal was given, the storm-troops galvanized into action, the men in forward positions hurling the hand-grenades along the trenches and the machine-gunners sweeping the narrow passages with fire.

" After a short fight we heard agitated voices from the other side, and before we understood what was happening, the first Englishmen came towards us with their hands up . . . We counted 150, and still they came. I went up to an officer and he conducted me to the company commander, a captain, who was lying wounded in a dug-out nearby. He was about 28 years old, with a clear-cut face. I introduced myself, and he raised his hand to his cap. He told me his name and gave up his revolver. His first words showed that I had a man to deal with. " We were surrounded." He could not rest until he had told his enemy why he had allowed his company to be taken prisoner so quickly.

" The British retired a little, and then an obstinate shooting match began . . . They resisted valiantly. Every traverse was contested. Mills bombs and stick-bombs crossed and recrossed. Behind each corner we found dead or still quivering bodies . . ."

By such tactics, the Germans advanced along the communication trenches and re-took part of the Hindenburg Line from the right-hand battalions of the 56th Division. Further to the left, near Tadpole Copse, a similar fight was in progress, but after an initial advance, the Germans were held back by units of the London Scottish and London (Kensington), and could get no further than their own original front lines.

By midday, the British position in the Cambrai salient as a whole was precarious. As a result of the breakthrough on the right, the Germans threatened to drive right across the base of the salient to Havrincourt. Their thrust had taken them forward up to three miles in places. But to the north and the west, despite the weight of the attack, they had not achieved the results they hoped for. And on the Bourlon-Moeuvres front, as stated in the British Official History of the battle: " The defence of (this) front against the repeated and determined assaults of the German masses, backed by a powerful artillery, may be rated as an outstanding British achievement in the war on the Western Front. The courage and endurance of troops who had confidence in their weapons and knew how to use them, the gallant and resourceful leadership of subordinate commanders, and the soundly organized and well directed artillery and machine-gun defence had combined to inflict upon Moser's divisions a bloody repulse which went far towards foiling the whole German plan."

Everything now depended on preventing the Germans from pushing across from the east, where they had already taken Villers Guislan and Gouzeaucourt. A breakthrough to Havrincourt and the Canal du Nord would completely cut off the seven British divisions in the salient, already hard pressed by frontal assaults, and would result in one of the worst disasters of the whole war. Such was the weight and speed of the thrust and so demoralized and ill-prepared were the British defences that little stood in the way of the Germans. But as a result of the superhuman efforts of the men of the Tank Corps, there were a few tanks, battle-scarred and mechanically unsound after ten days of fighting, but prepared to do their best. It was now time for them to come into action.

CHAPTER FOURTEEN

Return of the Tanks

WHILE the tanks were hastily being put into some kind of battle order at Fins and then ordered to head in the general direction of Gouzeaucourt, the first infantry and cavalry reserves had already arrived by shortly after midday. The ragged British line now extended along Welsh Ridge, bulged dangerously inwards to the west of Gouzeaucourt and Gauche Wood and on down to the Epehy-Villers Guislan Ridge, checking the German drive into the Fins valley. The 20th Hussars were the first to arrive, at the head of the 5th Cavalry Brigade which had been placed under III Corps command and ordered to secure Revelon Ridge. As the Hussars came over the high ground facing Gouzeaucourt, however, they met heavy fire and were forced to dismount and fight on foot. They moved to the right and linked up with the 11th Battalion Middlesex Regiment, which formed the left of Vincent's assorted force on Revelon Ridge.

Then came the first units of the Guards Division, which had been resting at Metz and was the only large body of troops available to make a counter-attack. Through a confusion in conflicting orders, only one brigade, the 1st, came into action. The commanding officer, Brigadier General C. R. Champion de Crespigny, had ridden on ahead of the troops into Gouzeaucourt Wood with his battalion commanders. Learning that the Germans had taken the village, he decided to attack at once without waiting for artillery support. By 12.30 p.m., the attack formation had been lined up, the 2nd and 3rd Battalions Coldstream to the right, the 1st Battalion Irish Guards to the left, north of the Metz-Gouzeaucourt road, with the 2nd Battalion Grenadier Guards in reserve. At the order to advance, the Guards swept down from the high ground towards Gouzeaucourt in perfect order. Immediately they came under heavy machine-gun fire from the German-held Quentin Ridge, but the well-trained troops deployed and pressed on, taking with them the dismounted Hussars on the extreme right.

" It was a magnificent sight," wrote Captain Dugdale, who witnessed the action from the ridge. " The arrival of the cavalry, fighting as infantry, gave us great encouragement."

One section of the Machine-Gun Corps, which had been holding the ridge before the counter-attack, had particular reason to be glad. The company they had relieved the night before had, as common practice, left their ammunition in the line to avoid carting the heavy boxes backwards and forwards. But the relieving company had been unable to find the dump and when the Germans had broken through to Gouzeaucourt and were trying to push on further over the ridge to Gouzeaucourt Wood, the machine-gunners were in a strong defensive position, with good guns—but without any ammunition. Not to be beaten, the commanding officer placed the useless guns in a prominent position and then ordered his men to " fire rapid " with their rifles. The bluff worked well to begin with and the Germans fell back before what they believed to be a well-held machine-gun emplacement. They were preparing to attack again when the Guards came up and counter-attacked first.

The first tanks of A Battalion, meanwhile, had arrived at the British line west of Gauche Wood and came under the command of Brigadier General Vincent's depleted 35th Brigade. At 2.30 p.m. four moved off towards Gouzeaucourt, without infantry support, while the remaining ten of A Battalion and twenty-two more of H and B Battalions headed directly for the village along the Fins-Gouzeaucourt road.

As the tanks appeared over the ridge, the fight for Gouzeaucourt was nearly over. The Guards had succeeded in pushing the Germans to the eastern edge of the village, taking many prisoners and recapturing the British field-guns and ammunition dumps that had been lost earlier that morning. The sight of the tanks finally clinched the battle and the Germans hastily retreated to Gonnelieu and Quentin Ridge, a mile to the east. There were insufficient reserves for the Guards to press forward their advantage that afternoon, but with the help of the tanks they consolidated the recaptured ground. Five of the tanks were lost by direct hits during the action.

The recapture of Gouzeaucourt and the holding of the front at Bourlon and Masnieres gave the British commanders some comfort at the end of the day. But the position was still dangerous and where the Germans had made their breakthrough, they still held the high ground along the Gonnelieu and Quentin ridges, threatening the next day to drive as planned across to Metz and Havrincourt Wood, cutting off the British salient. During the morning, alarmed at the reports he had received of the German advance, Haig visited Byng at his headquarters in Albert and promised additional reserves. Accordingly, arrangements were made to bring up the 21st and 9th Divisions of the First Army to reinforce the VII Corps and the 25th Division of the Second Army to help the III Corps. These troops would arrive in the area between December 1st and 4th; meanwhile it was up to Byng to use whatever forces he had to hold back the German attack. In view of the many artillery batteries that had been lost to the Germans, further guns were to be brought up by train from Flanders. And the French, whose help Haig had steadfastly refused when the original British attack looked like being a success, were now asked for assistance in case the Germans extended their attack to the right of the Third Army. General Petain arranged for two French divisions to come into action under Byng by December 2, if necessary, and two cavalry divisions were ordered to stand ready.

During the night, expecting the Germans to continue their attacks towards Metz on the following day, Byng issued orders for a counter-attack on the German position east of Gouzeaucourt with the aim of recapturing the old British line. The

Guards were to make for Gonnelieu and Quentin Ridge, while the objectives of the 4th and 5th Divisions of the Cavalry Corps, co-operating with the Guards, were Gauche Wood, Villers Guislan, and Villers Ridge. Tanks were to take part in both attacks. All the available vehicles were split up into two forces, the one, mostly of H Battalion, to attack with the Guards laying-up at Queen's Cross, to the west of Gauche Wood, while those of A, B and H Battalions, gathered in the hollow of Vaucelette Farm on the edge of Gouzeaucourt Wood were to take part in the cavalry attack. The tanks of E and G Battalions which Major Watson had managed to round up had run out of petrol on their way to the area and, as there were no fuel dumps nearby, were unable to take part in the operation.

When the Germans came to review their position at the end of the first day of their offensive, it was with the realisation that they had only achieved a limited success. The attack had simply run out of steam and because of bad communications and the fact that local commanders were so unused to troop movements in open country after three years of trench warfare that they were uncertain what action to take, great opportunities were lost. It was an almost exact parallel with the original British attack on the 20th; the same mistakes were made, the same chances missed. Rupprecht was critical of the move northwards by the 34th and 208th Divisions of the Busigny Group after being deflected by the resistance of Vincent's little force on Revelon Ridge. He felt this could easily have been overcome and a penetration made to the area south of Havrincourt Wood, as originally planned.

Also, the 28th and 220th Divisions of the Caudry Group had been checked north of Gonnelieu and outside la Vacquerie, which was still held by the British, and had been unable to advance on Metz. The attacks across the Canal de L'Escaut and that of the Arras Group against Bourlon in the north had also been largely unsuccessful. However, as Rupprecht stated that night, " if our success is not as great as we hoped, it has at any rate given the British a hard blow." For the following day, December 1, it was planned that the main attack by six divisions of the Busigny and Caudry Groups should aim for the high ground between Beaucamp and Trescault, taking la Vacquerie, Villers Plouich and Gouzeaucourt, while the Caudry Group should capture les Rues Vertes and advance as far as Couillet Wood valley. Zero hour was fixed for 9.30 a.m. But by then the British had already started their attack two hours earlier.

The morning of December was cloudy again, after a clear, mild night. The worsening weather kept most of the aircraft of both sides on the ground, and from this point on, air activity played little part in the battle. At 6.30 a.m., an hour before sunrise, the British attacking force of tanks, cavalry and infantry gathered to the west of Gauche Wood. Thirty-one tanks had been collected, twenty-two of H Battalion, seven of B, and two of A; all the others that had arrived from Fins and Havrincourt Wood the previous day, apart from those hit by enemy fire, had mechanical trouble and were unfit for action. Behind the tanks were two Cavalry Divisions, the 4th and 5th, and the 1st and 3rd Guards Brigades.

The attack on Gauche Wood was led by sixteen tanks of H Battalion, of which two of the section leaders were Captain Grounds and Captain Gerrard. As they moved forward to engage the German machine-guns hidden amongst the trees on the western outskirts, the 2nd Battalion Grenadier Guards charged at a run with fixed bayonets over a thousand yards of open country to grapple with the Germans on the northern edge of the wood, an action which took the Germans by surprise and succeeded by its very daring. Meanwhile, the Indian cavalry of the Ambala Brigade also came forward, the 18th Lancers to the right and Hodson's Horse to the left.

" There was a certain amount of opposition from the wood and the ridge on either side of it," wrote Captain Grounds in his report, " but with the number of tanks available, the machine-gun fire was finally silenced. The German field batteries were, however, active and during the crossing of the railway line we were fortunate in not losing any tanks. One tank in particular, commanded by Second Lieutenant Hulbert, bore a charmed life. In climbing over the small railway embankment it halted through engine failure on the top and was heavily fired on by a concealed German battery for what seemed like minutes. The ballast from the permanent way was going up in showers all round the tank, but fortunately no direct hit was received. Hulbert told me afterwards that he had never known his crew carry out orders so quickly and efficiently as they did during that pause on the top of the railway that seemed like an eternity, but was in fact only a few seconds."

A confused fight was soon taking place in the middle of the wood, in which the tanks, cavalry and infantry all participated. The Grenadiers had only two subalterns left, after losing eight officers and 151 other ranks during the charge on the wood, and so the British officers of the Indian cavalry took charge of clearing the wood. A great effort was made by the crews of those tanks which had been knocked out by artillery fire. Three of Captain Gerrard's section were disabled in this way, and his own tank, in which he had led the attack, was ditched. So he gathered the crews together and, having rescued the guns from the tanks, formed them into a Lewis gun section to fight with the infantry. Finding a German machine-gun and ammunition which had been captured earlier, he fought with this himself. Eventually, only seven of his officers and men remained out of the thirty-two who had started the action. Captain Grounds also formed a similar group after three of his tanks had been put out of action. He succeeded in capturing a trench and a large number of prisoners. Both men were later awarded the D.S.O. Another officer of H Battalion, Second Lieutenant Cecil Ewart Scott, received the M.C. in the same action for bringing the wounded members of his crew out of the tank while it was burning fiercely after receiving a direct hit.

The capture of the wood was completed by mid-morning, and while dismounted cavalry squadrons and the Coldstream Guards came up to secure the position, the surviving tanks went forward towards Villers Guislan. Three managed to reach the outskirts of the village, despite heavy artillery fire.

But the dismounted cavalry of the Lucknow Brigade, attacking from the south, were unable to move forwards to support them because of machine-gun fire and the tanks were withdrawn.

In his Despatch on the battle, Haig noted that: "Tanks were in great measure responsible for the capture of Gauche Wood. Heavy fighting took place for this position, which it is clear that the enemy had decided to hold at all costs. When the infantry and cavalry finally took possession of the wood, great numbers of German dead and smashed machine-guns were found. In one spot, four German machine-guns, with dead crews lying around, were discovered within a radius of twenty yards. Three German field guns, complete with teams, were also captured in this wood."

Once Gauche Wood had been taken, another four of the H Battalion tanks led the 3rd Battalion Coldstream Guards on a successful advance to the crest of Quentin Ridge, a move which in all probability would not have been possible without their support in protecting the infantry and knocking out many of the German machine-guns. But the tanks paid dearly for their action; three received direct hits and the fourth became ditched. The survivors from amongst the crews continued to fight on foot with the infantry.

Elsewhere, the attack was only partially successful. The remaining tanks which should have taken part were unable to do so. A number of them could not be made to start because of mechanical defects, others ran out of petrol and could not reach supplies, and a few simply lost contact in the general confusion with the units they were supposed to be supporting. Despite a dramatic charge by the 2nd Lancers, riding from Epehy towards the Targelle Ravine, during which many of the fleeing Germans were cut down by sabre and lance, the Mhow Brigade of the 4th Cavalry Division was unable to take Villers Ridge. And the 4th Battalion Grenadier Guards was beaten back when, without any tank support, they tried to recapture Gonnelieu. However, the British line had been pushed forward until it was just west of Villers Guislan and Gonnelieu and commanded an important position on Quentin Ridge. With the consolidation of the ground behind and the bringing up of fresh reserves, the immediate danger of a German breakthrough to Metz was alleviated. A vital part in the day's fighting was played by the Canadian Cavalry Brigade who, dismounted, established the line between Gauche Wood and Villers Guislan.

On the rest of the front, it was the Germans who carried out the attacks and the British who defended. To the north of Gonnelieu, a determined assault was made on la Vacquerie, after a heavy artillery bombardment. But the units of the Rifle Brigade and King's Royal Rifle Corps of 12th Division, assisted by the Guards, stood fast and despite severe losses, kept the Germans at bay. Next to them, on the left, the 20th Division did not find itself heavily engaged that day and there was little change in the line of battle, apart from a slight withdrawal across the Peronne-Cambrai road from the vulnerable trenches of the old Hindenburg front system. But further to the north, the 29th Division once again found itself bearing the brunt of the attack. Under the curtain of a furious artillery bombardment on Masnieres and Les Rues Vertes, waves of German infantry swept forward to the canal crossings. The first attacks were repulsed, but it then became apparent that the 86th Brigade, holding the town, was in urgent need of reinforcements. An appeal was sent to General Byng. But while, in reply, he stressed the importance of not giving up ground, he had no reserves to send forward. The divisional commander left the decision of whether or not to withdraw to the brigade commanders. Further heavy German attacks were made during the afternoon, but although these were also beaten off, a withdrawal became inevitable when no reinforcements were forthcoming. This took place later that night. Marcoing, held by the 88th Brigade of 29th Division, was now in an even more vulnerable salient. But rather surprisingly, the Germans had made no attack here during the day, except for some shelling and intermittent machine-gun fire. To the left, an attempt was made to advance on Cantaing on the 6th Division front, but this was repulsed.

The IV Corps front to the west, from Bourlon to Moeuvres,

again received heavy bombardment and infantry attacks from von Moser's Arras Group. In fact, fighting along the Canal du Nord had not ceased all night. But the Germans were unable to make much headway. During the evening, command of the Corps passed to General Fanshawe, and the V Corps relieved the headquarters. At the same time, the 61st (South Midland) Division came up to relieve the exhausted troops of the 12th and 20th Divisions and the 51st Division which had been hurriedly brought back when the German attack began, relieved the 56th Division.

December 1 saw the last action of the tanks in the Battle of Cambrai. By the end of the day, it would have been impossible to guarantee a single one arriving on the field again without the strong likelihood of it breaking down before even reaching the front line. The tanks had fought, some of them almost continuously, for most of the eleven days. They had achieved their purpose in making the original breakthrough. And then, during the first two days of the German counter-stroke, when their work was supposed to be over, a superhuman effort had been made to send them back into battle. It was an effort that played a major part in preventing a German advance across the base of the salient that could have resulted in one of the worst disasters of the war. Now, the Tank Corps could do no more. Of the 4,000 officers and men who took part in the battle, a total of 1,153 were either killed, wounded or missing. Of the 474 tanks, less than one-third returned to base, and these required extensive repairs. In fact, few of them were to see battle again, because by the time the tanks were next required, the following year, the Mark IV had been superseded by the more efficient and more heavily armoured Mark V, which also had the advantage that it could be driven by one man.

But the battle was not over yet. While the tank crews did what they could to salvage the ditched and broken down tanks which lay all over the battlefield, the Germans continued their attacks. By the evening of December 1, Marwitz, commanding the German Second Army, had to admit that the attack had " run itself out ". The tanks had played an important part in this, and there was also a shortage of ammunition and acute congestion on the roads in some parts of the front. Nevertheless, Rupprecht insisted that la Vacquerie, at least, should be captured. The following day was devoted to reorganisation and little fighting took place. Then, on December 3, came the last day of the main German counter-stroke. The attacks were heavy and restricted to specific fronts, particularly la Vacquerie and Welsh Ridge. After a day of fierce fighting, the Warwickshire and Gloucestershire battalions of 61st Division were forced out of la Vacquerie and back to the slopes of Welsh Ridge. And a heavy attack on Marcoing also forced a withdrawal to the outskirts of the village. During the next few days, the German attacks were limited, and concentrated mainly on improving their position on the slopes of Welsh Ridge.

Meanwhile, on December 3, Haig paid another visit to Byng at Albert. Although extra divisions were arriving in the area, the 25th from the First Army, the 9th from the VII Corps and the 16th (Irish) from the VI Corps, Byng estimated that he needed at least two more if the Marcoing-Bourlon salient was to be held. Haig had already discussed with Kiggell, his Chief of Staff, the day before a withdrawal to the Flesquieres line, as had been originally considered on November 21 before the decision was made to continue the battle. Now, he gave orders for this move to be made. In a telegram that evening to the Chief of the Imperial General Staff, Haig reported: "The present line could be held, but in view of the enemy's present activity it would use up troops which, in view of your instructions and the man-power situation, I do not feel justified in devoting to it. My available reserves to meet serious attack are very limited, and the troops need as much rest as possible after their strenuous exertions since April. Owing to this, combined with the state of man-power and the loss of troops already sent to Italy, I have had to ask Petain to hold reinforcements ready near my right in case the enemy's attacks are continued and extended. I see no prospect of being able to take over the French line while the present situation continues, nor can I despatch further troops to Italy unless the War Cabinet decides that risks which I cannot recommend are to be taken here. The

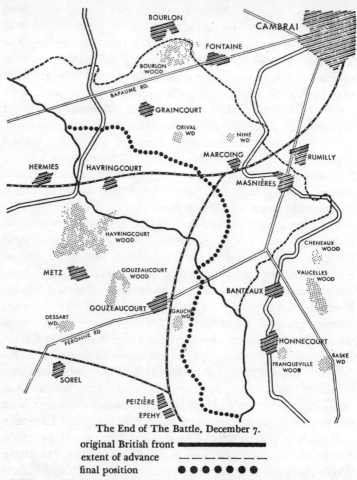

The End of The Battle, December 7.

original British front	━━━━━━━
extent of advance	─ ─ ─ ─ ─ ─ ─
final position	●●●●●●●

withdrawal from the Bourlon salient will probably be carried out tomorrow night."

The Third Army order for the withdrawal, which relinquished Marcoing, Nine Wood, Noyelles, Cantaing, Bourlon Wood and ridge, Anneux and Graincourt to the Germans, was issued at 9.30 a.m. on December 4 and began that night. Unfortunately, someone forgot to tell the Tank Corps, whose crews were still engaged on salvaging their tanks and repairing those that had broken down. The first they knew of it was when, to their astonishment, infantry and guns and equipment began streaming past them in the darkness. Luckily, the evacuation also took the Germans by surprise and little interference was made. The tank crews had no option but to abandon their disabled tanks and struggle back as best they could with whatever gear they could carry.

On the morning of December 5, the Germans continued their bombardment on Marcoing, Nine Wood and Cantaing, and it was not until the afternoon that air observers reported that the positions had been evacuated. This day was, in fact, fine after so many days of bad weather and poor visibility, and many aerial combats took place. The Germans began to feel their way forward with great caution, while the British artillery began to open fire on the positions they had just left. Skirmishes still took place on some parts of the front where the advancing Germans met the British rearguard troops, but there was no heavy fighting. By the morning of December 7, the withdrawal had been completed. The new British line, the "main line of resistance for the winter", corresponded roughly with the old Hindenburg Support line, running from a point about one and a half miles north-east of la Vacquerie, north of Ribecourt and Flesquieres, along the Flesquieres Ridge, to the Canal du Nord about one and a half miles north of Havrincourt. It was between two and two and a half miles in front of the original British line held at the start of the battle. On the other hand, the Germans had taken virtually the same amount of ground by their attacks to the south-east and their line now extended along Welsh Ridge, in front of la Vacquerie, Gonnelieu and Villers Guislan, and down to a point south-east of Epehy where it joined the Hindenburg front system again.

Some localised fighting took place during December 7, both sides being extremely wary of each other. The Germans thought that the tanks might make another attack, the British thought that the Germans might launch a big offensive to regain their position on Flesquieres Ridge. But both sides had exhausted themselves and were incapable of making any serious attack. During the battle, the British had employed fifteen infantry divisions and five cavalry divisions —which altogether amounted to more than a quarter of their total strength on the Western Front—and three tank brigades. Against this, the Germans had engaged twenty infantry divisions. The balance in ground taken and lost was maintained when the final count of casualties and prisoners was taken. Including the Tank Corps and the Royal Flying Corps, the Third Army losses were reported to be 44,207, including 6,000 prisoners taken during the first day of the German counter-attack when 103 field-guns and howitzers and 55 heavier pieces were also lost. The German total in killed, wounded and missing amounted to between 45,000 and 53,000, of which over 10,500 were prisoners taken during the first few days of the British attack; also, 142 guns, 350 machine-guns and 70 trench mortars were captured.

On the evening of December 7, a fierce blizzard swept over the entire Cambrai front. Heavy falls of snow covered the crumbled ruins that were all that was left of most of the villages, the shell scarred woods, the hulks of wrecked tanks, and the trenches that had become graves for so many. The sporadic fighting between weary troops on both sides petered out. It was a fitting end to the Battle of Cambrai; the first great tank battle which had ended with honours even like so many other battles of the Great War but which nevertheless marked a turning point in the history of warfare.

CHAPTER FIFTEEN

Aftermath

THE final result of the Battle of Cambrai was a cruel disappointment. What had happened to the stirring victory of November 20, which had set the church bells ringing throughout Britain? After taking the Germans by surprise during the first attack, how was it that the British had equally been caught on the wrong foot by the German counter-attack? People at home suspected that the generals had failed again, and Haig's reputation, already low, fell to the lowest ebb of his career. He had hoped for one final, dramatic success with which to end the third year of the war, to set against the failures of his Flanders campaign. He got his victory on November 20, only to have it snatched away from him at the last minute. The War Cabinet wanted to know why, and demanded a full and immediate report on the battle from Haig.

On December 18, Haig telegraphed a summary of his report to Sir William Robertson, Chief of the Imperial General Staff, in order that the facts, as he saw them, could be put before the House of Commons, where the Members of Parliament were in a critical and angry mood. This summary was mainly based on Byng's own conclusions which were, briefly, that the Third Army had not been taken by surprise by the German counter-attack, and that the reverse following the breakthrough in the Banteux Ravine was due to ill-trained junior officers, NCO's and men. In the light of evidence available even then, this was a patent distortion of the truth. It was typical of the times to lay the blame against those who were not allowed to answer back. But Haig accepted this and added only that the divisions concerned had not been relieved since the battle started and the men were naturally very tired.

This explanation seemed a little too glib even for the Imperial General Staff and they came back to put a number of specific questions to Byng. For instance, why had no reinforcements been sent up to that part of the front when the Germans attacked? Byng answered that no-one had asked for any, and insisted that he and his commanders were satisfied that sufficient troops had been available to prevent the breakthrough. In a further full report on the whole operation, sent on December 24, Haig confirmed Byng's testimony and found no reason to criticize any of the commanders. This report and others by the commanders of the 12th, 20th and 55th Divisions was studied by Robertson and other Army leaders. They endorsed Haig's findings—they were hardly in a position to do otherwise without causing a public outcry—and the nearest they felt able to go towards a criticism of those in higher rank was to "sense a certain lack of efficiency in subordinate leadership". They emphasized that intensive training was needed by all the Armies in France.

There was such a strong public feeling at the time, voiced by Members of Parliament and the Press, that the War Cabinet felt compelled to seek the opinion of an independent military authority. They chose the widely-respected General Jan Smuts. He was given all the reports—all those from the divisional commanders and above, that is—and asked for his conclusions. He was in an impossible position. What could be gained by blaming those in command? And by doing so, the resulting lack of confidence would detract from the war effort. So, ignoring as everyone else had the fact that Lieutenant General Snow, the VII Corps commander, had given warning of the German counter-attack and had asked for reinforcements and had aroused no response from Third Army headquarters on either count, Smuts came down on the side of the generals. He stated in his report: " The general disposition of our troops on that day (November 30) was quite sound, as appears from the fact that the two principal attacks of the enemy at Bourlon Wood and near Masnieres were both beaten back with great slaughter, and in the third and smaller attack to the right, in which the enemy had such remarkable success, the attacking and defending forces were fairly equally matched, two of our divisions (the 12th and 55th) being opposed to two enemy divisions with elements of a third. That under such conditions of virtual equality in numbers the attack should have succeeded is most surprising, not only on general grounds, but because all our experience in this war points to the great advantage of the defensive. . . . The short time taken for the enemy to reach Gouzeaucourt proves that there was some very serious breakdown and that the opposition met with could not have been serious. . . . Higher Command, Army, or Corps command were not to blame—everything had been done to meet such an attack as actually occurred. The breakdown may be due to either of two causes; first, that the subordinate local commanders actually in command on the scene of action lost their heads, allowing the situation to degenerate into confusion which spread to the rear and the neighbouring units; or second, that the trouble was still lower down with the junior officers, NCOs and men."

Smuts said he preferred the second explanation.

And so the whitewashing went on, to protect arm-chair generals who in the main had little conception of what the front line was like—and had no intention of going there to find out. One of those infantrymen so blamed was J. H. Everest, whose experiences during the German counterattack have already been described earlier in this book. During the two days when he and his fellow soldiers were being pushed back by the Germans, they had no water to drink and no food to eat. At the end of the second day, while waiting in a trench for a renewed attack, Everest went up to his company commander and asked for permission to search for water. " My request was refused," Everest wrote later. " Nevertheless, I went over the top and found some water in a mud-hole, thus ending two days of torture." Shortly afterwards, Everest was wounded and found himself in the Australian General Hospital at Abbeville. There were a number of other Cambrai wounded in the hospital as well. From one, Everest learned what the " mud of Ypres " was really like.

" While I and others were taking supplies into the line at Ypres," the man told him, " we waded through mud all the way. It was very necessary to keep following the leader strictly in line, for one false step to the right or left sometimes meant plunging into dangerous and deep mud-pools. One of our men was unfortunate enough to step out of line and fall into one of these mud-holes. Knowing from past experience that quick action was needed if we were to save him from quickly sinking, we got hold of his arms and tried to pull him out. This did not produce much result and we had to be careful ourselves not to slip in with him. We finally procured a rope and managed to loop it securely under his armpits. He was now gradually sinking until the mud and water reached almost to his shoulders. We tugged at that rope with the strength of desperation in an effort to save him, but it was useless. He was fast in the mud and beyond human aid. Reluctantly, the party had to leave him to his fate, and that fate was—gradually sinking inch by inch and finally dying of suffocation. The poor fellow now knew he was beyond all aid and begged me to shoot him rather than leave him to die a miserable death by suffocation. I did not want to do this, but thinking of the agonies he would endure if I left him to this horrible death, I decided a quick death would be a merciful ending. I am not afraid to say therefore that I shot this man at his own most urgent request, thus releasing him from a far more agonising end."

This was Flanders and it was conditions like these that led General Kiggell, in his first visit to the front in 1917, to break down into tears and cry, " Good God, did we really send men to fight in that? " The men did go and were willing to endure the appalling miseries that ensued. But the most bitter pill of all on top of all this was to be blamed for their commanders' own mistakes.

However, the report by Smuts did not end the critical mutterings at home, even though Lloyd George's government expressed full confidence in Haig and stated that it it was not in the national interest that there should be a public debate on the breakdown at Cambrai. Shortly afterwards, Haig was compelled to hold a Court of Enquiry in France to go into the evidence yet again. The Court assembled at Hesdin on January 21, 1918, and during the next nine days, evidence was take from 25 witnesses. The commanders of the three divisions principally concerned were there. But neither Byng nor his Chief Staff Officer felt inclined to appear, contenting themselves with sending General Staff Officers as representatives. And also notably absent were the two key figures in the whole controversy, Lieutenant General Pulteney of III Corps, who had rejected the request by VII Corps for an artillery bombardment against the Germans while they were gathering on the night before their attack, and Lieutenant General Snow who, as commander of VII Corps, had been ignored by Third Army headquarters when he gave warning of the impending attack. The Court of Enquiry made some attempt towards justice. It appreciated the difficulties and the fact that the 55th Division was stretched to the limit to hold 9,000 yards of front. But its findings still laid most of the blame on the troops and carefully avoided any criticism of the higher commanders, even though the Third Army representatives condemned themselves by agreeing that Villers Guislan and Gonnelieu should not have been described as " strongly defended localities ".

In retrospect, Cambrai was by no means the worst failure of the year. Although the ground won and lost by the end of the battle evened itself out equally, the British position on Flesquieres Ridge was better than that held by the Germans along the lower slopes of Welsh Ridge. The initial success had struck a great blow against German morale and in tying up twenty German divisions during the fighting, this had considerably relieved the dangerous situation in Italy, following the defeat at Caporetto. The Tank Corps had finally proved itself and learned new tactics that were to pay dividends during the battles of the following year. And the new artillery tactics of unregistered shooting had successfully outdated the lengthy bombardments which had preceded nearly every previous British attack. The fact that the battle had not lived up to the initial victory had its seeds in the rather vague plan for exploitation by the cavalry. The planning of the first breakthrough was admirable, and credit is due to Byng for his willingness to use the tanks in the way recommended by Fuller and the Tank Corps staff officers. But in relying on the cavalry to exploit the success by pushing north of Cambrai, the hand of Haig was evident. Even after the experience of the previous two years, Haig still dreamed of " riding into Berlin on horseback ", and nothing could shake this from his unimaginative mind, not even the wholesale slaughter of men and horses by machine-guns. They needed some kind of protection, and the fact that this was now given by a new kind of " iron horse "—the tank—was something he only dimly grasped.

The specific failure of the cavalry at Cambrai was due to poor leadership and the inability of local commanders at the front to take advantage of immediate situations as they occurred because they were under direct control from a headquarters miles in the rear. But even without this handicap, it is difficult to see how they could have carried out the exploitation laid down, and in view of the vagueness of the instructions given, the planners probably sensed this as well. The great hope was for a German rout, and this very nearly occurred. But one incident during the first hours of the attack prevented this and turned the scales—the needless hold-up at Flesquieres, due simply to the stubbornness of General Harper in not permitting his 51st Division to follow the tank tactics used by every other division. The delay itself was only slight, but it had the effect of causing the advance to lose momentum, at a time when Rupprecht and his commanders were considering a general withdrawal. As Hindenburg later wrote in his memoirs: " By neglecting to exploit a brilliant initial success, they had let victory be snatched from them, and indeed by troops which were far inferior to their own, both in numbers and quality. Moreover, Haig's command seemed to have failed to concentrate the resources required to secure the exploitation in case of success. Strong bodies of cavalry assembled behind their triumphal leading infantry divisions failed, even on this occasion, to overcome the last line of resistance, weak though it was, which barred the way to the rear and flank of their opponents. The British cavalry squadrons were not able to conquer the German defence, even with the help of their tanks, and proved unequal to decorating their standards with that victory for which they had striven so honourably and so often."

And General von Moser, also writing of the battle, said quite simply that, " the British failed because they, luckily, had not the dozen or two dozen divisions necessary to exploit the undeniable success of November 20."

Fuller was of the same opinion. " The battle came to a halt because there was not a single tank or a single infantry unit in reserve. Though planned as a decisive attack, the battle was in reality no more than a raid—for without reserves, what else could it be? It was, as I had foreseen, a 12 hours affair, and a few days later I remember General Franchet d'Esperey entering my office and asking me a series of questions on what we had done. At length he said, 'And what were your reserves?' I answered, 'Mon general, we had none,' upon which he exclaimed, 'Mon Dieu,' and with true French politeness turned on his heels and fled the room."

Another who preferred the idea of the "super-raid" is Frederick Elliot Hotblack (Major General retired), now the only survivor of the original Tank Corps headquarters at Bermicourt—which he remembers chiefly as always being cold—and who was at Cambrai the first Reconnaissance Officer the Corps ever had. " We just did not realise the depth of the German defence," he says, " or how quickly the Germans could bring up reserves." But he recalls how difficult it would have been for Haig to have ordered a withdrawal on November 21 or 22. The Allies had been starved of a success for so long that there was great pressure on Haig from both the Government and the Press to continue what seemed to be a real victory.

The lack of reserves was undoubtedly a vital factor at Cambrai, but it can be over-emphasized. When they were needed towards the end of the battle, Haig found it possible to bring up another five divisions from other sections of the front, even though it meant reducing the forces being sent to Italy. And more would have been available, had it not been for Haig's antipathy towards the French. He only informed Petain of the attack a few days beforehand; even so, the French offered a complete Corps of two infantry and two cavalry divisions. But Haig refused the offer. So there were more reserves available; but the Higher Command were not willing to make use of them for the initial attack. This perhaps betrays the fact that at the time, neither Haig nor Byng had any real faith that the tanks would be able to achieve the success they did. As Swinton had remarked on the first day of the battle, " I bet that GHQ are just as much surprised by our success as the Germans."

Despite that success achieved during the morning of November 20, it fell considerably short of what had been planned. The mistakes made were mainly due to an inability to understand and exploit a fight in open country—understandable perhaps after three years of stagnant trench warfare. From November 21 until November 27, when the British offensive was closed down, the Third Army was engaged in an arduous and costly struggle for positions it should and could have taken on the first day. The confidence of the Germans increased, as well as their strength—facts under-estimated by Haig when he decided to continue the fight for Bourlon. He took a risk, and lost. If it had succeeded, his future career and reputation might well have been radically different.

The German counter-attack on November 30 suffered from the same faults as that of the British. The momentum of a first, brilliant drive forward was not sustained, again due to an inflexibility in unaccustomed fighting in open country and confused communications. The Battle of Cambrai became one of the most evenly balanced battles in history.

Whatever it did not achieve, Cambrai proved beyond any doubt the value of tanks. The Tank Corps came through with flying colours and even Haig and others at GHQ were convinced But incredibly, there were still doubters in the War Office. After Cambrai, when Stern was putting through an order for 4,000 tanks for 1918, they accused him of lumbering them with useless vehicles and reduced the order to 1,350. This still did not prevent the tanks from playing a major role in the final battles of the war. To begin with, they were largely responsible for checking the German advance following Ludendorff's big offensive in March. It was during one of these battles, at Villers-Brettoneux on April 24, that the first-ever tank versus tank action took place. The Germans by then were equipped with small numbers of their A7V tank, a huge, clumsy affair that carried a total crew of eighteen. It was too cumbersome to be very effective —in fact, only fifteen were ever built—although when used, it created the same effect on the British infantry as the British tanks had on the Germans. But when the two sides met tank against tank for the first time, three British Mark IVs against three German A7Vs, it was the Mark IV that won the day, with only one of the German tanks succeeding in getting away. From then onwards, the Germans preferred to use captured British tanks for their operations. Another big success for the Tank Corps came on July 4, when at the Battle of Hamel, sixty Mark Vs led the 4th Australian Division in a brilliantly successful lightning attack. This more than vindicated the tanks in the eyes of the Australians, who had been sceptical ever since the fiasco at Bullecourt the previous year. And then, on August 8, came the Battle of Amiens in which 420 fighting tanks, basing their tactics on those used at Cambrai, led ten British, Australian and Canadian infantry divisions to win the decisive victory of the war. After Amiens, the Germans had to recognise that they could not hope to win the war and everything that followed was in the nature of minor tactics. It was the German Army's "black day", and the Kaiser's plaintive comment was that, "it is very strange that our men cannot get used to tanks." But the controversy about tanks was not over. It continued for long after the war was ended—in fact, virtually until the beginning of the Second World War when the Germans, always conscious of what they had been taught at Cambrai, turned the tables and gave their teachers a bitter lesson in return on how to use tanks successfully.

In looking back on the conduct of Cambrai, as well as other battles of the Great War, by no means all the blame can be laid on the shoulders of Haig and his advisers. There were many commanders like General Harper who were deeply suspicious of the tanks—or anything new for that matter—and who fought the war as if it was their division, or Corps or brigade, against the rest. Rivalries and jealousies flourished and added to the confusion which existed anyway because of ill-organized communications. The tragedy was rooted in the system, hardly defensible in peace-time but fatal in war, which ensured the promotion of military leaders far more through a natural progression of rank and seniority than of talent. And everything was done to maintain the theory of delegation of command, even when it meant Higher Command standing back and not intervening while mistakes were being made if, in doing so, it meant questioning the authority of a senior commander. And in return, the lower commands accepted without question strategies and tactics which they often knew to be wrong.

There are dangers in criticising with too much hindsight. But there were men at the time who saw the mistakes and warned against them beforehand—although little notice was usually taken of them. The struggle of the tank pioneers, both in getting the vehicles built and then ensuring that they were used to the best advantage, is a case in point.

The question, "What else could the generals have done?" is often asked. To repeat Winston Churchill's words: "I answer, pointing to the Battle of Cambrai, this could have been done. This in many variants, this in larger and better forms ought to have been done."

Epilogue

IT takes no more than fifteen minutes today to drive from Trescault to Cambrai. As the road winds over the top of the ridge and down towards Ribecourt, the whole battlefield gradually becomes visible. There is the dark green mass of Havrincourt Wood to the left, where the tanks lay hidden that early morning in November, and then the village on the slopes leading down to the Grand Ravine —still nothing more than a narrow, dried-up stream bed. Ribecourt is in the middle of the valley, then the ground rises again to Flesquieres Ridge which the Germans held for so many hours and where so many tanks were destroyed. Behind this are visible the chimneys of Marcoing and away in the distance one can just see the three church spires which give Cambrai its name as "the city of the three churches". To the far left, the dense, brooding wood of Bourlon still dominates the ridge overlooking the road leading past Fontaine to Cambrai.

Very little has changed. The villages and farms have all been rebuilt of the same mellow brick so that they look as if they have remained undisturbed for centuries. The hills and ridges that were fought for so desperately reveal themselves to be nothing more than gentle, undulating slopes. The sinister "sunken roads" of the battle-maps are no more menacing than Sussex lanes winding between high hedgerows. There is a stillness and peace over the rolling countryside. The only movement is a suddenly alerted partridge rising skywards. Or a farmer toiling in a distant field. For the earth is good here, and the once barren fields of matted grass are now laid out with well-tended crops of wheat and sugar-beet. At last, there is water in the Canal du Nord, and the canal was opened to barge traffic in 1966. During the final stages of construction earlier that year, workmen found several caches of German rifles and helmets buried in the foundations from the time that the canal formed part of the Hindenburg Line. It is this kind of discovery, and an occasional scar in the ground where there was once a deep trench, that brings back a memory of the ravages of war. This, and the cemeteries.

They stand at places where the fighting was fiercest, such as Ribecourt, Flesquieres, Marcoing and Fontaine. The first indication of their presence is a little green signpost of the Imperial or Commonwealth War Graves Commission standing beside the road. One follows an arrow pointing down a narrow path which leads either into open fields or to the top of a low hill. At the end of the path is the cemetery. There are more than a dozen in this area, in which are buried many of those who died in the battle. Each one is enclosed by a low stone wall and is shaded by tall cypress trees which stand on either side of a simple stone cross. All are nursery-tended with dedication. Through a low iron gate, the grass is always cut short and the borders kept neat and flowers brighten the long rows of graves. The little rounded headstones stand erect, bearing the names of those who are known or believed to be buried here. Their regimental emblems are cut in the face of the stone—the Tank Corps, Gordon Highlanders, Fort Garry Horse, Newfoundlanders, and many others. Their names are mostly ordinary British names. And they are young, between 19 and 23. Many of the headstones are blank, inscribed simply to " A Soldier of the Great War ", for the shell-torn bodies were often unidentifiable. In some of the cemeteries there are the graves of German soldiers as well. Their headstones are square-cut instead of rounded—that is the only distinction here. A plaque in each cemetery records the fact that this land has been given in perpetuity to Britain and the Commonwealth by the people of France in gratitude to the men who fell. In a stone alcove in the wall nearby there are two books. One lists the names of those buried in the cemetery. The other is a visitors' book. People from all over the world have signed their names here, but most are from the local villages—the elderly who remember the war and come to sit in quiet reflection, the young children who are brought by their schoolmasters to put flowers on the graves. Occasionally there is the name of a visitor from Britain or Canada or New Zealand. Under a column set aside for remarks are such lines as, " I was wounded near here," or " they answered England's call," or, simply, " félicétations " on the upkeep of the cemetery.

One stands in front of the rows of headstones and it feels a bit as a commanding officer must feel when standing in front of his troops to take a parade. The stones stare back, silent, perfectly regimented. One recalls all the heroic words and moving poetry that has been written about these men. But in the stillness, where only a gentle breeze rustles the tall cypresses, and in the unpretentious surroundings of well-cut grass and clusters of primulas and forget-me-nots, they seem to have no place. There is a greater simplicity here that is timeless and knows no language. One is almost an intruder. Many of these men fought and died bravely. But such was the waste and needless slaughter on the Western Front that the over-riding feeling is that these were simply the unlucky ones. They have no great message to pass on, even as to the futility of war. It is for the living to learn that for themselves. All these men wish for now is to be left in peace.

The road passes through the little villages and on into the city of Cambrai. Today, it is a quiet market town, with its roots deep in a historic past. It has known many occupations by hostile forces. The Romans were here, and the Normans, and the Hungarians, and the Flemish. And, during the past two world wars, the Germans. Twice the city has been almost destroyed. The first time was in 1918, when the Canadians were making their way forward to liberate the city. The second time was in 1944, when the railway sidings and the airfield were major targets for Allied bombers. These destructions have left their mark. The city is rebuilt now, with many modern houses and buildings. The population is a third larger than it was in 1914. But Cambrai has never really regained its prominence as an industrial centre, particularly for the weaving of cotton fabric which gave rise to the term "cambric." Attempts are being made to develop new industries in order to combat a growing unemployment.

When the great tank battle of 1917 began, there were few civilians left in Cambrai. The young men were either serving with the French Army, or had been rounded up by the Germans as forced labour to construct the trenches and fortifications of the Hindenburg Line. Many of the women and older men had managed to escape before the Germans occupied the city on August 26, 1914. A few women remained to look after the shops of their menfolk—or simply because they had nowhere else to go. One of these was Marie Denoyelle, who had come to Cambrai ten years before as a dressmaker. She is now 80 years old and still lives in Cambrai. It is an effort for her to remember what happened during those far-off days. Many of her memories are blurred with those of the second German occupation during the last war, which she also lived through. But she remembers the guns suddenly and unexpectedly opening up on that November morning and the growing excitement of the civilians as the sound of battle came nearer and it seemed that liberation was at hand.

"It seemed almost too good to be true when the Germans left the city that morning," she recalls. "But the English never reached Cambrai." It was a cruel disappointment. Later in the day the Germans came back, and they were to remain for nearly another year. Of the sufferings of the civilians during the occupation, the lack of food, the German requisition of goods for what was called "monkey money" because it had no value, the curfew which lasted from 7 p.m. to 6 a.m., and the the fact that during the night householders had to keep their front doors unlocked so that the German soldiers could enter with an excuse of looking for spies and men on the run although in reality it was to look for valuables to loot, Marie Denoyelle remembers little. It was common practice for the soldiers to demand money as protection against such intrusions. On one occasion, she paid this from a carefully hidden little hoard of gold coins. But in error, her house was looted by other soldiers. The two soldiers concerned gave her the money back, apologising for the mistake. This one kind act at a time of constant suffering and indignity was so unexpected that for her, this memory stands out above all others. " The two soldiers—they were so polite," she says simply.

Confirmation that the Germans did in fact evacuate Cambrai soon after the attack started comes from Max Vanlerberghe, who owns an antique shop in the main square. He was not born until just after the war, but his mother, Hortense Vanlerberghe, ran the shop all through the German occupation while her husband was away fighting with the French Army. She died several years ago, but Max remembers clearly the stories she told him about her experiences at that time.

" The Germans were in a complete panic," he says. " Then they all left and the city was empty for about six hours. Before they went, they looted all they could find. My mother took all the jewelry and silverware from the shop and hid it in the oven of the baker's next door. The Germans did not find it."

As the tanks came nearer, Hortense Vanlerberghe and the other civilians gathered eagerly in the deserted streets waiting for the British troops which they expected to see come marching up the road from Fontaine. But then, gas clouds began to drift over Cambrai. They came from German gas-shells, after the wind had suddenly changed direction. " My mother and everyone else had to go into the attics of their houses and keep pads of cotton wool over their faces," he recalls. " Many of them were very ill afterwards."

Like many others in Cambrai, Max Vanlerberghe has made a special study of the battle that came so near to bringing

liberation at that time. He has a collection of old battle-maps
and diagrams and can accurately describe the course of the
battle. He has been host to many British and Commonwealth
regiments visiting the battlefield for Cambrai Day, especially the Canadians for whom the battles of that period have
a special significance as marking the beginning of their
modern army, and he has a particularly warm feeling for the
Fort Garry Horse, who presented him with their regimental
flag.

"The young people today have no interest in these things,"
he says. "They say the first war was the war of their grand-
fathers and the second, the war of their fathers. The wars
have no meaning for them." Then, after a pause, he adds,
"it is better that way."

If Cambrai is remembered by the men of the Tank Corps
as the coming of age of the tank, then Bovington Camp, near
Wool, is their spiritual home—and has been ever since 1916
when the rolling hills of gorse and stunted pines of this part
of Dorset became the Corps headquarters and tank training
ground. It was from here that many of the first tanks left to
take part in the campaigns on the Western Front, and even
today, deserted and overgrown with weeds, there is still the
railway siding where they were loaded onto freight trains
to take them to the Channel ports and over to Boulogne. In
the days when the tanks were still secret, the men were
ordered first to practice this loading operation by heaving
great concrete blocks onto the trains—and one can only guess
at their thoughts and remarks about the strange ways of the
War Office brass before they knew the purpose of the operation.

In 1924, a Tank Museum was established at Bovington.
Pride of place went to the first tank of them all, "Big Willie,"
"His Majesty's Landship Centipede," or "Mother," as it
was variously known. And then, in 1940, this priceless relic
was broken-up by an over-enthusiastic officer—for scrap
metal. It was a fate suffered by many other of the Great War
tanks that remained at that time, including those which had
been placed as monuments on village greens in Kent and

other counties. But " Little Willie " is still at Bovington and can be seen by the many visitors who come to the museum each year, together with examples of all the tanks that have been made since. And outside the building, aged now but still hugely solid and awe-inspiring in a way that no tanks built since have been, are three of the Great War tanks. One is actually a survivor of the Battle of Cambrai.

Every year, on November 20, the men of the Royal Armoured Corps and particularly the Royal Tank Regiment from which the Tank Corps originated, celebrate Cambrai Day, wherever they may be. A recent letter in a local Gloucestershire newspaper recalled that " even in the dark days of the 1939-1945 war, Cambrai Day was still celebrated annually by a day off from work, a chicken dinner, free cigarettes and beer, served by the officers and senior NCOs." But for none does it have more meaning than those survivors of the battle still living—men like Frederick Hotblack who will recall the words of Hugh Elles: " Tomorrow the Tank Corps will have the chance for which it has been waiting for many months . . . I leave the good name of the Corps with great confidence in their hands."

Sources

IN addition to the many eye-witness accounts and both official and unofficial documents on which this book is based, reference has been made to the following books and publications: *Official British History of The Battle of Cambrai*, by the Committee of Imperial Defence; *The Tanks*, by Captain B. H. Liddell Hart; *The Tank Corps*, by Major Clough Williams-Ellis and A. Williams-Ellis; *The Times History of the War; The World Crisis 1914–1918*, by Winston Churchill; *Der Tankschlacht bei Cambrai*, by the German Reichsarchiv; *Der Englische Panzerangriff bei Cambrai am 20.11.1917 und seine Lehren für die Gegenwart*, in the Zeitschrift Militärwissenschaftliche Rundschau; *Die Schlacht bei Cambrai*, by Paul Freybe; *Eyewitness*, by Lt. Col. E. D. Swinton; *Tanks 1914–1918, the Logbook of a Pioneer*, by Lt. Col. Sir A. G Stern; *A Company of Tanks*, by Major W. H. L. Watson; *From Chauffeur to Brigadier*, by Brig. Gen. C. D. Baker-Carr; *Rolling into Action*, by Captain D. E. Hickey; *The Tank in Action*, by Captain D. G. Browne; *Memoires of an Unconventional Soldier*, by Maj. Gen. J. F. C. Fuller; *The Tank Corps Book of Honour*, by Major R. F. G. Maurice; *Evolution of the Tank*, by Rear Admiral Sir Murray Sueter; *Narrative History of G and 7th Tank Battalion*, by the Royal Tank Regiment; *The Battle of Cambrai*, by Maj. Gen. H. D de Pree; *Langemark and Cambrai*, by Captain G. Dugdale; *The First Battle of the Tanks*, by J. H. Everest; *The Part Played by the British Cavalry in the Surprise Attack on Cambrai, 1917*, by Maj. Gen. T. T. Pitman (from The Cavalry Journal); *A Narrative of Cambrai*, by Brigadier P. C. S. Hobart (from documents held by the Royal Armoured Corps Tank Museum at Bovington); *The Tank Battle of Cambrai*, by the Air Historical Section; *Ludendorff*, by Karl Tschuppik; and many divisional and regimental histories.

Many people helped to make this book possible, but particular thanks are due to Major Kenneth Macksey (author of *The Shadow of Vimy Ridge*), Maj. Gen. F. E. Hotblack, Major S. Storbeck (Assistant Military Attaché, German Embassy), Maj. Gen. N. W. Duncan and his colleagues at the Bovington Tank Museum, Mr. A. King (the War Office librarian), and the staff and officials of the Public Record Office and the Imperial War Museum.

Index

HESAP PLUSEN   PLEASE BRING THE BILL

HESAP BOOK
(PUSULASI)